NOAA'S ARK

the Rise of the Fourth Reich

Being a History of Lies, Deception, and Administrative Abuse

by Gary Gentile

I0039080

Bellerophon Bookworks

Bellerophon Bookworks
3 Lehigh Gorge Drive
Jim Thorpe, PA   18229

Additional copies of this book may be purchased from the same address by sending a check or money order in the amount of $20 U.S. for each copy (plus $4 postage per order, not per book, in the U.S. Inquire for shipping cost to other countries). Alternatively, copies may be ordered from the author's website and paid by credit card:

http://www.ggentile.com

Picture Credit
The front cover photograph was taken by the author.

In the event of the author's demise, provisions in his will guarantee continued publication in perpetuity.

International Standard Book Numbers (ISBN)
1-883056-47-0
978-1-883056-47-6

First Edition

Printed in U.S.A.

TABLE
OF
CONTENTS

Subterfuge 101
The Death of Denial

Miscast Authorization

In 1972, Congress passed the Marine Protection, Research, and Sanctuaries Act (MPRSA), the purpose of which was to create marine sanctuaries in order to "preserve, restore, or enhance areas for their conservational, recreational, ecological, research or esthetic values in coastal waters."

Areas that warranted such a designation were those that were "necessary to protect valuable, unique, or endangered marine life, geological features, and oceanographic features. Areas to complement and enhance public areas such as parks, national seashores and national or state monuments and other preserved areas. Areas important to the survival and preservation of the nation's fisheries and other ocean resources. Areas to advance and promote research which will lead to a more thorough understanding of the marine ecosystem and the impact of man's activities."

The primary goals of the MPRSA were "to enhance public awareness, understanding, appreciation and wise use of the marine environment" and "to facilitate to the extent compatible with the primary objective of resource protection, all public and private uses of the resources of such areas."

By 1974, no areas had yet been designated as marine sanctuaries. In fact, the proposed guidelines and the delegation of authority for the MPRSA were still undergoing review, and the National Oceanic and Atmospheric Administration (NOAA) was still ironing out "the procedure by which areas may be nominated as marine sanctuaries and the concepts, policies, and procedures for the processing of nominations and the selection, designation, and operation of a marine sanctuary."

This bureaucratic cart-before-the-horse routine – pass the law first, then decide how to implement it regardless of its ramifications – was to become NOAA's modus operandi.

The law was so vague and overbroad that it harbored the potential for vast and dire consequences. Of twenty-two "states, agencies, organizations and individuals" that submitted opinions about the proposed guidelines, only four "were wholly favorable as to the nature and content of the guidelines as they appear in the Federal Register on March 19, 1974."

The other eighteen entities voiced objections and/or suggestions for revision. There was great concern about the excessive authority that NOAA was being granted by this blank-check policy of undefined law, and how differences were to be resolved between NOAA and those who protested its policies once they were emplaced.

In addition to this administrative quagmire was a major issue of international significance that placed the MPRSA on shaky grounds; or, in this case, on wavy waters. Specifically, Title III of the MPRSA contradicted the Geneva Convention on the High Seas, of which the United States was a signatory member. According to international law, no nation may exercise authority beyond its territorial borders.

Yet the Marine Sanctuaries Act (Title III of the MPRSA) extended NOAA's jurisdiction to the continental shelf: more than a hundred miles into international waters. The State Department noted its objection to this part of the Act as a case of "creeping jurisdiction." Several legislators were quick to point this out.

Notwithstanding this High Seas piracy, NOAA was so eager to extend its controlling interest beyond the three-mile territorial border into adjacent international waters that it ignored the legal deficiencies of the Act by petitioning for the creation of the Monitor National Marine Sanctuary: a one-mile-diameter circle that would be centered on John Ericsson's famous Civil War ironclad, which had been discovered the previous year.

This first marine sanctuary was illegal on other grounds (or waters) too. As noted above, the MPRSA was enacted to safeguard marine organisms and natural formations from the pressures of civilization. Nowhere did the act mention the control of shipwrecks. In its opening bid for the acquisition of submerged real estate, NOAA shoved these illegitimate obstacles aside, and pressed for control of the *Monitor*.

Might Makes Right

Congressional representative John Breaux articulated the fallacy of the Monitor NMS: "Wrecks on the continental shelf beyond the territorial sea are not owned by the United States, according to international law. The 1958 Geneva Convention on the Continental Shelf provides the applicable rule, from which the marine sanctuaries program may not deviate."

Not only did the MPRSA establish a wrongful precedent as far as national policy was concerned, but it laid the groundwork for future shipwreck acquisition under the guise of sovereign prerogative. If NOAA could seize the *Monitor* simply by dint of its discovery, it could also seize Spanish treasure ships that were being worked by commercial salvors who had made enormous investments of time and money in searching for them: a situation similar to nationalizing a business or corporation after it began to show a profit, or snatching one's home when it was determined to have value as a tourist attraction.

In the event, NOAA later *did* seize a number of Spanish treasure ships, when it created the Florida Keys NMS. NOAA ousted the rightful owners, and divested them of salvage protection that had been guaranteed to them by international Admiralty Law. But in 1975, no one yet imagined that NOAA was a corrupt administration that was bent on domination of the underwater world and all its valuable assets.

The Environmental Protection Agency prepared an Environmental Impact Statement which was supposed to address these and other relevant objections. But so strong was the sentiment toward preventing non-government encroachment of the *Monitor* that the EIS ignored the relevant legal issues and concentrated its efforts on refining management procedures. Lip service was paid to international law by stipulating that "the regulations will not apply to foreign nations or vessels."

The great underwater land grab was on: only the first of many of NOAA's territorial violations to come.

Eminent Domain

So little did the EPA understand the hostile marine environment in which the *Monitor* lay, that its statement read, "During the period of more than a century since the *Monitor* sank, the chemical, biological, and mechanical agents contributing to its deterioration have reached a state of comparative stability which, in effect, reduces the rate of further deterioration."

Any honest archaeologist will contradict that statement. Hurricanes and fierce northeasters constantly take heavy tolls on shipwrecks. Saltwater corrosion is an ongoing process that never reaches a state of equilibrium until no more structure or original material remains.

Despite rational objections, illegalities, and violation of the avowed purpose of the MPRSA, the political climate was ripe for the establishment of marine sanctuaries which NOAA desperately wanted to create and perpetuate.

As the *Monitor* was available and supposedly in need of "protection" (NOAA's euphemism for "control"), enough influential people were found who were willing to dispense with the dictates of law and logic, and to lobby for the *Monitor's* inclusion in the Marine Sanctuaries Program.

The grip of politics was nearly as ironclad as the vessel it sought to shoehorn into a program in which it did not fit. For NOAA, acquiring the *Monitor* could mean scientific prestige and increased Congressional funding: a magic goose that could lay more than one golden egg.

Therefore, on January 30, 1975, the *Monitor* was

duly designated the first National Marine Sanctuary. At the time, no one understood that this territorial demand was equivalent to Hitler's invasion of Poland, and that world domination was soon to become NOAA's newfound objective.

The Start of a Dictatorship

Along with the designation came restrictions that were so stringent that none but those who were favored by NOAA could hope to share in the *Monitor* experience. In order for an American citizen to gain access to the *Monitor*, one had to submit an application of proposed activities:

"Each proposal must be reviewed as a minimum by individuals competent in the discipline of marine archaeology, naval history, oceanography, and other relevant disciplines as appropriate, including but not limited to engineering, anthropology, geology, metallurgy, physics, chemistry, biology, naval architecture."

Copies of the proposal would be appropriately circulated, and, "Each reviewer will be given a 30 day period for review."

Otherwise, "no person subject to the jurisdiction of the United States shall conduct, nor cause to be conducted, any of the following activities in the Sanctuary; (a) anchoring in any manner, stopping, remaining, or drifting without power at any time; (b) any type of subsurface salvage or recovery operation; (c) any type of diving, whether by an individual or by a submersible; (d) lowering below the surface of the water any grappling, suction, conveyor, dredging or wrecking device."

Furthermore, "the Act authorizes the assessment of a civil penalty of not more than $50,000 for each violation of any regulation."

The irony of these restrictions and punishments is that they applied only to American citizens: the very people to whom the *Monitor* was most noteworthy. As noted above, "the regulations will not apply to foreign nations or vessels." This exclusion meant that any citizen of any foreign country was free to do anything he wanted with the *Monitor* – grappling, diving, dredging, salvaging, even demolishing with dynamite – because the wreck lay in international waters where American law had no jurisdiction, and because foreign nationals were not bound by the laws of the United States unless they stood within American borders.

John Newton, leader of the expedition that discovered the wreck, commented, "The *Monitor* belongs to and has been paid for by the public."

Yet NOAA excluded that very same American public from appreciating and enjoying "all public and private uses" of the *Monitor*, as was prescribed by Congress when it enacted the MPRSA.

The first American citizen to be singled out for exclusion from appreciating firsthand the shipwreck that is arguably the most historic one in American naval history, was this author.

Innocence Aboard

In the 1980's, I commenced work on a lifelong project: my multi-volume encyclopedic Popular Dive Guide Series. I expected to spend the next several decades on diving and conducting historical research on every available shipwreck off the U.S. eastern seaboard. To complete this goal I had to plan years in advance.

I started thinking about diving on the *Monitor* during the 1983-1984 winter writing season. As the 1984 diving season dawned, I began what I thought in my naivety would be a simple process to procure the necessary permit to dive on the *Monitor* that summer. It seemed like a simple task.

I was already familiar with the permitting process of the National Park Service. For many years I had backpacked and climbed mountains in National Parks. In each case I signed in at the ranger station, explained what trails or routes I intended to take, picked up a copy of the park regulations, and went on my merry way with the fond wishes of the ranger to enjoy my visit.

Not so with NOAA. When I submitted my first query letter, I had no idea that I was going to spend the next eight years fighting NOAA for the right of all Americans to see for themselves the iconic shipwreck that illegal aliens could see without permission: lawsuit engagements that eventually cost me thousands of hours and tens of thousands of dollars.

I described my clashes with NOAA in exacting detail in *Ironclad Legacy: Battles of the USS Monitor.* There is no need for me to reprint all of it here, especially as there is so much more information to impart in the present volume. I will only outline NOAA's machinations as they relate to the origin of its lies, deception, and administrative abuse, leaving it to the reader to empathize with my frustration in dealing with a bureaucratic mentality that held American citizens in contempt – a mentality that continues to this very day, as the remaining chapters in this book will amply demonstrate.

The Loud Sound of Silence

I wrote to NOAA in January 1984. My letter was ignored; perhaps it was lost in the mail.

I wrote again in March. My letter was ignored; perhaps it got mislaid.

I wrote yet again in the spring. Anticipating the courtesy of a reply, I chartered a boat, signed up participants, and made plans for the expedition.

I wrote several times during the summer. In compliance with the law, my dive buddies and I were forced to visit alternative destinations.

By autumn it was too late to dive on the *Monitor* that year, because hurricane season was in full swing. I wrote yet again, taking a different tack that was intended to provoke a response: I submitted a letter of intent in which I proclaimed my determination to dive on the wreck regardless. I couched my language in no uncertain terms.

The adult-to-adult approach had not worked; the adult-to-child approach did. My latest letter resulted in a phone from a NOAA spokesperson. The call lasted more than an hour. NOAA-S started the conversation by announcing contradictorily that it did not respond to correspondence of a hostile nature. It then explained the complicated permit procedure and review process, and admitted that photography could in no way damage the resource.

I requested a copy of an accepted proposal to use as a template. Instead, I received an outline of subject headings that I should flesh out, and a copy of the 1982 Monitor NMS management plan. (The date of this plan is important; I will refer to it later.) The cover letter was signed Edward M. Miller, Sanctuary Project Manager.

By the time I received this letter (in December), nearly a year had passed since I first began my *Monitor* project.

A Year on Hold

The letter contained no explanation of what the academic subject headings meant, or any hint of how each subject should appear in its final form. The subjects were totally inappropriate for my purpose of taking photographs: "Research Design – the scientific questions to be addressed," a "Letter of Transmittal," and a detailed "Budget" with "sources of funding and amounts" and "reliability and commitment of funding."

I was contemplating a simple dive trip, not a multi-million dollar interdisciplinary science project. It seemed to me that Miller had sent a permit application that I would find impossible to fill out.

I followed the outline as best I could, paying particular attention to scuba equipment, wreck-diving techniques, and backup plans. I stressed that I wanted only to look at the wreck and expose some film.

The 30-day review time came and passed. Two months after I submitted my formal permit application, I wrote for a status report. No response. A month later I wrote again. Finally I got a phone call, the gist of which was that I must agree to having a NOAA observer onboard, and it would be nice to have a recompression chamber in case of decompression injury. Then the permit would be granted.

Were these the recommendations of the review committee? No, just an afterthought from Morgan Wells, the NOAA diving coordinator. What did the review committee say? A formal review process was not necessary because this was only a photographic expedition. Could I have a conditional permit stipulating the two additional needs to be met? NOAA-S would not commit itself, nor would it authenticate the recommendations by putting them in writing.

It was all word of mouth, over the phone, off the record. This was not an official denial; it was limbo. Nonetheless, I acceded to NOAA's requirement by obtaining the use of a recompression chamber.

I kept writing for clarification. NOAA kept refusing to answer my letters.

By the end of 1985 I was two years into the project, and nearly a year had passed since I submitted my formal permit application: a time span that seemed inordinately long in view of regulation guidelines that specified a 30-day review process.

By that time I had more than a dozen unanswered letters.

Miller officially denied my permit application on February 5, 1986. As an excuse for denial he created two artificial classes of divers: recreational and scientific or research. He arbitrarily defined recreational diving as no-decompression diving to less than 130 feet: a pigeonhole that was a training standard, not a physiological limitation. To be a scientific or research diver I was required to have a NOAA certification, which NOAA would not let me have.

To suit NOAA's purpose, Miller refused to recognize a class of divers whose training and experience exceeded those of what he termed recreational diving. Miller refused to accept my logbook documentation of more than 600 open-water decompression dives, and more than 50 dives equivalent in depth to that of the *Monitor*.

In short, every time I satisfied one of NOAA's requirements, Miller invented another one. This wily carrot-on-a-stick device could go on forever. Miller and Wells were creative in conjuring new requirements that I might not be able to meet. First they requested resumes of all prospective divers, then they requested – that is, they made it a requirement – that every diver have a medical examination.

This latter requirement I viewed as another scheme by Miller to inflate the cost of the expedition so much that it would not be economically feasible, as everyone was paying his own expenses.

It now became mandatory that my permit application be submitted "90 days prior to commencement of planned operations to allow sufficient time for review." So far only Miller and Wells had reviewed my application. Now the review process was back in the picture, but it was tripled in time – despite the 30-day stipulation in the management plan.

I submitted several letters of protest. One of the new requirements was the location of my base my operations. As I did not know the position of the wreck site, I requested the loran coordinates, so I could determine where to dock the charter boat. Miller refused to furnish this crucial piece of information. In the same breath he warned me not to dive on the *Monitor* without a permit.

This was the height of absurdity: Miller threatened me with reprisals if I did not stay away from a specific spot in the ocean, but refused to tell me the location of that spot.

Still on Hold

I did not give up. Over the next two months I prepared my second permit application. What two years before had been a simple request, and a year afterward an eleven-page application, now became more than a *hundred*-page dissertation. I followed Miller's outline and left no question unaddressed. Twenty pages of text described the objectives of the expedition, the equipment to be used, the methods and techniques of underwater photography, and a detailed research design.

I purposely dated my permit application April 1, 1986: April Fool's Day. Miller took four months to devise a way to deny my permit. "Your request for a permit to dive in the Monitor National Marine Sanctuary has been denied due to violations of safety standards set by NOAA, the U.S. Navy, and the commercial diving industry."

This decision was based solely on the recommendation of one person: Morgan Wells. He took the tack that because he and NOAA divers, Navy divers, and commercial divers lacked the ability to dive to 230 feet, so did the rest of the world.

The irony of this trumped-up justification was that during the summer when I could have been photographing the *Monitor*, I photographed *deeper* shipwrecks that lay within a few miles of the ironclad. Those wrecks did not happen to be part of NOAA's exclusive domain.

Furthermore, "the stated photographic objectives were met in 1979." If this statement were really true, NOAA would not have had the need to organize another survey of the site ever again, which eventually it did – many times over.

Of course, by this time I realized that logic had nothing to do with denial. I appealed Miller's decision to NOAA in the mistaken belief that obstructionism existed only at the bottom of the totem pole. I did not understand at that time that the conspiracy rose through the ranks of NOAA all the way to the top.

Affirmation of the denial came from Peter Tweedt: "The only justification you offer in support of your request is that you have successfully conducted similar dives in the past."

What else was necessary? The proof of the pudding was in the eating, as my grandmother used to say.

I requested a hearing before an Administrative Law Judge. Tweedt: "Since you did not request a hearing when you filed your appeal, you waived your right to a hearing in this matter."

As 1986 drew to an end, I was no closer to diving on the *Monitor* than I had been three years earlier. I had spent one entire just getting NOAA to answer my query letters, and two years waiting on responses from my two permit applications. I seemed to be at a dead end.

A Federal Case

Through the divers' grapevine, attorney Peter Hess heard about NOAA's time-lapse stonewalling of my photo trip to the *Monitor*. When I met him at a diving get-together, he professed an interest in my case because he was specializing in maritime law. I brought him up to date on my three-year saga. He suggested that we take the case to court; he was willing to represent me.

In the early months of 1987 we collaborated on writing a complaint. We filed the complaint on April 15.

In addition to alleging that the denial of my permit was arbitrary and capricious, and that criticisms about safety did not take into consideration my "experience and expertise in shipwreck scuba diving," the suit raised several additional issues about NOAA's conduct. For example, Miller's letter "inadvertently revealed his lack of impartiality and bias against Plaintiff's permit application in that it described an ambitious NOAA photographic project on the *Monitor* shipwreck site scheduled for the summer of 1987: a project whose media impact would be significantly compromised by the granting of a permit to conduct a rival photographic survey."

(This despite Miller's claim that "the stated photographic objectives were met in 1979.")

We also alleged, "This impartiality is further evidenced by the appended requirements made after the original requirements had been met, only to have additional inapplicable demands being made of Plaintiff."

There was also the question of improper delegation of authority. According to federal code, Miller was not authorized to deny the permit; that responsibility fell to Administrator Anthony Calio. Nor was Director Tweedt authorized to rule on the appeal; that was the job of Secretary of Commerce Malcolm Baldridge. It appeared that Miller was directing his own little fiefdom.

In summation, "Upon information and belief, Defendant NOAA's true purpose in denying the permit had little to do with safety concerns: it was as much intended as a bar to Plaintiff – and to any subsequent applicant whose proposal might compete with NOAA's own research and publication designs."

NOAA denied the charges and assigned a battery of lawyers to defend its position. In its initial defense motion, NOAA supplied the court with the official administrative record: copies of the documents that supported its case, my permit applications and voluminous correspondence, Miller's responses (both of them), denial letters, and half a dozen pages of internal memoranda.

Curiously missing were the comments of the technical review committee which, according to Monitor NMS regulations, was required to review all *Monitor* permit applications. This deficiency was evidence that Miller was running the Monitor NMS autonomously, the way he saw fit, and not in keeping with federal regulations.

After all, Miller himself had written with respect to the *Monitor*: "An intricate system of research proposal review was initiated that represents an unusual degree of cooperation between federal, and state agencies and individuals who are recognized experts in their field. Each proposal is sent to the Office of Ocean Management of the National Oceanic and Atmospheric Administration (NOAA), the cognizant federal agency for marine sanctuaries, who in turn sends the proposal to the Division of Archives and History of the State of North Carolina who distributes it to more than thirty recognized professionals in the fields of archaeology, oceanography, history and other related disciplines for critique and comment. The State of North Carolina collects the reviews and forwards the proposal to interested federal agencies such as the Smithsonian Institution and the Naval Historical Center for further review. After the review on this level, NOAA collates all the comments and either grants or denies a permit."

Where were all these reviews that Miller was obligated to obtain?

Furthermore, NOAA's records contradicted Miller's comments with regard to safety: "Diving 'regs' were not promulgated under the APA, rather they are really guidelines. Can be modified by 2/3rds vote of NOAA Diving Safety Board." (APA is the Administrative Procedures

Act.) This meant that Wells did not possess sole discretionary authority to deny my permit on grounds of safety.

NOAA itself recognized the deficiencies in its diving regulations and decompression tables. When NOAA published "Recommendations For Improved Air Decompression Schedules for Commercial Diving," it stated, "the use of the *U.S. Navy Diving Manual* may not be suitable for use as a standard for commercial diving operations." Despite NOAA's own warnings, it denied my permit application for supposedly violating standards which the agency itself recognized were "antiquated and unsafe."

We filed a discovery motion: the standard procedure that compelled a defendant – especially a democratic government agency whose official papers were a matter of public record – to disclose documents that had been withheld from the plaintiff.

We also prepared twenty-four pages of interrogatories, the answers to which would enlighten the court on the lack of consideration that my permit application received. I contended that Miller shelved my permit application, that he did not circulate it for review as was mandated by federal law, and that he kept it a well-guarded secret from his superiors until I wrote to them directly when I filed for appeal.

NOAA protested vehemently. It countered the interrogatories and discovery motion by claiming that the court should make a ruling based not on all the evidence that existed, but only on the evidence that the agency submitted: selected facts instead of all the facts. This is like asking a math student to give the correct sum for a column of numbers, but letting him have only half the numbers.

Astonishingly, the judge fell for the gambit. Without hearing the testimony of any witnesses, he threw the case out of court for lack of evidence: the very evidence that NOAA refused to divulge.

Thus ended lawsuit number one. Another year was wasted.

The Harassment Blind

By June 1987, I was focusing my attention on North Carolina, and stepping up survey work for my proposed two-volume set about shipwrecks off that State.

NOAA-S called me on the phone and accused me to scheming to sneak-dive on the *Monitor* without a permit. It reminded me of the $50,000 fine that it would love to impose on me for defying regulations; and that failure to pay the fine could result in a prison sentence.

I denied all charges and laughed it off. Later I learned that NOAA was spying on me and keeping in touch with my activities. At the end of one day's diving, an officer of the Marine Fisheries Service accosted me in a manner that was brusque and accusatory. He brought up the *Monitor*. "We heard you were going to dive it no matter what. We've been watching you ever since you came around the cape, to see if you'd go near it."

He then informed me that not only Marine Fisheries but the Coast Guard was tracking my movements. "We're keeping tabs on everything you do."

Later, when I mentioned these unpleasantries to my fellow divers, suddenly they recalled that National Seashore park rangers had quizzed everyone about the details of their dives, with great regard given to depths, dates, and destinations.

Some of the guys who frequented the nightlife establishments found themselves the objects of overt interest to off-duty female rangers, who questioned them about their diving activities. These women made it a point to seek them out each night, and to pump them for information about me and my activities; they had much to gain by their phony propositions. Pursuant to the Marine Sanctuaries Act, NOAA was authorized to "pay a reward to any person who furnishes information leading to an assessment of a civil penalty, or a forfeiture of property, for a violation."

With NOAA's attorneys trying so hard to keep its records out of court and from public scrutiny, with NOAA-S threatening me with imprisonment and monetary reprisals, with Marine Fisheries, the Coast Guard, and park rangers watching over my activities, I at last realized the depths of NOAA's commitment to persecute me.

Applications Galore

I was not idling on the legal front. After the federal ruling was issued, I submitted a third permit application which I knew NOAA would deny, but which was intended merely as an administrative step toward filing an appeal. Hess and I drafted the application with this specific goal in mind. Facts that we wanted to make part of the official record we appended to the application.

For example, I included National Park Service material on deep diving in Isle Royale National Park. Although the *Kamloops* lay at a depth of 260 feet – 30 feet deeper than the *Monitor* – the NPS did not preclude scuba diving on the wreck. (To prove this point, I dived all the way to the bottom of the *Kamloops* while breathing air.) The NPS did not require a permit, a resume, a medical examination, or a recompression chamber. It required only that visitors sign in at the ranger station when they arrived at the park: name and address. It did not even require proof of identification. They took visitors at their word.

NOAA refused to acknowledge this information before, using the rationale that because it had not been submitted as part of my permit application, the existence of such accepted practices in an equivalent federal agency could be ignored: this despite NOAA's admission that it was the responsibility of its Diving Coordinator to remain "abreast of new diving techniques and innovations."

According to Monitor NMS regulations, NOAA now had ninety days in which to issue or deny the permit. If we filed immediately for a hearing before an administrative law judge, NOAA was required by law to assign a court date within thirty days. Yet *a year and a half* passed before NOAA denied my permit.

During that time I constantly requested status reports, either by letter or by phone. My letters went unanswered. Miller refused to comment over the phone. By this time I had *fifty-one* unanswered letters on file. I complained to my Congressional representative, Robert Borski. He wrote in my behalf, and received a reply from "Joseph A. Uravitch, Chief."

Uravitch made no attempt to rectify the situation. Instead, he dug in NOAA's heels. He claimed that my flood of letters "has served to delay the processing of this application." I failed to grasp the logic of his statement.

Uravitch twisted the regulations to suit NOAA's purpose: "A *minimum* of ninety (90) days is requested for review. There is no limit imposed on the time allotted for review." This was not true, but if it were, NOAA could take years or decades or centuries to review an application.

Uravitch: "Your third proposal is undergoing thorough programmatic and legal review and you will receive this agency's response when this review is completed. I expect that you should receive your response shortly. To report on the status of the review, the NOAA Diving Office submitted its findings on October 18, 1988, and my office is compiling the review comments and will be issuing a review document to support the agency's final decision concerning your permit application."

"Shortly" turned out to be five months. Subsequent document acquisition, via the Freedom of Information Act, revealed that the Diving Office findings that Uravitch alluded to were not issued until June 8, 1989 (more than four months *after* Uravitch's letter was dated); that the "thorough" review consisted of *only* the Diving Office findings, and nothing else; and that *not a single* other review comment was ever solicited, either prior to or subsequent to the writing of the letter: the so-called "compiling" was purely imaginary. No other reviews were sought, either from within or from outside of NOAA.

One might wonder how so much absence of activity could take so long.

Most of Uravitch's comments were either irrelevant or self-serving. But Uravitch's whitewash proved that the conspiracy to exclude the American people from sharing the *Monitor's* history went all the way to the top. Miller's whim coincided with NOAA's official aspiration.

Other requests pursuant to the Freedom of Information Act were denied outright. One that I appealed exposed NOAA's disregard for the law. Whereas initially I was informed that the requested documents did not exist, upon appeal it was ascertained that *thirty-four* documents did in fact exist. However, NOAA found loopholes to exempt all but three of them from release.

When I questioned Miller about what I could do to make my permit application acceptable, he refused to respond. He left it to me to discover ways to write an acceptable application. So I played a game of pin-the-tail-on-the-donkey by submitting *eight* additional applications during the eighteen months that number three was supposedly under review.

Each new application was different. I proposed to breathe a variety of gas mixes that included helium to replace nitrogen (trimix and heliox) in order to reduce or eliminate nitrogen narcosis), and I proposed to breathe a variety of decompression gases (nitrox and oxygen) in order to reduce the decompression penalty. I proposed the use of underwater communications equipment, both hardwire and wireless.

I got really cute by submitting one proposal in which the divers would abide by NOAA's 130-foot depth limitation. I described how a boat could drift over the wreck with divers hanging onto a suspended line, never venturing deeper than 130 feet. Because visibility in Gulf Stream waters often exceeded 100 feet, the divers could see and photograph the wreck from above. This method did not violate any of NOAA's diving regulations, making it impossible to deny on grounds of safety.

NOAA made no response to any of these proposals.

Better yet, I submitted one application that involved no divers at all. The idea was to conduct side-scan sonar and proton magnetometer surveys of the wreck site and adjacent debris field. NOAA spent seven months cogitating over that one. When the agency was unable to conjure a justification for outright denial – one that would hold up in court – it requested additional information. Of the fifty-two questions that it wanted answered, a few were even reasonable.

Finally I received permit number UMNMS-01-89 to conduct my proposed remote sensing survey. The numbering system meant that it was the first permit to be issued in the Monitor National Marine Sanctuary for 1989. Diminishing the success of finally breaking through NOAA's impregnable permitting barrier was the long delay in issuing the permit: it did not become effective until September 30, 1989: well after the prime weather window and in the middle of hurricane season.

NOAA's strategy of procrastination finally came to an end. My third diving application was ultimately denied on June 9, 1989. The other seven diving applications were totally ignored.

My Day in Court

Hess wasted no time in requesting a hearing. NOAA continued its dilatory tactics by waiting until August to respond with a statement whose stupidity boggles the rational mind: "Please submit a written statement of the reasons for the appeal." The ploy was obvious: NOAA wanted to postpone the hearing until all possibility of mounting an expedition in 1989 was lost.

Hess submitted three reasons: (1) NOAA's diving standards were antiquated and not in keeping with the standards of other federal agencies, such as the NPS, which vouchsafed, "Visitors should be allowed to take risks, and push the bounds of personal safety." (2) I and my fellow wreck-divers were "wrongfully and improperly classified and judged against a sport, or novice diving standard." And (3) "The administrative officials who participated in the permit denial process were non-disinterested, bore a personal antipathy toward Mr. Gentile, and had ulterior and capricious motives for denying the applicant access to the Monitor Marine Sanctuary."

NOAA vigorously protested our request to subpoena Miller and question him under oath: an option that I had been denied in federal court. As the sole person in charge of the sanctuary ever since I submitted my first diving request, only he could shed light on the early stages of the five-year ordeal. NOAA went down kicking and screaming on this point, first with written opposition, then with oral argument, going so far as to claim that an Administrative Law Judge did not have the authority to issue subpoenas.

The judge thought otherwise. He ordered Miller to appear in court and take the stand.

A few days prior to the hearing, Marilyn Luipold, NOAA's courtroom attorney, sent us copies of the material that she was submitting for the record. Hess tasked me with reading through a stack of papers that measured several inches in thickness, and annotating anything that might help to bolster our case.

Several hours later I found the key fact that would clinch victory!

It was in the 1983 Monitor Management Plan. The reason we were unaware of this fact when we filed the federal lawsuit was due entirely to Miller. In 1984, he cunningly sent me a copy of the outdated 1982 plan instead of the revised 1983 plan, in which the pertinent fact was published. Apparently, Miller did not let Luipold in on his deception and cover up.

I will not elaborate on the day-long hearing that went into overtime. Those who are interested in the fine details can read all about it in *Ironclad Legacy*. The intent of the present volume is to reveal instances of NOAA's lies, deception, and administrative abuse. Keeping that in mind, I will mention only a few significant testimonial occurrences in order to demonstrate that NOAA's defiance of truth was not subject to change under oath in a court of law.

Wells stated that he kept abreast of "new diving techniques and innovation" by attending professional meetings and reading journals, not by diving or by participating in diving operations. He revealed no familiarity with the NPS policy of allowing visitors to dive to 260 feet on the *Kamloops*. He admitted that he let my third permit application sit on his desk for more than a year, even though he had nixed it the first two times around, and "It did not take a lot of thinking."

My star witness was Miller. Because he had treated me with such disdain by not answering queries and by dragging his feet with my applications, ALJ Hugh Dolan told Hess, "You may treat him as a hostile witness."

In addition to safety, NOAA cited damage to the resource as another pretext for denial. I pre-empted that issue by showing underwater footage of the 1979 NOAA expedition, in which NOAA divers trampled all over the wreck because they did not wear fins, but trod on wreckage and dragged heavy hoses and communication cables wherever they went.

Against this clear evidence, Miller reluctantly admitted, "The Sanctuary probably did not have any objections to a diver taking photographs of the *Monitor* . . . because the photographs would have no effect on the resource."

Miller insisted that the ninety-day time allotment to review applications "is simply a guideline," despite a written statement to the contrary in the regulations.

In order to preclude diving, Miller tried to paint a bleak picture of conditions on the wreck. For example, he stressed the fact that on one occasion during a NOAA expedition, visibility on the *Monitor* was zero, and because of that single and unusual instance implied that my proposal to take photographs was impossible to accomplish.

For another example, he tried to make it seem that the current always "ripped" across the wreck, contending that a diver "would be blown along the bottom like a piece of tumble weed."

Getting a straight answer from Miller was more difficult than taking pictures in the dark. For example, it took two pages of dialogue transcription just to establish the *Monitor*'s depth.

Miller gave long rambling answers that strayed so far off the track that at one point the judge was so confused that he had to stop Miller's babbling and readdress the question. To give the flavor of Miller's incoherence and abstruseness, consider his insistence on having an on-board recompression chamber, and what relevance it had to denying my permit. To abbreviate seven pages of wandering and murky testimony:

Hess: "Did you not state in a letter to Mr. Gentile that he would have to obtain the use of a recompression chamber aboard the diving vessel, and did he not comply with that request?"

Miller (after three pages of obfuscation and two interventions by the judge): "When Mr. Gentile asked me, hey what do you think of my diving procedures, I point blank said, hey the big deficiency here is the lack of no on-site diving chamber. Several months later he writes back and says I have a one man chamber lined up. Then I said, hey did you read the NOAA diving manual. What does the NOAA diving manual say?"

Hess was eventually able to establish that nowhere does the NOAA diving manual state that a chamber of any kind was a prerequisite for diving.

During his discourse on chambers, Miller meandered off the subject and pleaded that my initial application did not include a medical exam. "In fact, Mr. Gentile has never submitted a diving medical examination. So, if we had gone beyond the issue of safety of diving on scuba air to that depth, that would have become an issue."

This was precisely the opening that Peter was looking for. "You are saying, then, that had for some reason we obtained approval or an overruling of the NOAA diving coordinator's disapproval, then you would just disapprove it subsequently on different grounds?"

Miller: "I would have recommended that consideration of disapproval."

Hess: "In other words, what you are saying is every time he meets one of your requirements, you are going to create another one?"

Miller: "No, I am not saying that."

Hess: "How come you did not include that reason, the lack of a diving medical examination, in the original disapproval if that was a reason? Why is it not in the record?"

After several red herrings, the judge intervened and put Miller back on track: "Never mind the editorial comment. Listen to him [Hess] and answer the question objectively, without personal comment or otherwise. Now, can you answer the question?"

By now Miller was so flustered and agitated that he continually interrupted Hess before his questions were complete; several of his premature responses had to be stricken from the record.

Dolan: "Ask the question again."

Hess: "Nowhere in the administrative record do you mention that this permit was being denied for lack of compliance with providing diving medical examination reports. In fact, Mr. Gentile testified that at considerable time and expense each of the proposed divers submitted these sorts of medical examinations. You just testified, however, that the absence of those medical examinations was another reason that you could give to deny the permit. My question is, why is that not in the administrative record anywhere? Why is that just becoming an issue now?"

Miller: "I think the lack of information in the proposal that would, we would go back to ask for additional information, ask him to take the medical compliance. I do not think it was disqualifying. What we are talking about is what disqualified his proposal. He has been insisting on diving to 230 feet on air when we have been insisting No. According to the standards that NOAA and the United States Navy has set, and the standards that NOAA follows as an Agency, you have to make a decision based on some standard. The standard just happens to be the U.S. Navy decompression chambers."

Now, through some form of convoluted logic and ungrammatical sentence structure, we were back to decompression chambers.

Miller talked himself around so many circles that he even claimed that I could not have photographed nearby wrecks west of the *Monitor* (where I testified the conditions of weather, current, and visibility were similar) because, "That would be pretty close to the axis of the Gulf Stream, or right on the other side. You cannot be west of the *Monitor*. It is too deep. You are off the continental shelf."

Land is west of the *Monitor*. The continental shelf is east.

We were holding in abeyance the crucial fact that added icing to our case. We wanted to trump Wells with it because he was NOAA's diving coordinator, but the judge jumped the gun and brought the fact to light serendipitously and, in the event, far more dramatically.

Unlike civil and criminal courts, in an administrative law court the judge is permitted to question witnesses for his own clarification, and for clarification of the administrative record. After Hess excused Miller, the judge exercised that privilege.

Dolan: "You have testified to a number of other people, or organizations. You ran through the dates very fast. I would appreciate it if you would just give me a list to the best of your recollection of who, what, when where dove on the *Monitor*, to the best of your knowledge."

As sanctuary manager, this was a question that Miller should have been able to answer with authority. "Diving on the *Monitor*?"

Dolan: "Yes, regardless how it was done."

Miller reeled off dates and summaries in chronological order. In 1977, divers conducted stereo photography. The purpose of the 1979 expedition was "An archaeological excavation in the forward portion of the ship, in the captain's cabin. The divers went through an intensive diving medical exam at Duke University."

Dolan: "Did they do photography?"

Miller: "Extensive."

Dolan: "Where is that?"

Miller: "NOAA made a film of it. It has been widely distributed through the school system and libraries. It is in the NOAA library and in over 200 public publications, I'd say, based on – "

Dolan: "Okay. Move on to the next after 1979, next

expedition."

Miller then described the 1983 expedition.

Dolan: "Was there photographic data collected there?"

Miller: "Everything is always photodocumented on site." About the 1985 expedition, he said, "We towed instrumentation through the water column. No diving." About the 1987 expedition: "We used a remotely operated vehicle called a Deep Drone. It is basically a platform from which we operate. It had all the instrumentation on board that we could take photographs without any concern of decompression or any of those other concerns. The photography was quite good."

(What happened to zero visibility and totally black pictures?)

Dolan: "Now, that is the extent of the examinations of this wreck that you aware of?"

Miller hesitated, glanced at me, then said, "That is correct."

Dolan (after a few more questions and answers): "To your knowledge, has anyone ever dove on that wreck from the surface down, scuba diving?"

Miller: "No, sir."

Hess leaped to his feet as soon as the judge dismissed Miller. "Your Honor, I would like to bring to your attention a deficiency in Mr. Miller's testimony. Specifically, when you asked him had there ever been any scuba diving in the Monitor National Marine Sanctuary." He cited the 1983 Management Plan that the judge had in front of him. "Your Honor, if you would allow me. 'R.V. Calypso, June 9-14, 1979. Sponsoring agency Cousteau Society. Participants, Cousteau Society. Purpose to photograph the *Monitor* with movie film to be used as a segment in a one hour television special.' . . . In sum, divers using scuba descended to 210 feet and made a decompression dive on the *Monitor*."

Miller had committed the unpardonable sin of courtroom conduct: he had not only committed perjury, but he had lied directly to the judge.

Dolan to Miller: "You are familiar with that?"

Miller: "Well, I was not involved with that, and I had forgotten about that expedition."

(Miller was not only one of the reviewers of the Cousteau Society permit application, but he had assisted in redrafting the proposal.)

Miller: "NOAA actually issued a permit for that expedition."

Dolan (astounded by the revelation): "That appears to be a standard scuba dive that was made."

Miller: "Well, they used the Jacques Cousteau research vessel. I believe it was on container scuba air."

Dolan: "Again, this exhibit says, 'Divers using standard scuba equipment to send it 210 feet to the wreck, staying 10 minutes at that depth, then ascending at given rates, and decompressing at approximately . . . ' and going on. They had a permit to do that?"

Miller was forced to admit, "That is correct."

The rest is anticlimactic, but for the record I want to show that Miller did not stop perjuring himself just because he had been caught in that monstrous lie. When Hess asked about my mixed gas proposals that were still pending, Miller said, "I have never received a mixed gas proposal from Mr. Gentile."

Hess refuted this blatant lie immediately. When he produced copies of the various proposals, Dolan asked Miller, "Are you aware of that?"

Miller: "Oh, yes."

Hess: "So you have received applications from Gary Gentile to dive the *Monitor* on mixed gas?"

Miller (grudgingly): "Right."

The witness was excused. NOAA's courtroom antics did not end until 8:30 that night.

Distemper

At this point it is important for the reader to understand that NOAA's *Monitor* skullduggery was not an isolated event. It stretched from the bottom of the barrel (Miller and Wells) to the top of the heap (Tweedt and Uravitch) and invaded all levels in between. NOAA's insidious actions constituted an administrative *mindset*.

This self-centered and anti-public sentiment may have originated with illegal and contemptuous usurpation and subjugation of the *Monitor*, but once NOAA learned how deftly it could circumvent or violate the law without suffering recriminations, its all-consuming temper quickly escalated to a perverse pathology that tended to subvert civil service in deference to self-gratification. The remainder of this book will demonstrate how pervasive this arrogance has become, and how NOAA's initiative to use and abuse the citizenry for its own nefarious purposes keeps growing worse.

NOAA treats the natural resources that are under its "protection" as possessions on which to capitalize. Its principal watchword is "exploitation."

Case Closed

Dolan ordered NOAA "to furnish copies of the application for permit and the diving plan relating to the Cousteau expedition." What I had been requesting for five years, Dolan got within a week. He sent photocopies to Hess and me: more than a hundred pages of correspondence, inter-office memoranda, formal proposals, cruise logs, and follow-up dispatches. Little wonder that Miller had refused my requests, for the evidence was exceptionally damning.

Not only had the Cousteau Society been granted a permit for non-research purposes (photography only), but it had received the permit within 30 days of submission! Worse yet but, as noted above, the review committee of which Miller was a part helped to redraft it. There was no stipulation that necessitated medical evaluations of the divers.

In her 29-page closing brief, Luipold made light of the Cousteau expedition by devoting only four sentences to it. She added insult to injury with regard to NOAA's year-long procrastination in handling each of my several applications, by writing, "the stately pace of bureaucratic decision making is well known."

She also resorted to NOAA's usual transgressive method of dealing with embarrassing issues: she submitted a "Motion to Extend Time for Decision and Proposed Schedule for Submissions," claiming, "this extension is necessary to provide each party a reasonable opportunity to submit exceptions to the recommended decision, and supporting reasons for such exceptions."

This was an extraordinary admission on her part. Not only was she trying to further retard the stately pace of the administrative process, but even before the judge had time to collate the voluminous material at his disposal, she already knew that she would want to make exceptions to his ruling.

Luipold did not get her extension. Judge Dolan duly issued his decision on November 30, three days late due to an unavoidable delay in the shipment of pertinent documents. He declared, "The inordinate delay in the processing of appellant's requests is not explained by Agency Counsel's expression respecting 'the stately pace of bureaucratic decision making.' the situation here is better described in the presidential phrase about being left twisting in the breeze."

Dolan: "I recommend that the Agency determination to deny the permit requested be reversed."

Not only that, but there was an unexpected bonus. In addition to concluding that "the standards adopted for Agency use by NOAA and/or the United States Navy may not be imposed upon the public sector merely because the proposed activity is to be carried out within a Marine Sanctuary," he also remarked for all posterity that "the appellant and other staged decompression divers are not sport or novice divers. Their training, experience, and certifications reflect a substantially greater proficiency."

This pronouncement established a legal precedent that could be cited in future cases in which the government sought to ban an activity because of safety considerations.

Dolan then quoted the Idaho Law Review: "A venturesome minority will always be eager to get off on their own, and no obstacles should be placed in their path; let them take risks, for Godsake, let them get lost, sunburnt, stranded, drowned, eaten by bears, buried alive under avalanches – that is the right and privilege of any free American."

Immediate Aftermath

Luipold jumped a rung in the administrative ladder and convinced NOAA's Deputy Assistant Administrator John Carey to grant a 30-day extension. Her 21-page brief in this regard contradicted the meaning of the word.

She did not find a few exceptions to Dolan's recommendations; she took exception to each and every one of them. For instance, she claimed that safety considerations had "evolved" since the Cousteau expedition. This was jingoistic legalese for NOAA's indulgence in arbitrarily changing the rules to suit its purpose. Yet she submitted no documentation to substantiate her allegation.

Luipold pooh-poohed Dolan's admonition that Wells had an "unalterably closed mind on matters critical to the disposition of the case" by claiming that "near-total control of access to the wreck site is considered necessary."

She also tried to introduce new evidence: archaeological research guidelines, which outlined the format for the submission of research applications. Hess was quick to note that I had repeatedly requested these very same guidelines since 1984: "The appellant cannot be held to standards set forth in a document maliciously denied him."

Carey tried to wiggle out of the corner that his subordinates had painted him into. Although the archaeological "guidelines do not appear to have been cited by the Agency in its denial for Agency decisions, nor do they seem to have been made available to Mr. Gentile when he was preparing his applications . . . I have chosen for the purposes of this case to treat them as part of the record."

Carey was forced to admit some damning evidence, to wit: ""There are no internal NOAA procedural requirements for handling reviews or requests for approval."

And: "The NOAA Diving Regulations are in fact internal agency guidelines on diving safety. . . . Nowhere does it say that these diving safety rules apply to non-NOAA activities or divers or that they are binding on applications to dive in Marine Sanctuaries."

Carey was also forced to admit that the NOAA Diving Manual clearly stated, "The recommendations and guidelines contained in this Manual are not intended to replace judgement [sic], expert opinion or the application of knowledge and technology that may become available after publication."

Finally: "Mr. Gentile and others who can demonstrate similar levels of fitness and experience should be allowed to employ Mr. Gentile's proposed diving methods under permits granted pursuant to these research proposals."

NOAA's public affairs office played down the case in a sterilized press release, which stated simply that NOAA had "reversed a previous decision," as if the longstanding denial of public access was a matter of small potatoes, and not a monumental substantive dispute that was contested by a considerable amount of expensive, high-visibility litigation. This was typical NOAA pretense.

Nonetheless, Carey condescended to grant the issuance of Conditional Permit MNMS-01-90 to me. The abbreviation means that this was the first permit to be issued for 1990; it was signed into effect on February 12, 1990.

The permit was conditional in that additional information was requested on my photographic objectives, and that my proposals had yet to be sent to "appropriate state and Federal preservation agencies" for approval. I thought that this was yet another gambit to ultimately deny the permit on some trumped-up grounds.

I was shocked to learn that the head of the Advisory Council of Historic Preservation, which was in charge of reviewing my proposals, did not even know the location of the *Monitor*. She thought it was in Florida!

In the meantime, NOAA denied my proposal to drift

over the wreck on a weighted line "because, based on our knowledge of physical conditions in the Sanctuary, e.g., turbidity and cloudiness of the water, we do not believe proposal 5 will result in photos or videos of even minimal quality, clarity, or usefulness."

NOAA's beliefs were irrelevant. Such an expedition would not cost NOAA anything, would not damage the resource, and would not violate any of NOAA's safety concerns. Why should NOAA care if I wanted to waste my money on such a venture? This was just another example of NOAA's unreasonable attitude toward what the agency believed to be unwarranted invasion and public incursion into its privately held territory.

All my mixed gas proposals were also approved. Along with my air dives, I could – and did – conduct some mixed gas dives on the *Monitor* that summer.

NOAA Absurdities Never End

I will not endeavor to describe the successes of my *Monitor* expedition. I want to touch only upon those issues which, in keeping with the theme of this book, demonstrate NOAA's lies, deceptions, and abuses: with regard to administrative misconduct as well as to failures in logic.

The first instance of failed logic occurred before my expedition left land. Ervan Garrison, NOAA's newly appointed archaeologist, called me on the phone and urged me to place rulers on the hull in order to provide scale for my photos and video footage.

As an archaeology major in college, I knew that Garrison's suggestion made perfect sense.

Uravitch "overruled" this accepted scientific procedure because it would entail "touching" the wreck in the most literal definition of the word. "Touching, possessing, moving or injuring, or attempting to touch, possess, move or injure, the Wreck, its artifacts or any other Sanctuary resource is prohibited."

Strike one against the cause of science: the cause that NOAA was supposed to support.

This ban was ridiculous in light of the activities that

NOAA conducted on its 1979 expedition, in which heavy metal grids were placed on the fragile structure, in which divers trod on the hull and dragged umbilical hoses all over the wreck, scraping and snagging, and in which extensive excavations were made into the body of the hull.

In the event, the NOAA observer who accompanied my expedition inspected the divers' wetsuits after every dive, in an attempt to discover a speck of rust or a smudge of marine encrustation on the neoprene. It found none.

Additionally, NOAA bracketed my expedition with a pair of its own expeditions, the purpose of which was "to document the site prior to and after this year's research activities." NOAA was hoping to dig up dirt (in a figurative sense) that could be used as ammunition to deny future scuba diving permits, as well as to implement $50,000 fines. NOAA lost on both counts.

Instead, NOAA confirmed the very circumstance that I had been warning it about for years, but for which it refused to take action: irreparable damage from anchors and scallop dredges. NOAA ignored my recommendation to mark the wreck site with a buoy as a way to ward off fishing boats. Now, NOAA found that the wreck had sustained considerable damage since its previous survey: the collapse of the midship bulkhead, a portion of the lower hull, and adjacent supporting frames and hull plates; the disappearance of several feet of the armor belt; plus bent frames and cracks in hull plates and the armor belt.

NOAA's ambush had backfired. Instead of incriminating me, it underscored my complaints about NOAA's stupidity and lack of scientific acumen.

If my fellow divers and I had damaged the wreck in the slightest amount, I have no doubt that NOAA would have advertised that fact on billboards. But after NOAA ascertained that we did no damage whatsoever, the truth of the situation was withheld from the media.

On a different front, NOAA's Advisory Council of Historic Preservation complained bitterly about imposed time constraints. Whereas NOAA received approval of my proposal nearly three months before deeming to let me know about it, NOAA submitted its entrapment proposal only two days prior to the onset of its boat's departure, then proceeded immediately to conduct the expedition without the Council's approval.

According to the Council's complaint, "The Council is very concerned that NOAA's 'normal' way of doing business is becoming an expectation of expedited review."

On-site Harassment

On my expedition's first day at sea, NOAA-O complained that the charter boat flew a diver-down flag but not an alpha flag. The flags signal slightly different meanings: the diver-down flag is required by dive boats to alert nearby mariners that a diver is in or under the water, and that they must not approach closer than 100 feet for fear of running over the diver; the alpha flag is required by vessels whose movements are restricted by, for example, being at anchor or without motive power. When either of these flags is flown, the signal is not mere suggestion, but law that is enforced by the U.S. Coast Guard. No vessel may approach a vessel that is flying either flag without express permission from the captain of the flag-flying vessel.

NOAA-O insisted that I fly an alpha flag, so that night I bought one from the local marine supply store. The next day we flew both of them, one atop the other. I was conducting a drift decompression next to the boat when I heard the high-pitched whine of an approaching speedboat. I glanced up just in time to see the sleek hull of a cigarette boat zoom by practically overhead, its spinning propeller blades only a few feet above my head. The speedboat left a rooster-tail wake that rocked the dive boat, shook the divers in the water, and stretched taut the surface-supply oxygen hoses that we were breathing from. The regulator was nearly yanked out of my mouth. If anyone lost his grip on the down-line and lost buoyancy control, he could have been chopped like suey by

Subterfuge 101   37

the propeller, or paralyzed for life by missing decompression.

I was trapped under water by a decompression ceiling that exceeded an hour, so I could not ascend to the surface to see what was going on: a good thing, as the outlaw speedboat made another close pass. All I could do was stay deep, hang on tight, and let lunatic events unfold.

The boat belonged to the National Marine Fisheries Service (a branch of NOAA). It was operated by a Marine Fisheries officer, and it was transporting an armed NOAA enforcement agent who had been called to the scene – by, it later developed, the NOAA observer who was on my charter boat at the time.

After making his high-speed passes, the officer requested permission by radio to board the *Quiet Waters.* Captain Roger Huffman denied the request on the grounds of safety: standard operating procedure in a situation of this nature, when the location of divers could not be accurately ascertained, and when those divers might surface anywhere at any moment. Huffman requested that the agent belay boarding until after the divers were safely aboard.

The NOAA agent found this unacceptable. He insisted that we prepare to be boarded.

Gene Peterson acted as diving safety officer whenever I was in the water. His job was to oversee topside support, ensure safe conditions, and act in my stead as liaison with NOAA-O. Peterson was also a Coast Guard licensed ocean operator. As the speedboat approached, he got on the radio, explained the circumstances, and *demanded* that the boat maintain the safe distance that was prescribed by law. Quite an argument ensued.

The NOAA agent proclaimed arrogantly that NOAA law enforcement activities overrode obedience to common sense, Coast Guard regulations, and international law. He claimed that we were interlopers in a National Marine Sanctuary: not true, because by this time we had drifted outside the sanctuary border.

Peterson absolutely forbid the boat to approach because it would compromise the safety of decompressing divers. He appealed to the NOAA observer. After all, if there was already one NOAA representative onboard – one who had in hand a permit that sanctioned the project – why did another one have to interfere?

NOAA-O should have been the prime interlocutor in this dialogue, yet it refused to take part in the dispute that it had created.

The Marine Fisheries speedboat drew close. The NOAA agent positioned himself on the bow. Gene stood on the gunwale and shouted him off. The thick fiberglass bow of the speedboat rammed the wooden hull of the *Quiet Waters*. Splinters flew, but fortunately no planks were sprung. The agent leaped aboard. He put his hand on his pistol and made threatening gestures. NOAA-O stood by quietly and watched it all happen. Peter Hess captured the entire escapade on videotape.

The NOAA agent claimed that he had been tipped off about our diving operations on the *Monitor*. This took no amount of detective work; I had published the dates in the Local Notice to Mariners. Besides, his informer stood less than ten feet away from him. The two NOAA agents conversed. After half an hour of small talk, the NOAA agent called back his boat.

Now Peterson tried to prevent him from leaving, again because of the possibility of running over decompressing divers. Steve Cummings, support diver that day, brought down a slate with a message to stay deep while the speedboat returned for the pickup.

By the time I got out of the water, the NOAA agent was gone. I lashed into NOAA-O with loud incriminations, making sure to mention that NOAA had violated the very alpha flag that NOAA-O had forced me to buy.

NOAA-O's comment? "I'm only here as an observer."

Interagency Whitewash

Both Gene Peterson and I filed official complaints with the Coast Guard – which NOAA likes to refer to as its "partner" – about the NOAA agent's flagrant disregard for safety during the boarding incident. Wild and irresponsible boat operation is supposed to be taken seriously, especially when human lives are endangered, but in this case the Coast Guard responded by addressing NOAA directly:

"The Coast Guard does not have the authority to investigate allegations of negligent vessel operation by another federal agency. Therefore, I have notified the complainant that his letter has been forwarded to you for investigation of the incident."

Asking NOAA to investigate its own irresponsibility is like asking Jack the Ripper to be his own judge and jury. The outcome was predictable: a total whitewash.

NOAA's Spendthrift Measure

On my first dive to the *Monitor* I discovered an intact glass lantern globe in the stern debris field. I videotaped and snapped still photos of the artifact. I told NOAA-O about the find, and offered to retrieve it before it was broken or swept away by the current.

NOAA-O declined my help. After my expedition ended, NOAA chartered a large surface support at the cost of $10,000 per day, and spent two days recovering the item by means of a remotely operated vehicle. A simple job that I could have done for free. Instead, it cost American taxpayers $20,000.

The NOAA Merry-Go-Round

The day after I got home from the People's Expedition, as I called the photo trip that I organized, I submitted a permit application to photograph the *Monitor* in 1991. I did this with such immediacy not because of an overzealous desire to ensure my return, but due to comments that were made by NOAA-O and the NOAA law enforcement agent who boarded the boat.

Several times throughout the project NOAA-O alluded to plans in the works to rewrite sanctuary regulations in order to preclude public access in the future.

When the NOAA agent boarded the boat, Hess informed him that we had a permit to dive on the *Monitor*. The agent replied, "Yeah, well, we're gonna see that no one ever does again."

I reasoned that by submitting a permit application before any such action could be taken, my permit could not be revoked retroactively. I changed the date on my computer file and printed an identical version of the application that had already won in court.

It was important to send the message to NOAA that the issues at stake were not forgotten, that public access to the sanctuary must be guaranteed forever, and that future applicants must not be put through the bureaucratic ringer the way I had been.

This time NOAA took only six weeks to *deny* my Twelfth Proposal for Performing Underwater Photography on the USS *Monitor*. The denial letter consisted of only four sentences, two of which were introductory. "Permits are only issued for research or salvage operations (15 CFR # 924.5). It has been determined that your proposal does not come within the scope of permitted activity under # 924.5 and is therefore denied."

This was the same evil scheme that NOAA had invoked numerous times over previous six years: whenever I satisfied one demand, NOAA created another one to justify denial. I had overcome the safety pretext, so now NOAA claimed that photography did not qualify as research – although, when NOAA took pictures of the wreck it *did* qualify. In other words, only private sector photography did not qualify.

No intelligent reader can fail to grasp NOAA's true motivation. Once again, if there was any doubt that the original safety dispute was anything but bureaucratic chicanery, this latest denial demonstrated superbly NOAA's true intent.

Rather than being honestly relieved about the resolution of safety and liability issues, NOAA hunkered down and conjured a different way of excusing denial on as-yet uncontested grounds. NOAA may even have had *more* than one joker up its collective sleeve; perhaps it was playing only one card at a time, and keeping others in reserve for future courtroom go-arounds: a continuation of its gimmick of creating new demands whenever

I satisfied a previous one.

Concurrent with my denial, NOAA filed a notice in the Federal Register to revise "site management conditions" as another way to deny public access – despite the larger context of the MPRSA "to enhance public awareness" and "to facilitate all public and private use of the marine environment." If NOAA got its way, the *Monitor* would continue to be an exclusive club for NOAA members only. Others need not apply.

NOAA had nothing to lose by going to court. All its expenses were paid by the taxpayer. The only downside for not prevailing was that it would be forced to do the job that it was mandated by Congress to do: allow the citizenry to enter is private playground.

The November 2, 1990 hearing was every bit as costly, complicated, and time consuming as the previous one, and every bit as meaningful. Court convened in the same room we had used before, with the same judge.

Another Day in Court

This was my third lawsuit against NOAA. Having lost the federal case and won the previous administrative case, I was batting 500.

Hess made the opening statement: "Mr. Gentile reapplied for a permit to continue his research on the *Monitor* with another expedition in the summer of 1991. This agency, prior to reviewing even one frame of video footage or one photographic still resulting from the 1990 expedition, determined without any consultation with the permit applicant that his work did not constitute research. The critical issue, then, in this proceeding is what constitutes research."

Whereas before I produced three expert witnesses to testify about modern deep-diving practices in the wreck-diving community, this time I produced two: a recreational diving symposium organizer and an archaeologist.

Brian Skerry was president of the Boston Sea Rovers. He testified about my past participation in the club's annual symposium, and my next scheduled appearance in which I was going to feature slides and video footage from the People's Expedition. With an attendance of several thousand people, this manifested a prime example of "enhancing public awareness."

Dan Koski-Karell was an archaeologist who conducted the proton magnetometer survey on the People's Expedition. He also advised me and my fellow divers on proper archaeological method with regard to establishing the provenance of artifacts (particularly the lantern globe), and the value of sequential photography to demonstrate the process of deterioration. He also laid the groundwork for conducting corrosion studies and ultrasonic thickness tests which, while not part of the present proposal, were intended as future objectives once we got the stumbling block of NOAA's obstructionism and exclusivity out of the way.

NOAA's first witness was Susan Durden, the newly appointed "Regional Manager for the Atlantic and Great Lakes Regions in the Sanctuaries and Reserves Division, previously named Marine Estuary Management." Her position in the NOAA hierarchy was a step above sanctuary manager. She readily admitted that issuing another permit to me "would effectively set a precedent for recreational diving," and that "it would be very hard for us to . . . control access to the site."

She also admitted that NOAA used photographs and videotape "as a tool for scientific research."

To this admission, Hess responded, "So your pictures are good for scientific research, but ours aren't?" After Durden gave a typically obfuscating bureaucratic answer, Hess elaborated, "Then you do agree that some photographs and some videos may be useful in scientific research?"

Durden: "Yes."

Hess followed this line of questioning to its logical conclusion by asking how NOAA had determined that *my* photographs and videotape possessed no scientific merit when NOAA had never seen them. For this she had no answer. Yet she admitted that my permit application had been denied without reviewing the images.

Subterfuge 101

The reader must understand that a condition of my permit was that I submit to NOAA, at my own expense, duplicate copies of every photograph and all videotape footage that my fellow divers and I shot: including images that would normally be discarded in the editing process as substandard; the videotape footage could not be edited. I collected and duplicated every photographic still and every foot of videotape, had everything copied, and forwarded it to NOAA, but by that time my Twelfth Proposal had already been denied.

I showed some of the videotape footage in court in support of my case. Despite Miller's dire warning about zero visibility – one of his testimonial exaggerations in the previous case – we had exceptional visibility: 100 feet or better. My photographs and videotape footage showed the *Monitor* in startling clarity.

In relation to my Twelfth Proposal, Durden made the astounding remark, "I believe that this could potentially cause irreparable harm to the resource."

Hess asked for elucidation: "Would you say that, from your review of the evidence that we presented, the videotape in particular, that there was in fact no evidence of any harm whatsoever to the resource by the particular Applicant's photography?"

In addition to my photography and videography, NOAA had its own images from its follow-up expedition to recover the glass lantern globe. NOAA's footage showed no damage from free-swimming scuba divers.

Durden: "I don't believe, from the things we looked at today, that I could in any way make a statement relating to that."

Hess: "Well, let's put it this way: If you were to compare the sorts of activities which Mr. Gentile conducted this past summer with the activities that were conducted in 1979, which entailed walking through the wreck, dredging it and laying metal grids on top of it, wouldn't it be fair to say that that sort of activity by NOAA had a far greater potential for harming the wreck?"

Durden: "As a non-scientist, I also would not attempt to make a judgment on that."

NOAA's other witness was Ervan Garrison, the NOAA archaeologist who had recommended the placement of rulers on the wreck as a way to provide scale for my photos. When NOAA's higher-ups overruled his recommendation, it went a long way toward ensuring that my images would have less scientific value than might otherwise have been the case.

In other words, NOAA intentionally established the rules of conduct in order to reduce the value of my images. This was proof that NOAA was less interested in archaeology of the site than it was in controlling it.

For the record, Hess submitted a NOAA document entitled "Suggested Photographic and Videotaping Priorities for the July 1990 Reconnaissance," which NOAA created in June after the first of its two-part sting operation. Based on the June observations, it indicated certain areas of the wreck that should be photographed in greater detail.

Hess: "Was a copy of this document ever provided to Mr. Gentile, who you knew was going out to photograph the *Monitor* in the beginning of July 1990?"

Garrison: "No."

Hess: "Didn't you think it was important for Mr. Gentile to know what the photographic and videographic priorities were on the *Monitor*?"

Garrison: "I don't think that we need to presuppose what his priorities are, that our priorities are the same."

Thus NOAA ignored a prime opportunity to suggest that I create imagery that could have proved valuable to the resource. Had NOAA made such a suggestion, it would have been tacit to admitting that my image making was archaeologically useful. This was more proof of NOAA's ulterior motive of control, which superseded its interest in scientific research.

To Hess's question about whether "the NOAA expedition was to get before and after shots of the wreck to see what, if any, impact the 'sport divers' had on the *Monitor*," Garrison said simply, "Yes."

Concerning the disparate treatment of permit applicants, NOAA initiated its own 1990 proposals over the telephone, and did not submit a formal written proposal until all the bugs had been worked out. As Garrison phrased it, "You are almost the judge and jury."

Almost?

When asked to explain how photographs were used as a tool in archaeological research, Garrison replied, "It is very important for documenting the site. Archaeology is a very destructive science and it tends to destroy that which it studies so that our photographs and drawings and any image that you can have of the excavation or study is warranted."

Hess referred to photographs that I took of the engine, brass hand-wheel, and revolution counter – all of which were unique. "We you able to, with your submersible, pass through the engine room of the *Monitor*?"

Garrison: "No."

Hess referred to the written report in which I described my penetration under the hull where it was supported by the displaced turret. Hess: "Were you able to circumnavigate between the turret and the collapsing hull or deck plating of the *Monitor*?"

Garrison: "Obviously not."

Thus we established that free-swimming scuba divers had been able to reach places, make observations, take photographs, and shoot videotape that NOAA had been unable to do by means of cameras that were mounted on removely operated vehicles (ROV's).

The last and very significant point that Hess made concerned NOAA's future budgetary constraints, making it "unlikely that there would be a visit to the *Monitor* Sanctuary by NOAA next summer."

Garrison: "It is entirely possible, but I can't speak to it with any certainty."

In light of my permit denial, no NOAA trip meant no photographs at all the following year. As Hess put it, "If Mr. Gentile were to go out there and get images in 1991 similar to those that he got in 1990, and these were the only images taken of the *Monitor*, would that not be . . . more beneficial for the long-term study and management of the Sanctuary than their complete absence?"

Garrison would allow only, "It might be."

My batting average dropped from 500 to 333.

The ultimate irony came afterward, when NOAA eventually got around to reviewing my photographs and videotape footage. NOAA found my images so stunning that it requested permission to publish them in brochures and periodicals. They chose the most dramatic image for a 2-foot-by-3-foot poster that promoted the Monitor NMS, and which was distributed for free to schools and libraries.

Yet NOAA did not reverse its position about the merit of private sector photography.

Lawsuit the Fourth

By losing the case I gained support. Congressional support.

NOAA's bad press put the agency under Congressional scrutiny. Hess and I aided and abetted the cause by keeping our respective representatives fully informed of ongoing events: Robert Borski (mine) and Tom Carper (his). Also in the loop was Norman Lent, the representative of Howard Klein, who was executive director of the American Sport Divers Association. Both Carper and Lent held seats on the Merchant Marine and Fisheries Committee, which controlled NOAA's purse strings.

The next proposal differed radically from the previous twelve. In order to break association with my name and my photographic objectives, we submitted the permit application in Hess's name, and changed the objective from photographic to scientific.

Hess proposed to conduct two disparate corrosion studies, and he proposed to continue these tests on an annual basis. "Discrete areas of the shipwreck will be targeted for non-destructive galvanic measurements which are intended to indicate the rate of corrosion occurring there, and ultrasonic measurements which ought to indicate the percentage of true iron (as opposed to organic encrustation and overlying corrosion product) remaining at that particular location."

For comparative photography to be more effective,

we asked NOAA to forego the ban on "touching" the wreck so we could place rulers and plastic grids on the encrusted structure. Furthermore, we wanted to "fan" sand off partially exposed artifacts in order to photograph them better; then, rescue those artifacts that were in danger of being lost or destroyed by environmental factors.

This proposal was a tough nut for NOAA to crack. Each research objective possessed valid scientific merit. Pursuant to a FOIA request, I learned that sanctuary manager Irene Byron (who took control after Miller's dismissal) wrote to Durden, "Mr. Hess's proposal contains goals from NOAA's past expedition operation plans."

To wit: the corrosion engineers who performed the 1987 studies for NOAA specifically recommended the need to "conduct diver-assisted ultrasonic thickness (UT) testing at representative locations on the armor belt, turret, and other areas of interest."

The NOAA censor redacted the following and most damaging sentences, and it took nearly a year to obtain an unredacted copy of Byron's memorandum: "I will assume Mr. Hess will appeal a denial of his proposal and point this out. It can be defended that we have changed our management goals most notably in the rejection of complete recovery of the wreck."

This was additional proof that NOAA considered scientific research on the *Monitor* to be subservient to maintaining absolute control over its dominion.

Instead of denying the permit, on July 23, 1991, Durden wrote seven pages of carefully worded comments that criticized point by point every single one of the proposed objectives. She ended by stating her willingness to "accept modifications to your proposal if you wish to pursue this."

I had already gone this route with Miller, and recognized her dalliance for what it was: a way to consign the proposal to limbo. No denial meant no hearing. Already Durden's stratagem resulted in missing the 1991 diving season, thus giving NOAA another year in which to close any loopholes that might allow the public to have access to the wreck.

Hess filed for an administrative appeal anyway.

Durden claimed that not only had she not denied the permit, but that she did not have the authority to deny it. This was ridiculous considering that Miller, the lowest totem on the pole, had denied my permits: first single-handedly, then by conspiring with Wells. Furthermore, NOAA had successfully defended Miller's authority to do so in federal court.

NOAA fumbled with this catch-22 for three months before issuing an "official" denial. A month later, NOAA claimed that, although it had not done so before, it was required to notify the public of hearings via the Federal Register. "The regulations also state that the hearing should be held 'no later than 30 days' on receipt of the request for an appeal. The time frame in the regulations does not allow sufficient time for notice of the public."

This paradox was another of NOAA's machinations. NOAA based the date of "receipt" not at the time of the first request (in July), or even the second (in August), but on the issuance of NOAA's ultimate denial letter, at which time NOAA automatically filed for an appeal in Hess's behalf. It must have made sense to someone!

In the event, the hearing was not held until February 13, 1992: more than six months after Hess's first request, and more than two months after NOAA's official denial. The result of this inordinate delay allowed time enough for me to appeal the FOIA request in which Byron's incriminating statements had been redacted, and to obtain full disclosure.

In the meantime, however, NOAA conjured up a joker to trump our ace. In a word: methodology.

Despite the testimony of our corrosion engineer, David Johnson, NOAA claimed that the research design was incomprehensible to the only two people who wrote opinions about the proposal: Byron and Garrison, neither of whom possessed the necessary expertise nor sought it out.

Johnson testified that free-swimming divers could perform the corrosion tests with a delicacy that was not possible at the ramming speed of the remotely operated vehicle that NOAA employed.

Despite a day-long hearing and testimony that filled more than 300 pages of transcript, NOAA rested its case on semantics. NOAA wanted the proposal to contain separate paragraphs to distinguish "research design" from "methodology," so that both reviewers could differentiate one from the other without getting confused about which was which, and how much detail applied to each. This time, the putative lack of methodology was NOAA's sole rationale for denial.

The reader must be wondering what happened to Miller's "intricate system of research proposal review" in which "more than thirty recognized professionals in the fields of archaeology, oceanography, history and other related disciplines" were supposed to "critique and comment" on every proposal.

Certainly some of these so-called recognized professionals would have possessed the education, knowledge, intelligence, and background to distinguish research design from methodology, both of which were little more than different wordings of the same concept. Instead, NOAA relied on the incompetence of the only two individuals it assigned to review the proposal.

ALJ William Ogden ruled in favor of NOAA, and Carey confirmed the ruling.

The batting average went down to 250.

"They Came from Shangri-la"

NOAA's victory was Pyrrhic and short-lived.

I was fighting NOAA with a double-edged sword: one edge on the legal front, the other one on the political front.

Shortly before the fourth case went to trial, NOAA attended a budget hearing before the House Merchant Marine and Fisheries Committee, at which Congressional representative Norman Lent loudly criticized NOAA's mishandling of the *Monitor*.

The NOAA representative at that meeting characteristically professed complete ignorance of the entire issue of public access, claiming that the wreck was too deep for divers to reach. As I had dived on the wreck in 1990, either he lied in the hope of misleading the Committee, or his information was two years out of date.

Lent's persistence paved the way for further action.

As soon as Carper received word of Carey's ruling, he called NOAA to arrange a special meeting in his office: the lion calling the prey into his den. NOAA had no choice but to acquiesce to his demand; nor could NOAA forestall him the way it was used to forestalling me. The meeting was held less than two weeks after NOAA's ruling was issued.

I have no idea what was said at that meeting, but I did get some glimmerings from Carper's explanatory letter: "Much of our discussion focused on the process through which research permits were awarded. However, we also talked about the timeframe for the release of a revised management plan."

The revised management plan was nearly two years behind schedule. Coincidentally, if the reader wishes to believe in such coincidence, the rough draft was published and circulated for public comment one month after NOAA's meeting with Carper.

NOAA's procrastination worked to our advantage because, due to our lobbying efforts, the *newly* revised plan now contained language which conceded that access to the *Monitor* for non-research purposes – that is, for photographic and/or recreational purposes, such as simple sightseeing – was being considered.

Also coincidentally, one *week* after the meeting between Carper and NOAA, Hess received a phone call from a NOAA representative who said that, adverse ruling notwithstanding, NOAA was now willing to help to revise the latest proposal in order to meet "regulatory criteria."

Hess and I may have lost the battle, but ultimately we won the war.

X Marks the Spot

NOAA did not give in easily. Although the Congressional exchanges took place in April, bureaucratic foot-dragging withheld permit approval until July 22, 1992. If the delay was intended to prevent us from chartering a boat, procuring lodging, and acquiring personnel and equipment for an expedition that calendar year, the thinly veiled artful dodge failed.

We mounted an expedition for September.

In the meantime, while the *Monitor* shed another layer of rust and became a little less substantial, and while NOAA was performing legal gymnastics to keep American citizens from involvement with their maritime heritage, my worst fear was realized.

A fishing boat dropped anchor on an unmarked set of loran coordinates with a fathometer rise of fifteen feet. The anchor snagged wreckage, the anchor line went taut, and fishing lines went over the side. At 3 a.m., a Coast Guard patrol boat arrived and informed the skipper of the fishing vessel that he was hooked into the *Monitor*.

The skipper was ordered to weigh anchor and accompany the cutter to port, where a citation would be issued and a full report would be made. The anchor, however, was caught in the wreckage.

The vessel drove forward, drifted, maneuvered to the side, and drove forward again, all in a vain attempt to free the anchor from entrapment. The flukes were caught under the port armor belt, slightly forward of the displaced turret. When the anchor finally broke out of its entanglement, it dragged over the armor belt, along the hull adjacent to the engine room, and across the propeller shaft and skeg. It left deep red gouge marks where the steel flukes cut through the encrustation and exposed the naked, rusting iron.

The anchor also hooked the skeg hard enough to break the single attached leg of the A-frame from the underside of the after deck, displace the skeg to starboard, peel off the iron plating where the skeg was attached to the keel, and drop the now-unsupported skeg until the unattached leg of the A-frame came to rest on the seabed some five feet below.

This incident occurred because NOAA refused to mark the location of the sanctuary.

NOAA's knee-jerk action was *not* to install a warning buoy on the wreck so that mariners could avoid it, but to urge for stiff fines and increased surveillance: an enforcement mentality rather than a scientific or archaeological approach: more proof that NOAA's principal ambition was control rather than study and preservation.

As of this writing, more than two decades after this destructive incident, NOAA still has not marked the wreck site with a warning buoy.

Continued Access Difficulties

After eight years of litigation ending in Congressional intervention, at which time the law was laid down with finality, one might have thought that continued public access to the *Monitor* was assured. Such was not the case.

NOAA devised a permitting system that was so cumbersome and fraught with conditions that few people possessed the knowledge or tenacity to complete an application that satisfied NOAA's demands. Visitors were prohibited from diving on the site if their only reason for doing so was to appreciate the iconic shipwreck in person; they had to perform some kind of underwater work that NOAA considered useful: "useful" being a subjective concept that gave great latitude to NOAA in denying permits.

This meant in effect that visitors had to work without pay; worse, they had to pay for the privilege of working for NOAA. This was contrary to the purpose of the MPRSA.

In my subsequent proposals I stressed still photography and videography as ways to record the location of exposed artifacts. NOAA's employment of remotely operated vehicles (ROV's) prevented close approach to the wreck for fear of entangling the ROV's operating cables. These cables connected to ROV to the support vessel on the surface, but the catenary was always at risk of snagging on wreckage. An ROV could hover above the wreck or pass around its perimeter, but it could not settle down into the interior where small artifacts lay.

Despite NOAA's adversarial posture with regard to public access, my subsequent expeditions led to some interesting reversals in NOAA's attitude and priorities.

Bringing Home the Bacon

In 1993, I discovered a nest of U.S. Navy mustard bottles in a collapsing storage area of the *Monitor*. Some of these bottles were still corked and contained their nasty-smelling contents. I captured images of these bottles on film and videotape. The film had to be processed, and the images would not be available for weeks. But that night I showed the videotape footage to the new sanctuary manager, John Broadwater.

Broadwater made an on-the-spot executive decision that later must have turned the heads of his recalcitrant superiors in the NOAA hierarchy. As I had established provenance of the delicate glassware photographically, he asked me if I would forego my planned photographic objectives in order to use my precious bottom time to re-cover some of the artifacts: those that were most at risk of being lost or damaged by storms: upcoming hurri-canes and fierce winter northeasters.

I agreed. My team and I recovered a china dinner plate, a pair of brass oarlocks, and a handful of mustard bottles.

Armed with the existence and precise location of these military relics, in 1994 NOAA funded a $2 million dollar expedition to recover more artifacts from the same area. NOAA's method of retrieval was a submersible that was equipped with manipulator arms.

The expedition was a dismal failure.

NOAA probably has a plethora of excuses as to why the expedition failed to achieve its objective, but the bot-tom line is that not a single artifact was recovered. Two million dollars was poured down the drain with nothing to show for it.

On my expedition a few weeks later, Broadwater pleaded with me to recover more artifacts. By this time in the evolution of my photographic proposals, I had convinced NOAA to allow me to place grids consisting of lightweight PVC pipes at pre-selected locations on the wreck. Each length of plastic pipe was marked in twelve-inch increments that provided scale for the objects to be photographed and videotaped. I also placed plastic rulers next to individual items such as glass bottles.

My team and I had spent a great deal of time in preparing for the expedition: fitting out the pipe grids, choosing locations, pre-assigning jobs, and so on. We were already task-loaded. Nonetheless, we agreed to recover artifacts after we placed our grids and performed the initial still photography and videography in order to establish provenance.

The end result was that we recovered *dozens* of bottles: not just more mustard bottles but hair tonic bottles and pepper bottles of assorted shapes and sizes. Plus we obtained still and moving images of each item in situ prior to removal, with everything to scale and with its provenance firmly established.

As I noted near the beginning of this chapter, my grandmother used to say that the proof of the pudding was in the eating. I have proved my point sufficiently enough to satisfy all but the most jaded and contemptuous individuals: recreational divers can perform valuable services in rescuing relics that are in imminent peril from loss and obliteration as a result of inevitable shipwreck collapse.

NOAA could do no better with its multi-million dollar outlays. And sometimes it did worse.

Suppression

My original intention was to write a chapter about the *Monitor* and include it in *Shipwrecks of North Carolina: from Hatteras Inlet South.* I postponed publication in anticipation of reaching a conclusion to my protracted litigation with NOAA. Time languished as NOAA kept prolonging its assault against public access to the Civil War ironclad.

I wanted to get the book in print, and follow it soon

afterward with the companion volume: *Shipwrecks of North Carolina: from the Diamond Shoals North.* All the time I was conducting historical research on North Carolina shipwrecks, I was also expanding my *Monitor* research. During the course of the latter, I learned a great deal more about the *Monitor* than had ever been published in books about the subject; so much so that the reams of primary source materials that I accumulated over the years could no longer be reduced to the size of a chapter: not even one of mammoth proportions.

As a result of these factors, I decided to pull the *Monitor* chapter out of the Popular Dive Guide Series, proceed with publishing the two North Carolina volumes, and write a separate book that dealt exclusively with the *Monitor.*

I divided the resultant book into two halves. The first half included a biography of *Monitor* inventor John Ericsson, comprehensive descriptions of the *Monitor's* inception and construction, a minute by minute account of the Battle of Hampton Roads and its months-long aftermath, and a detailed description of the *Monitor's* loss in a storm off the coast of North Carolina. The second half was about my eight-year travail with NOAA.

Thus was born *Ironclad Legacy: Battles of the USS Monitor.* The two halves were approximately equal in length, and included all the battles of the famous ironclad: not just the naval battle against the CSS *Virginia* (ex-USS *Merrimac*), but the environmental battle against nature as well as the bureaucratic battle against NOAA.

The book was sold across the country in book stores, dive shops, and maritime museums. Two retailers that are of interest here are The Mariners' Museum in Newport News, Virginia, and the National Park Service, which administered the Cape Hatteras National Seashore. The Mariners' Museum sold *Ironclad Legacy* in its gift shop. The NPS sold the book in two museum gift shops on the Outer Banks of North Carolina: the Wright Brothers National Memorial, in Kill Devil Hills; and the Cape Hatteras Lighthouse, in Hatteras.

These museums were prime locations that related

directly to the subject matter of the book: Newport News was located a few miles from the site of the famous Battle of Hampton Roads; the Outer Banks was located alongside the Diamond Shoals, where the *Monitor* sank.

By the time NOAA entreated me to rescue artifacts that it had been unable to recover, NOAA was expanding its association with The Mariners' Museum. NOAA donated money to enlarge the facilities, with the ultimate goal of designating the museum as the location of the main *Monitor* exhibit. Eventually, millions of dollars of NOAA financing resulted in a partnership in which NOAA was the principal shareholder of the *Monitor* exhibit.

After NOAA assumed corporate control, The Mariners' Museum stopped stocking *Ironclad Legacy* for sale to the public.

NOAA entered into a similar arrangement with the National Park Service. NOAA allowed the NPS to display *Monitor* artifacts in the Cape Hatteras Lighthouse museum. Afterward, the NPS ceased selling *Ironclad Legacy* at both its Outer Banks museum gift shops.

The Invisible Man

In February 2013, NOAA released its "Monitor National Marine Sanctuary Final Management Plan and Environmental Assessment." The following statement appears on page 44: "In 1990, for the first time, NOAA issued research permits to private dive groups who dove to the *Monitor* using conventional scuba equipment."

This statement is part lie and part deception. The lie is that it neglected to reference the permit that NOAA issued to the Cousteau Society in 1979.

The deception relates to the circumstances under which NOAA "permitted" members of the public to dive on the wreck. The way the statement is worded, the reader is led to believe that NOAA willingly advocated scuba diving on the *Monitor*, as an act of altruism; instead of having been forced to tolerate public access by the order of a judge in a lawsuit which NOAA hotly contested but lost. Missing is all mention of NOAA's consistently hostile and adversarial attitude and conduct, and six years of NOAA's heated obstructionist maneuvering to prevent the very activity that it now takes credit for initiating – and which for two more years NOAA tried its damnedest to prohibit.

NOAA's duplicity goes deeper than the *Monitor*. In the Final Management Plan, the phrases "maritime heritage" and "cultural heritage" appear in literally *scores* of places. The Plan stresses time and time again the need to promote awareness of the *Monitor's* unique history. The Plan goes as far as to articulate an Education Action Plan, whose avowed purpose is to educate the public about all activities relating to the *Monitor*.

Yet NOAA has gone to incredible lengths to expurgate all knowledge and awareness of its intractable efforts to thwart public access to the wreck site. None of its current publications mentions the bitter court battles that resulted from NOAA's hard-core stance in this regard, or NOAA's dilatory and filibustering tactics as measures to stymie litigation, or NOAA's malfeasance in prosecuting the lawsuits, or NOAA's life-threatening harassment behavior once temporary access was obtained.

All of these proceedings are part of the *Monitor's* history. Yet NOAA avoids their affirmation like the plague, by keeping my name and involvement with the sanctuary under wraps.

NOAA is unrepentant; it has donned a false front by posing as a friend of the public, and by projecting a sanctimonious image that is contradicted by its verifiable record.

To predict NOAA's future conduct, one has only to study its past. NOAA has not changed its stripes. Its campaign promises are empty; they are contrived to achieve a selfish goal at the expense of the American people who, by means of meticulous censorship, have purposely been kept in the dark about NOAA's nefarious deeds.

The Monitor NMS website has been sanitized. A search of the website reveals a conspicuous absence of my name and the four court cases that were ultimately responsible for enabling public access to the wreck. As a result of sweeping these important truths under the carpet, NOAA affects an appearance of respectability that is belied by eight years of disreputable conduct, and by a constant continuation of lies, deception, and administrative abuse, as the remainder of this book will clearly show.

Subterfuge 201
Expansion as a
Territorial Imperative

Blowing the Whistle

In 2007, I started quarterly publication of a free on-line newsletter that was an extension of my website (http://www.ggentile.com). Visitors to my website were informed about the purpose of the newsletter – to provide up-to-date news and events primarily about wreck-diving – and were encouraged to subscribe.

The list of subscribers grew quickly and exponentially to more than one thousand. In addition, subscribers forwarded my newsletters to friends and fellow divers. Eventually I published my newsletters in book form. Thus the number of recipients of my diving news and events reached many thousands of people in the recreational diving community: my targeted audience.

At the time, I was involved in conflicts with NOAA with regard to the Stellwagen Bank NMS. (For details, see Subterfuge 301: "The Stellwagen Bank Robbery.") These conflicts led me to renew my investigations of NOAA. Serendipitously, I unearthed a non-publicized NOAA document that was entitled "Our National Marine Sanctuaries Strategic Plan 2005-2015."

The publication date of this 15-page document was April 2005. The plan outlined literally hundreds of ways and means for NOAA to augment its control over all matters marine. For example, one of the goals that NOAA hoped to achieve over the next ten years was to "designate new sanctuaries."

Another was: "By 2015, 1200 additional shipwrecks identified and evaluated within national marine sanctuaries demonstrating historic potential for the existence of shipwrecks."

Yet another was the establishment of "Sanctuary Advisory Councils" (of which more will be written later).

The word "expansion" was not used in NOAA's Strategic Plan, but the announced goals begged the question: where did NOAA expect to "find" twelve hundred additional shipwrecks if not by increasing the amount of territory that was under its control, either by creating new sanctuaries or by extending the borders of existing sanctuaries? The implication was clear: during the next decade, NOAA intended to annex one thousand two hundred shipwrecks that were presently in the public domain because they resided in international waters where the United States held no jurisdiction.

Further research led me to some remarkable findings. An eight-fold expansion was already underway in the Thunder Bay NMS. Next on NOAA's agenda was a pair of other expansion projects: doubling the size of the Stellwagen Bank NMS, and a *thousandfold* increase in the boundaries of the Monitor NMS.

NOAA planned to expand the one-mile-diameter of the Monitor NMS to cover all the shipwrecks on the Diamond Shoals and along the Outer Banks.

Because Congress had placed a hold on the formation of new sanctuaries, these proposed expansions were the only way in which NOAA could supplement its territorial prerogative.

In my newsletter for February 2009, I announced NOAA's intention to expand the Monitor NMS. The truth about NOAA's hidden agenda touched off a storm of protest, especially from my subscribers in North Carolina. Recreational divers feared that their favorite dive sites would be placed off-limits. Dive shop owners and charter boat skippers feared that they would be put out of business.

Regulations in the Monitor NMS prohibited access of any kind without a hard-to-obtain permit. If such regulations applied to every shipwreck off the coast of North Carolina, divers could no longer visit local shipwrecks, and fishing party boats would not be allowed to take their customers to wreck sites: the only place where bottom dwellers could be found in any quantity. Thus the

secret expansion program portended an economic catastrophe to which NOAA was unsympathetic.

I received a flood of mail in response to my declaration. Some people did not believe that my information
was correct; others did not *want* to believe that my information was correct. NOAA had made no public an-
nouncements about strategic plans to expand the size
of the sanctuary. When queried, NOAA vehemently denied that any such strategic plan existed.

This meant that by the time I published my newsletter, NOAA had been deceiving and lying to the public for
four years.

It Pays Not to Advertise

NOAA employed several tactics to keep its strategic
expansion plan out of the public eye. Although it was required by Congress to hold public meetings in affected
areas whenever it proposed the establishment of a new
sanctuary, or when it proposed changes to an existing
sanctuary, it was under no Congressional requirement
to overly advertise the times, locations, and purpose of
these meetings. Not until the first week of December
2008 – three and a half years after putting on paper its
plans to seize 1,200 shipwrecks – did NOAA announce
these required meetings.

One of the five meetings was held out-of-state. None
of the meetings was heavily promoted. As a result of
keeping the general populace largely in ignorance of the
meetings and the reason for holding them, attendance
was poor: generally no more than a handful of curious
citizens who spotted the back-page notice and wondered
what NOAA meant by the word "expansion."

Those few who did attend received precious few answers to their questions, and the answers that they did
receive were not honest and forthright: NOAA's answers
were contrived to conceal the truth rather than to eluci-
date it. NOAA speakers rushed past the mention of
plans to expand the Monitor NMS in its effort to extend
its control over all the shipwrecks in the vicinity of the
Diamond Shoals of North Carolina.

This was the reason why some divers and anglers did not believe the ominous tidings in my newsletter. NOAA had sought to blindside them by claiming that the meetings were nothing more than casual checkups on the status quo of the sanctuary. The only new information that NOAA imparted was that it might seek to "protect" a few other shipwrecks in the area. NOAA did not elaborate on how it intended to "protect" them.

Prejudice and Criticism

Once the cat was out of the bag, public protest became the watchword. Leading the pack were Bobby and Renate Edwards. They owned and operated a fishing and recreational diving concession called Atlantis Charters, in Atlantic Beach, North Carolina. Because their charter business would be negatively impacted by the proposed expansion and restrictive regulations, they seized the torch that I had ignited, and took it upon themselves to raise awareness of the issues that were being burned at stake.

The Edwards' delved into NOAA's recent activity as it pertained to the Monitor NMS, and used their website to publish what they called a "timeline of events." These were events that seemed merely spiteful when they occurred, but assumed greater significance when viewed later in hindsight, in light of NOAA's newly-discovered hidden agenda.

On July 7, 2008, NOAA issued a press release to announce a forthcoming three-week dive trip to "study the wrecks of three German submarines sunk by U.S. forces in 1942 off the coast of North Carolina during the Battle of the Atlantic."

According to David Alberg, who was now the superintendent of the Monitor NMS, "This expedition is the first part of a larger multi-year project to research and document a number of historically significant shipwrecks tragically lost during World War II, including U.S. and British vessels and merchant marine vessels. The information collected during this expedition will be crucial to efforts to preserve these historic sites."

The U-boats that they intended to "study" at this time were the *U-85*, *U-352*, and *U-701*.

"Two of the U-boats, *U-352* and *U-85*, have been severely impacted by salvage operators and souvenir hunters since their discovery more than three decades ago. *U-701* is relatively intact but also has begun to show signs of damage from illegal salvage attempts. The sub was discovered by recreational divers in 1989 before being covered by sand and rediscovered in 2004."

NOAA's blatant attempt to blame recreational divers for the lack of intactness of the *U-85* and *U-352* was without foundation. The agent almost exclusively responsible for the poor state of hull integrity was Mother Nature. The sea is a corrosive environment in which submerged wood and metal must eventually succumb to the normal processes of decay and deterioration. Wood rots; metal rusts.

In addition to the accepted forms of gradual destruction – from saltwater acidity, wood-boring mollusks, electrolytic reduction, microbial action, mineral deposition, and so forth – are such catastrophic events as fierce northeasters and tropical hurricanes. Wave action batters shallow-water shipwrecks while deep ground swells pound deep-water shipwrecks to pieces. Wood and metal hulls are badly abraded by the sandblasting effect of speeding currents that churn up sand and propel this and other particulate matter against everything in its path.

Recreational divers can neither provoke corrosion nor accelerate its natural progression. Yet Alberg's slanderous comments contrived to incite the non-diving public – who was kept ignorant of the natural forces of devastation – into castigating recreational divers as the causative effect that was responsible for initiating and aggravating the U-boats' ongoing degradation. His comments clearly demonstrated his and NOAA's contempt for the people whose fascination for historical shipwrecks was so profound that it drove them to travel hundreds or thousands of miles to visit the sites at their own expense.

In an article that was published two weeks later, Tane Casserley – who was cited as "the national maritime heritage coordinator for NOAA's Office of the National Marine Sanctuaries" – stated, "What we want to stop is the looting and souvenir hunting that goes on."

Allegations were made that recreational "divers are even said to have removed the skeleton of a German sailor from a sunken U-boat in the area."

Joseph Hoyt, touted as a NOAA maritime archaeologist, was quoted thus: "A lot of [recreational] divers, if they find a skull, or remains, will decide that others want to see it, so will move it out and bring it up on deck."

Alberg: "They [recreational divers] are going to a grave and looting a grave."

Besmirching the reputation of recreational divers constituted an undeserved smear campaign in which unsubstantiated statements could be used to rouse public ire on NOAA's behalf. What Alberg, Casserley, and Hoyt neglected to mention to the press was that the worst U-boat looters and destroyers were not recreational divers but the U.S. Navy. These facts had been published and were well documented, yet NOAA's representatives chose to withhold this information from the public and their Congressional representatives.

The Real Culprits

As one egregious example, in the late 1980's or early 1990's (the precise date has been concealed), the U.S. Navy conducted a clandestine salvage operation on the *U-85*. The goal was to recover a torpedo that was stowed inside the outer skin but outside the pressure hull. The torpedo in question – a G7a T1 compressed air model – weighed 3,369 pounds. A salvage vessel with heavy-duty lifting machinery was needed to raise an object that weighed nearly two tons, (including slings, hardware, and miscellaneous lifting apparatus).

I remember seeing this torpedo in place in the 1970's. I photographed it in the 1980's. I noticed its absence in the 1990's. The recovered torpedo was placed on display for Navy personnel to see: a place that is not readily accessible by the non-uniformed public.

The act of salvage did considerable damage to the hull structure in the vicinity of the torpedo's stowage location. Metal plates were either torn and shredded or missing. A previously covered section of the pressure hull was exposed to the ravages of the sea.

There is no way to determine how many less obvious souvenirs the Navy divers looted when they absconded with the torpedo.

But the grossest U-boat stripping operation that has ever been conducted in American waters took place on the *U-352*. Once again the perpetrator was the U.S. Navy. This time the Navy was not selfishly motivated. This enormous undertaking was performed at the insistence of Senator Lowell Weicker, a Republican from Connecticut. After hearing that the U-boat contained unexploded ordnance – that is, 88-millimeter projectiles and "live" torpedoes with supposedly intact warheads – and that recreational divers visited the site on a regular basis, he exerted his senatorial influence to enjoin the Navy to survey the wreck in order to assess its potential danger to human life.

The Navy dragged its collective feet for a year and a half. After all, the long-forgotten explosive devices were stowed deep in the interior of the pressure hull or inside sealed torpedo tubes. Finally, in the summer of 1980, senatorial will presided, and the Navy was ordered to mount a major salvage operation in order to satisfy Senator Weicker's elaborate demands.

After exhaustive administrative preparations that included the accumulation of equipment and the assignment of personnel, the USS *Hoist* (ARS-40) got underway on May 27, 1980 for an operation that lasted six full weeks. For two days and nights, working around the clock, the *Hoist* towed a side-scan sonar fish over four different positions that were annotated in Navy historical records. "However, no probable contacts were made."

It was not until May 29 that the "decision was made to ask the Squadron to make arrangements for commercial assistance from Morehead City in locating the submarine."

Voila! What insight. Instead of wasting wages and enormous quantities of fuel, someone thought of the obvious: ask the skippers who ran their boats to the wreck on a daily basis. "Using loran charlie navigation, *Atlantis II* located and buoyed off *U-352* within 20 minutes."

Initial diving operations (on scuba) consisted of tying a series of radar buoys to the bow, conning tower, and stern of the hull, in order to determine its heading (which was northeast), so that a six-point mooring could be established. This set-up job took two days.

On May 31, the first survey was conducted. Wearing MK 12 Surface Supplied Diving System with three hundred feet of hose, and taking photographs with a UDATS camera, it was ascertained that "the submarine is at rest on a sandy bottom, with a 65-75 degree starboard list. Divers reported soundings of 110 feet at the stern and amidship, and 116 feet at the bow. A variety of sea life linger in the vicinity of the submarine, including a school of barracuda. The forward 30 feet of the bow hull section is broken and down at an angle of 30 degrees. The entire submarine is heavily encrusted in barnacles, 75 percent of the decking is missing and only structural framing remains attached to the pressure hull. Approximately 20 per cent of the starboard hull is submerged in the sandy bottom, and an air lift or falcon nozzle could be used to remove this sand to gain access for a complete hull inspection. As previously mentioned, the submarine's outer shell is badly deteriorated and all that remains is the structural framing attached to the very accessible pressure hull which is in good shape. Because of the 65-75 degree starboard list, divers were unable to determine whether or not the two starboard forward torpedo tube outer doors are opened. Number two torpedo tube (upper port tube) is broken in half and number four tube (lower port tube) is intact but divers were unable to confirm that presence of torpedoes. Although the external survey revealed that no torpedoes are stowed topside on the maindeck, a torpedo warhead was discovered wedged in the deck framing approximately 30 feet forward of the conning tower, above the forward torpedo room. The warhead is intact with exploder removed. The forward torpedo loading hatch is open and the hatch cover is missing. Divers passed survey of conning tower to continue looking aft. The messdecks hatch and after torpedo loading hatch are both open and both hatch covers are missing. Divers reported that after torpedo loading hatch is blocked by two six inch diameter pipes, possible vents. Divers moved further aft and determined stern torpedo outer door is opened and approximately 2.5 feet of a torpedo extends out the stern tube."

They also found a single 88-millimeter shell in the sand some twenty-five feet off the starboard side.

The next day, divers found that "the upper conning tower hatch is open and is lying on the bottom of the conning tower. The lower conning tower hatch, which allows access into the control room, is partially open. Divers reported that the ready service aft of the 88mm gun mount is completely deteriorated. Only the gun mount base remains intact . . . divers entered the forward torpedo room through the forward torpedo loading hatch and began the internal search. Divers reported the forward torpedo room contains a considerable amount of mud, sand and silt. The presence of unexploded ordnance could not be determined at this time. However, two horizontal HP air flasks were identified extending between frames 26 and 37 on the port side, partially covered by mud and sand. A violet colored Petroleum Oil Lubricant (POL) product is present in the overhead with a depth of approximately 8 inches. A square water tight door (door missing) provides access between petty officer's compartment and the forward torpedo room. At about frame 45 within the petty officer's compartment, an approximate rectangular shaped 18 inch by 24 inch hole passes through the pressure hull in the overhead and into the sea. Upon completion of the brief internal survey of the forward torpedo room and the petty officer's compartment, divers prepared for the X-ray of the stern torpedo. The radiation exposure device is heavy and required two divers to horse it around into position. . . . An exposure was taken and the preliminary picture indicated the torpedo is unarmed."

On June 2, divers commenced the removal of mud and sand from the forward torpedo room in order to "make the final determination as to the presence of unexploded ordnance" by implanting a jet. Bad weather, strong currents, and hard-packed mud conspired to make this a difficult and time-consuming job. Not until June 11 were they able to excavate down as far as the deck plates. Furthermore, it was possible that more torpedoes might be stowed below the deck plates. "Several divers attempted to release the inner torpedo tube locking device using a 36 inch aluminum pipe wrench, but were unsuccessful."

Then came a couple of days of bad weather, one day of good, a couple more days of bad. "Probing by hand in the bilges revealed no evidence of any torpedoes/unexploded ordnance in the excavation. Four air flasks, extended between frames 26 to 36, were positively identified within the forward torpedo room. Two lie end to end along the port side bulkhead and two lie end to end along the starboard side bulkhead."

June 17: "The lower port torpedo tube was found to be cracked and the battery section of a torpedo was visible. The lower port torpedo tube is cracked approximately 3 to 4 feet outside of the pressure hull which would indicate the torpedo is broken in the center section."

Also, "Alongside the starboard quarter, approximately 10 feet from the submarines side, divers located the end of a torpedo center section. . . . Divers confirmed this torpedo was without an exploder."

June 18: "Two torpedoes were located in the bilges and confirmed, one directly underneath the port side air flasks and a second approximately 8 inches to the right of the first (as facing the bow). Both torpedoes are without exploders." The next day they found two more torpedoes in the bilges.

Part of June 22 was spent exploring. "In the vicinity of the CO's cabin there is approximately 3 feet of clearance between the mud and sand level and the overhead. There is also a considerable amount of mud and sand in the mates compartment and the officers mess."

June 23: "Tubes one and four were drilled and probing revealed the presence of a torpedo in each tube. The two new torpedoes bring the total to ten torpedoes located thus far. . . .

"Divers reported the galley is approximately 2/3 full of mud and debris. The galley hatch door leading forward is present and partially open. Divers proceeded forward into the mates compartment and reported the space is approximately half full of mud and noticeably clear of debris, and that there is approximately five feet of clearance between the mud level and the overhead. A circular watertight hatch opens into the mates compartment and provides access into the conning tower control room. Divers then back tracked and proceeded aft through the engine room. However, the extreme starboard list, combined with the mud, debris and the port and starboard engines, made transit of the engine room very difficult. Divers continued through the engine room space and into the after torpedo room to investigate the two bars obstructing the after torpedo loading hatch. Investigation revealed the two bars appear to be securely in place and will probably require removal to allow easier access into the torpedo room. Like the forward torpedo room, the after torpedo room is full of a considerable amount of mud and debris. To complete a comprehensive survey all mud and debris will have to be excavated."

The next day they proceeded to torch through the bars, but then found that in MK II gear they could slip between them. After much excavation and time lost to bad weather, the determination was made on July 1 that no torpedoes were stored in the after torpedo room. Then they partially excavated the galley, where they removed the deck plates, and the CO's cabin. No unexploded ordnance was located.

July 3: It was decided that any remote removal of the exploder from the torpedo in the stern tube is not considered a practical course of action." The next day, "divers completed external excavation of sand alongside the entire length of the starboard side of *U-352*. No additional unexploded ordnance was found. However, communications problems developed with MK12 hats and diving had to be secured."

When it developed that replacement communication assemblies were unavailable, survey operations were terminated.

July 6: "Divers discovered all 88MM and loaded them on board. Divers then placed the torpedo warhead section into a cargo net lowered to the bottom . . . lifted approximately 3 feet off the ocean floor and towed to a point 1500 yards away from the ship and submarine." Divers then attached an Incendiary Torch Remote Opening Device. "The first sign of the warhead burning was a large amount of smoke and bubbles on the surface. Approximately 5 minutes after commencing the burn, the warhead became buoyant and ascended to the surface engulfed in flames. The warhead was recovered and lifted onboard along with 5 lbs of raw explosive and 7 lbs of residual."

By July 7, the salvage operation had completed its objective. Navy divers had made 137 dives for a total bottom time of 361 hours. A summary report stated that they had found numerous rounds from the ship's gun and an unexploded torpedo outside the submarine, as well as eight torpedoes inside the hull (seven in the forward torpedo room and one in a stern torpedo tube.

Inexplicably, the report failed to mention the torpedo that was trapped outside under the starboard hull. "The torpedoes in the forward room do not pose a hazard as long as left undisturbed, i.e., if restricted from access they will not explode spontaneously but the torpedo in the aft tube does constitute a hazard as it can be approached from outside the hull."

The recommendation was made that the torpedo in the after tube be burned by ITROD, while gratings could "be welded on the entrances to the submarine to prevent access and accidental detonation of any of the torpedoes inside the hull or their associated exploders, six of which could not be located and could be anywhere inside the vessel."

The results of the survey were pondered for a year. Navy divers returned to the wreck on June 18, 1981, stayed nine days, and made 67 dives. Using ITROD, they succeeded in burning the torpedo that was protruding from the stern tube as well as the one that was trapped under the starboard hull in the bow.

Then they proceeded to seal off the hatches. Instead of welding a grating across each opening, as recommended, they opted instead to emplace on each hatch a locking device that consisted of a steel T-bar that slipped inside the coaming and smooth circular plate on the outside. The circular plate had a rounded hole in the middle, for the T-bar bolt, and two half-moon cutouts on opposite sides: so the T-bar could be held in place while the nut was run down the shaft from the outside. The nut was then welded in place.

Double Standard

It is important to understand that this highly publicized salvage operation was not conducted in accordance with archaeological standards or guidelines. No archaeologist was on site to oversee the methodology that the Navy divers employed. Digging was not done in the painstaking manner in which fossils were habitually unearthed, but with a water jet.

In order to clear the bilges under the main deck, and to reach the lower torpedo tubes on the starboard side, divers removed more than ten *feet* of mud, silt, and sand from four major compartments totaling one-third of the length of the hull, or 70 feet. These compartments measured some 15 feet across. The cubic footage of the sand that was removed approaches 10,000 cubic feet (allowing for the curvature of the hull).

Sand weighs approximately 100 pounds per cubic foot. This means that more than 500 *tons* of thick overburden was spewed indiscriminately into the ocean out-side the pressure hull, then spread by itinerant currents for miles in all directions.

There was no collection sieve to separate human re-mains from other debris: skeletal material and cultural objects were expelled along with the rest of the junk, with no thought given to sanctity in any form. No one cared about exhuming German bones and body parts, then spitting them into the water column.

Yet this kind of "grab and bag" conduct not only re-ceived full U.S. government approval; it was authorized by the government, and for two years running. The only people who protested the wholesale devastation of the *U-352* were recreational divers; not NOAA, not any other U.S. agency or administration, and not the German gov-ernment. Then it was conveniently dismissed by NOAA when its representatives started bashing recreational divers.

Partners in Crime

As long as I am on the subject of the U.S. Navy, I will recount a more recent act of wanton destruction. NOAA proudly counts the U.S. Navy as one of its partners; per-haps as its most important partner. By this strong as-sociation, NOAA condones the Navy's practices and the manner in which it handles shipwrecks.

The 2000's found me working on my two-volume set of books about shipwrecks that lay off the coast of Mas-sachusetts. I worked in close coordination with Victor Mastone, the Director and Chief Archaeologist of the Massachusetts Board of Underwater Archaeological Re-sources. He shared information with me, and I shared information with him. He even directed me to survey the wreckage of a military aircraft that had crashed during World War Two. I surveyed the wreck, took photographs, and drew a sketch of the fuselage, wings, and salient features, including wing-mounted machine guns.

After spending five years on surveying shipwrecks off Cape Cod and in Boston Harbor, I published the re-sults of my work so that others could share my experiences: either vicariously by reading about them, or under water if they wanted to visit the sites in person. I provided detailed descriptions of the shipwrecks, and GPS coordinates to enable boat owners to locate the sites.

My most satisfying discovery was the wreck of the U.S. minesweeper *YMS-14*. On January 11, 1945, the *YMS-14* sank after collision with the U.S. destroyer *Herndon* (DD-638) in the near approaches to Boston's Inner Harbor. According to local lore, which I heard in the course of my research, the hull had been dredged out of existence during channel-widening operations in recent decades. The only remaining visible feature was the 4-inch deck gun, which had been dragged more than a mile from the original site of collision.

Nonetheless, Marcie Bilinski and I decided to make a concerted effort to search the seafloor for disparate parts of the wreck. We spent several days and many hours under water in sweeping the murky bottom by tying a line to an arbitrary location, and swimming in ever-widening circles.

We found unmolested debris fields and pieces of wreckage spread over a broad area. Although my sand searches were somewhat productive, Bilinski was the one who hit pay dirt. She found a large section of wreckage that, in her words, consisted of "white round things and tall things" which she did not recognize. After her return to the boat, I followed her guideline to the spot. I immediately recognized the "white round things" as depth charges. The metal containers had long since rusted away, leaving the degraded white explosive material exposed to the elements. The surface of the explosive material was scalloped in the same fashion that I had seen on depth charges on other shipwrecks. The "tall things" were the rudder posts.

On subsequent dives we learned that the entire hull lay buried under the sand, and that it was contiguous. We tied a permanent orientation line from bow to stern. Off this centerline we worked sideways on guidelines. This system enabled us to build a picture of the layout and associated wreckage. I made drawings and took photographs.

When my book was published, in 2008, I illustrated it with a photograph of one of the exposed depth charges. The picture and accompanying text reached military circles. The U.S. Navy then took it upon itself to demolish the shipwreck – without concern for historic preservation, without informing Mastone of its intentions, and without authorization from the Massachusetts Board of Underwater Archaeological Resources: the State agency that was responsible for maintaining the integrity of archaeological resources that existed in State waters.

Bilinski and I returned to the site afterward. We found that the wreck had literally been blown to smithereens. Navy divers had detonated so many pounds of explosives on the site that the area looked like a moonscape. The seabed had been unearthed by the blast, large boulders had been shattered and the pieces tossed great distances, and marine life had been obliterated.

One rudder post was missing. The other one was laid down horizontally by the explosion, and a deep pit was gouged out of the rocky substrate beneath it. The bottom contours were so altered that the broad patch of sand that extended outward from the shipwreck was totally gone; the seabed was a debris field littered with shattered rocks.

An important piece of America's past had been demolished. Hardly anything now remains of what used to be an historic landmark.

The largely eroded depth-charge remnants could not have exploded on their own. Nor could they have been of any use to terrorists. Explosive material deteriorates over time, the same way food rots and medicine goes bad – by means of chemical breakdown.

There is irony in this situation. Had the witchhunters at the Naval Historical Center caught an American citizen removing so small an item as an iron bolt from the blasted wreck, either before or after its destruction, they would have sicced the Naval Criminal Investigation Service on him – as they have done in the past – and prosecuted him for stealing what the Explosive Ordnance Division had intended to or failed to destroy.

Obscure Euphemism

Back to December 2008, and the public meetings that NOAA called "scoping" meetings. Four meetings were held at various locations in North Carolina; one was held in Virginia. The avowed purpose of the meetings was to examine public sentiment with regard to a Management Plan Review of the Monitor NMS.

One might wonder why the management plan needed to be reviewed, unless proposed changes were in the works. Yet NOAA representatives never uttered the word "expansion" at any of these meetings. At first they practiced deception by avoiding the subject. Then they lied outright by going as far as to deny that any such plan existed.

Instead, they discussed the possibility of "protecting" the three U-boats that NOAA had "examined" off North Carolina: the *U-85*, *U-352*, and *U-701*. Exactly *how* they intended to "protect" these U-boats was never mentioned. In fact, even to this day NOAA has never expressed any opinion about how it might go about protecting them. It bandies about the word "protection" as if its definition were simple and clear-cut, and lacked political ruse.

There *are* ways in which shipwrecks can be protected. They can be raised intact in the manner in which the *Glomar Explorer* raised the Soviet submarine *K-129*, and then immersed in an environmentally controlled liquid solution.

Barring that, a shipwreck that is left in place on the ocean bottom can be somewhat protected from the elements by building a coffer dam around it. This is only a stopgap solution because a coffer dam protects a shipwreck only from gross physical damage such as storm surge and deep ocean swells. To be fully protected, a shipwreck must be completely enclosed, and the seawater must be replaced with distilled fresh water with a pH of zero.

Cathodic protection can be implemented on metal-hulled shipwrecks by the installation of sacrificial anodes. This method requires the emplacement of galvanic anodes (blocks of zinc, magnesium, or aluminum) in numerous places on the hull.

Wooden-hulled shipwrecks can be partially protected by being coated with several layers of anti-fouling paint.

Yet NOAA has never suggested any of these possibilities, or any other kind of preservative treatment. So what does NOAA mean when its uses the word "protection?"

Fortunately, I do not have to answer that question. It was answered for me by a NOAA employee who participated in NOAA's 2008 dive trip to "examine" the three U-boats. This employee asked for anonymity in order not to jeopardize future employment.

Anytime NOAA uses the word "protect," read "control." Read "restricted access." That is, access only to NOAA employees and assignees. Read "no public access."

NOAA's grand scheme is about control: not just of the three U-boats, but of the 1,200 merchant vessels that were cited in its April 2005 Strategic Plan. And then some . . . But more on that later.

At these public meetings, any suggestion that NOAA might consider denying access to the U-boats – the way it fervently denied access to the *Monitor* – met with energetic responses that were unanimously opposed to any and all forms of restrictions. This makes perfect sense: what sane individual would agree to relinquish personal freedom?

Enter the Dragon

After my newsletter exposé was published on February 9, 2009, Bobby Edwards contacted me and asked me to authenticate my source material. He had attended one of NOAA's public meetings the previous December, where there was no mention of any plan to annex 1,200 shipwrecks. I told him about the National Marine Sanctuaries Strategic Plan, which by then was four years old.

Edwards acknowledged the veracity of my statements. He wasted no time in forwarding my newsletter to interested parties – divers and anglers alike – and, in order to put NOAA's relevant activities into perspective, he compiled his timeline of recent NOAA events, and published it on his website as a work in progress.

NOAA was now being tracked by the people who were the most adversely affected by expansion of the Monitor NMS. Immediately, NOAA offices received a barrage of telephone calls about its expansion plan. NOAA representatives vehemently denied that any such plan existed.

These denials did not hold water. Only four days after the release of my exposé, the Sanctuary Advisory Council for the Monitor NMS held a meeting (on February 13, 2009) in which one item on the agenda was a report from David Alberg and the Expansion Committee.

This begs the questions: what is the Sanctuary Advisory Council, how did it originate, and what is its purpose?

Stacked Deck

One of the objectives stated in the Strategic Plan of April 2005 was to "create, operate, and support community-based sanctuary advisory councils to advise sites and the overall program in the management of their resources, and to serve as liaisons to the community."

The first Monitor NMS SAC meeting was held on May 12, 2006. At that meeting NOAA made it clear that the purposes of SAC's were "to provide advice to the manager of a national marine sanctuary," and "to provide advice on sanctuary operations and projects, and the sanctuary designation process."

More important than these avowed purposes of the sanctuary advisory councils was the manner in which the councils were established: "The National Marine Sanctuary Program *appoints* members." Emphasis added.

Between April 2005 and May 2006, NOAA inter-
viewed prospective members and appointed those whose
orientation was most closely aligned with NOAA's goal
for expansion. The majority of these members were government employees.

Although the first Monitor NMS SAC meeting was
supposed to be open to the public, no public announce-
ments were made about the meeting's date or location.
This tactic limited attendance to those who were specifically invited to attend what was ostensibly a closed
meeting. Only two attendees were non-associational parties who had no affiliation with NOAA or other government agencies.

Among the twenty-six people in attendance, eight
worked directly for the National Marine Sanctuaries Program in various capacities, and three worked for The
Monitor Center at The Mariners Museum. To emphasize
bias, one representative of The Mariners Museum stated, "We work hand-in-hand with NOAA."

Nine other attendees were government historians or
archaeologists who were already working as consultants
for the Monitor NMS. Four non-government seats were
occupied by people who passed the interview process by
swearing allegiance to NOAA.

According to the "Monitor National Marine Sanctuary Council Swearing In/Oath," all SAC members "took
the following oath on May 12, 2006 at 3:09: I (speak
name) as a duly appointed member (or alternate) of the
Sanctuary Advisory Council established under the National Marine Sanctuaries Act hereby agrees [sic] to assist to the best of my ability in achieving the Sanctuary
goals."

According to the SAC charter, members were supposed to "facilitate communication between stakeholders and sanctuary staff," and "provide a forum to discuss and act upon locally important and/or challenging
resource management issues." Yet the oath makes it
clear that these pronouncements were mere lip service
that was intended to appease opposition.

More telling were the challenges that SAC was charged with overcoming: challenges that were stated explicitly in the minutes of the meeting. One was to "exceed legal authority." Another was "getting the 'right' person to effectively represent and communicate to and from their constituency."

In the latter case, the implication is that the "right" person was one who expressed no objections to NOAA's Strategic Plan to seize 1,200 shipwrecks that lay in international waters: shipwrecks with a clear pedigree of ownership.

Rigged Jury

At the next SAC meeting (on November 2, 2006), it was recorded that David Alberg "had the opportunity to meet with NC Congressman [Walter] Jones in October, where they discussed the public interest in modifying the MNMS to protect [read "control"] additional wrecks in the Graveyard of the Atlantic."

At this point there could not possibly have been any public "interest" in expansion of the Monitor NMS because the public knew nothing about NOAA's Strategic Plan to wrest control of 1,200 shipwrecks from their owners and from the public domain. That goal was kept strictly under wraps.

The only people who knew about NOAA's territorial demands were those who served in NOAA's administration and those who swore an oath to assist NOAA in achieving its goals, whatever those goals might be. Outsiders were kept in the dark.

Choosing members on the basis of compliance was equivalent to a prosecuting attorney selecting only victims of rape as jury members in the case of a defendant who was accused of sexual assault.

Incest Works Best

Despite NOAA's avowal to Congress, the Sanctuary Advisory Council was *not* "community based," nor was it intended to serve as a liaison with the community. SAC members were handpicked from non-community

sycophants whose primary job was to effect an appearance of legitimacy. It did this by reflecting NOAA's wishes in a perfect mirror image, as if the advice it offered
had originated from impartial council members instead
of from NOAA directives. In reality, NOAA told SAC what
advice to give.

SAC never – I repeat, never – gave advice to NOAA
that NOAA had not previously pronounced. Nor did it
ever disagree with anything that NOAA proposed. After
all, the members all swore an oath "to assist NOAA in
achieving its goals." They did not swear an oath to defend community objections.

SAC was never anything more than a group of specially appointed yes-men and -women. Its purpose was
to deceive Congress into believing that SAC was acting
in good faith as a referee between NOAA's "recommendations" and the public's civil rights.

It is important to observe that a NOAA representative
presided over SAC meetings.

Expansion Gets a Name (or Two)

At the SAC meeting that was held on November 9,
2007, NOAA went so far as to announce a name change
for the expanded Monitor NMS: the Graveyard of the Atlantic NMS.

At the May 16, 2008 SAC meeting, NOAA announced: "A team of divers will visit the U Boat sites
from July 6-24 to survey and document the sites for inclusion into the National Registry." This was one of those
instances in which NOAA was attempting to "exceed legal authority" by assuming control over property that
ostensibly belonged to a foreign government. (Again,
more on this later.)

Once again Alberg initiated a discussion about expansion of the Monitor NMS. Afterward, he coined an
expression that he reiterated ad nauseam through the
following years: "NOAA has no position on expansion at
this time." He may have said this to mollify the five "public guests in attendance," but his statement was nothing
more than cleverly worded misinformation that contra-

dicted the objective that had been set forth in the April 2005 Strategic Plan.

At the SAC meeting that was held on October 2, 2008, NOAA suggested another potential name for the expanded Monitor NMS: Battle of the Atlantic NMS. This was the first official indication that the annexation of shipwrecks was projected to go far beyond the Grave-yard of the Atlantic – that is, the international waters off the North Carolina coast – and would eventually include every shipwreck off the American eastern seaboard. (Yet again, more on this later.)

Lambasting Recreational Divers

Meanwhile, Alberg continued his diatribe against recreational divers, while extolling NOAA's questionable virtues with specific regard to U-boats.

For one example of his ongoing vituperation, consider the following accusation, which was quoted in newspapers on July 7, 2008: "Two of the U-boats, *U-352* and *U-85*, have been severely impacted by salvage operators and souvenir hunters."

Alberg neglected to mention that the "salvage operators" who were most responsible for destroying the integrity of the *U-352* were U.S. Navy divers; and that the "souvenir hunters" who were responsible for removing the greatest amount of tonnage from the *U-85* were, again, U.S. Navy divers.

He was also quoted as saying, "This expedition is the first part of a larger multi-year project to research and document a number of historically significant ship-wrecks tragically lost during World War II, including U.S. and British naval vessels and merchant marine vessels. The information collected during this expedition will be crucial to efforts to preserve these historic sites."

This latter quote was another way of saying that NOAA intended to control these wrecks by expanding the Monitor NMS and, in accordance with current regulations which it had no intention of changing, by denying access to those shipwrecks.

Misrepresentation

Sanctuary waters were muddied by other misleading remarks. The following declaration was worse than double-damning: "Mr. Bunch commented that overall any expansion of the sanctuary's interest in other shipwrecks was met with approval in general by the dive community and that he was optimistic if expansion ever becomes an option."

First, although James Bunch sat in the Recreational Diving seat, he did not represent the recreational diving community. By definition, a representative is *elected* by the people he is supposed to represent, in order to express their interests and anxieties. NOAA *appointed* Bunch to the Recreational Diving seat because he professed to be sympathetic with NOAA's shipwreck takeover; after all, he swore an oath "to assist to the best of my ability in achieving the Sanctuary goals." Bunch's quote simply regurgitated whatever NOAA stated and wanted to hear in return.

Second, the comment that was attributed to him did *not* reflect the viewpoint of the recreational diving community. In fact, it was diametrically opposed to the actual stance of the diving community. No recreational diver I have ever met favored NOAA's expansion plan.

Third, what did he mean by his statement, "if expansion ever becomes an option"? By this time, expansion of the Monitor NMS had been a strategic objective for three and a half years. Expansion was not just an option; it was a proclamation.

Fourth, and most important, Bunch did not make the statement that was attributed to him. I spoke with him at length about this quote. He assured me – and I believe him, having known him for many years – that he never said any such thing.

The NOAA recorder twisted Bunch's words to make it sound as if the dive community favored expansion. In actuality Bunch said that he approved *discussion* of expansion, but not expansion itself. In other words, if NOAA wanted to initiate a debate about whether the Monitor NMS should be expanded, he favored the solicitation of input from the fishing and recreational diving communities. End of story.

Bunch's true position was maliciously reworded to give the appearance of acquiescence.

Deliberate Falsehood

Jeff Johnson, Monitor NMS historian and program specialist whose surname was also spelled Johnston in official memoranda, "said that it takes about two weeks to get a permit turned around." This statement was so far from the truth as to be absurd.

Consider this message that Todd Baldi sent to me on December 12, 2007: "I have applied several times to secure a permit to the USS *Monitor*. I have read your book about the trials of getting a permit. Any suggestions/advice on how to proceed with the permit process? I have sent about 4-5 applications and basically gave me the complete runaround.

"I have been trying to get a copy of an existing approved permit application so I can model mine after it? [sic] Do you ever allow anyone to look at your permit requests? Any chance you would release a copy to me?"

My permit applications were a matter of public record. Not only were they submitted to NOAA and therefore accessible pursuant to the Freedom of Information Act, but they were also submitted to the court as evidence in my lawsuits against NOAA. Unfortunately, they were also outdated with regard to NOAA's newly issued permit application guidelines.

Because I kept my finger on the pulse of NOAA's activities, especially with regard to the Monitor NMS, I knew that more recent permit applications existed. So that Baldi would know how to frame his permit application in suitable language, I suggested that he submit a FOIA request for them. I recommended this route because, in light of Johnson's conscious obstructionism, I doubted that he would help voluntarily, and certainly not without extraordinary delay.

I also asked Baldi to provide more detail about his mistreatment by NOAA.

He responded a week later. "I am kind of sick of NOAA. My saga reads very similar to yours. I sent a request into them 3 years ago and they never responded. I called them everyday [sic] for a month and finally got an email from Jeff Johnson saying 'I have your dates penciled in.' When I responded back, he wrote me two weeks later saying he never received my permit application.

"I filed another permit, called daily again and they sent me another application for permit request with no mention of my second application. I sent a third about a year later and received a call from Joel Silverstein saying my permit had been turned down. That was really bizarre since Joel doesn't have any official affiliation with NOAA that I know of."

Collusion or Conspiracy?

Bizarre was an understatement. Silverstein was a recreational diver who had previously submitted a permit application which had eventually gained approval. He had organized a dive trip to the *Monitor*. His only affiliation with NOAA was as a successful permittee.

Silverstein could have learned about the denial of Baldi's application only if he were told by Johnson (or by someone else who had access to in-house records). Permit denials are not supposed to be shared with competing permittees.

Johnson never contacted Baldi personally about his application denial. It seemed as if Johnson had delegated this task to Silverstein. This was not only unusual; it was illegal, and it had no official standing.

Ironically, in response to Baldi's FOIA request, of the four approved permit applications that he received, two were copies of Silverstein's.

He also received "Guidelines For Submitting Applications For National Marine Sanctuary Permits and Authorizations." This tome was thirty pages in length: twice as long as my accepted permit application, and three times as long as Silverstein's. The complexity of the guidelines made it exceedingly difficult for the average applicant to submit an acceptable permit application: another way for NOAA to foil access.

The situation worsened. To frame the latest of his long series of permit applications, Baldi followed NOAA's permit application guidelines, and used the four approved applications as templates. He submitted a new permit application in due course.

On August 21, 2008, Baldi wrote to me: "NOAA has accused me of copyright violations using public domain documents. The madness never ends!"

Somehow through the machinations of NOAA, Silverstein learned about Baldi's latest permit application. Not only did Silverstein complain to NOAA, but he sent a stern letter of protest to Baldi for using what he termed "proprietary information."

Within minutes I replied to Baldi's message. Later that morning he replied to my email: "Why does Joel have access to my NOAA application? I had to file a FOIA request to get his application to model my own after. Yet after I file mine NOAA immediately forwards my application to him without my permission?!?!?! I don't understand why there is a double standard where he can see my stuff but no one can see his w/o a FOIA request.

"If he wants to see it, he can file his own FOIA request and get a copy of my application.

"As far as I am concerned, NOAA has said nothing to me yet. Only Joel had contact [sic] me. And Joel doesn't work for NOAA."

In the event, the heat was quickly reduced from a boil to a simmer. Silverstein acquiesced after Baldi sent him a copy of his permit application (as yet not approved), and found no usage of putative "proprietary information."

Even so, it was not until mid-November that Johnson informed Baldi that his permit application was in the queue for "HQ approval." And after that, another month passed before his permit application was officially approved. These unconscionable delays meant that another diving season was lost before Baldi would be able to dive on the *Monitor*. Thus he was forced to schedule his trip for 2009.

The manner in which NOAA mishandled Baldi's permit application was a factual case in point that belied Johnson's preposterous boast about a professed turnaround time of two weeks. Keep in mind that the Baldi debacle was currently ongoing – and had been in the works for *four years* – when Johnson spun his crock to SAC, on October 2, 2008.

To add insult to injury, from the time that Johnson made his "two-week" declaration, another two and a half *months* passed before Baldi's latest permit application – after a long series of similar applications – received official approval.

The actual turnaround time for Baldi was five years!

The Sunken Tanker Project

It must be stressed that the Sanctuary Advisory Council was not the autonomous entity that NOAA claimed it was. NOAA representatives presided over every meeting, and did most of the talking. SAC members made comments, but their remarks and observations never – not once – found fault with NOAA's objectives or strategic plans. Instead, the members parroted advice on how NOAA's plans and objectives could best be achieved, without any regard for the constitutional rights of the public to have a say in the matter.

Aaron Harmon told me that he attended one SAC meeting at which four *armed* federal agents were in attendance: certainly an excessive show of force on NOAA's part.

At the meeting that is still under consideration – October 2, 2008 – NOAA dragged yet another stratagem into the argument for expansion: "Mr. Alberg also explained the environmental threat the sunken ships pose to our Nation's coast."

Alberg's contention was that tankers that were sunk by enemy action during World War Two were filled with hazardous petroleum products that were just waiting to be released into the ocean and contaminate coastal waters when the hulls and tank compartment bulkheads rusted through or collapsed.

NOAA was not the first government agency to address this potential cause for alarm. The U.S. Coast Guard beat NOAA to the punch – by *forty-one years!*

During World War Two, Nazi U-boats sank hundreds of vessels off the coast of the United States: from the Canadian border to the tip of Florida and in the Gulf of Mexico. A great number of these vessels were fully-laden tankers. The two largest concentrations of vessels that were shelled or torpedoed in shallow water – that is, on the continental shelf – were located off the New Jersey coast and off the Diamond Shoals of North Carolina.

The Coast Guard's Sunken Tanker Project was triggered by the grounding of the *Torrey Canyon* off Cornwall, England, on March 18, 1967. The subsequent spill of oil on French and British shores stimulated global awareness of the inherent dangers of large-scale pollution from the growing fleet of supertankers.

Millions of gallons of oil contaminated the ocean, coagulated on beaches, and collected on the feathers of thousands of birds, which died as a result of the oily saturation. Suddenly, Americans remembered the Nazi campaign against coastal shipping. Media hyped these seaside shipwrecks as sunken powder kegs that were about to explode.

In direct response to this European environmental catastrophe, the U.S. government established a protocol to inspect "tankers sunk on the United States continental shelf by enemy action during World War II." The Secretary of Transportation directed the Coast Guard to conduct an exhaustive investigation of wartime casualties, and to provide logistical support for underwater examinations.

According to the Coast Guard's findings, "Of the 148 American tankers known to have been casualties of enemy action during World War II, 105 were attacked in the Atlantic or Gulf of Mexico. Of these only 27 had been sunk with petroleum cargo in less than 200 feet of water. . . . Each of the 27 tankers was then evaluated, taking into consideration such factors as: depth of water, type of cargo, whether or not there was an extensive fire or loss of oil by torpedoing or gunfire before sinking, distance offshore, and sea currents and physical conditions which would affect diving operations."

The Coast Guard selected four submerged tankers for preliminary investigation: the *Coimbra* (south of Long Island, New York), *Gulftrade*, *R.P. Resor*, and *Varanger* (all three off New Jersey). These initial targets were chosen by dint of the "expressed concern of the people of the area, high volume of marine traffic, extensive recreational beaches, high population density, significant recreational boating and fishing, and marine wild life."

According to the report that resulted from the preliminary research, these "tankers, most of which were carrying cargoes of petroleum products when sunk, were considered to pose a potential and substantial threat of pollution to the American shoreline should they still contain their cargoes and be in a position to release them as a result of the natural deterioration of their hulls."

The thesis for this last remark lay in the theory that the submerged cargo tanks had maintained perfect oil-tight integrity for twenty-five years, and might breakdown suddenly and catastrophically. Advocates of the theory imagined a procedure in which the tanks could be tapped like barrels of aging wine. A special tapping device was designed and constructed in the event that the theory was substantiated. The device could drill through a thick steel hull, then siphon the oil through a hose into a holding tank onboard a surface vessel.

The *Gulftrade* was picked as the first target of opportunity. In 1942, the hull broke in two after a torpedo struck amidships. The two sections drifted apart before sinking. The bow section was considered a menace to navigation because it sank in 60 feet of water; it was subsequently demolished by explosives. The stern section sank some ten miles away at a depth of 90 feet.

A Coast Guard spokesperson said, "We will take samples of the oil to see what chemical changes have occurred in it. We will also measure the thickness of the hull plating, and take samples of the fittings, such as piping."

Ocean Systems, a commercial diving outfit that was based in Louisiana, was contracted to furnish divers for the in-water work. The Coast Guard furnished the buoy tender *Sweetgum* as a diving platform.

The Sunken Tanker Project was a national news event. On the first day of the Project – August 14, 1967 – New Jersey's Congressional representative James Howard promoted the Project by holding a press conference aboard the *Sweetgum*. Also in attendance for the occasion was Donald Agger, the Assistant Secretary of the Department of Transportation. Howard alarmingly informed the press that "only the molasses-like quality of the coal tar and the 34-degree sea floor temperature seem to be preventing its spread to shore. A strong undersea storm, however, could start it on its way."

At best, Howard's limelight allegations were naïve and uninformed. At worst, they were ill-conceived attempts to scare or hoodwink the public into believing that their beaches were on the brink of environmental destruction. This dire prediction and rabblerousing rhetoric were contradicted by actual observations made by spear-fishers and wreck-divers, who had been exploring both parts of the wreck for years, and who had never found indications of oil. Nonetheless, the Project received extensive media coverage throughout the month of its operation.

The bow section of the *Gulftrade* was not slated for investigation because it had been thoroughly destroyed. The first survey was conducted on the *Gulftrade's* stern section. Commercial divers spent two days examining the wreckage, making eight dives in all. The conclusion that was reached by Project personnel, and that was entered into the expedition diary, was succinct: "No oil found, hull in poor condition, metal samples taken."

A Coast Guard memorandum noted, "Hull mostly demolished and spaces wide open."

Another memorandum stated, "Hulk open to sea, rivets eaten away permitting plates to separate, plates badly eroded. Three metal samples taken . . . for analysis . . . along with two rolls of video tape."

Yet another document stated that the divers "observed demolished w/cargo spaces open, rivets deteriorated allowing hull plates to separate; superstructure demolished earlier by COE." (COE stands for U.S. Army Corps of Engineers.)

Diver George Koch was more descriptive in his statements to the press. "From looks alone I couldn't tell you it was a ship. I don't see how it could contain any liquid now; it's so torn and twisted." He said that the only recognizable feature he found was a gear wheel, apparently from the engine room. Of 81,223 barrels of bunker C oil that the *Gulftrade* carried on her final voyage, he saw nary a drop. This came as no surprise to local recreational divers, who could have provided the same information for free.

Contrary to expectation, analyses of the recovered samples proved that metal erodes unevenly, creating thin spots and pinholes through which oil must have leaked long ago. Furthermore, this seepage did not occur all at once but over a long period of time. Oil that dripped into the ocean in such a manner was dispersed piecemeal without causing any kind of environmental damage.

Next on the Project list was the *R.P. Resor*, which lay at a depth of 130 feet. Hard-hat divers conducted an examination on August 16, 1967. According to an interim report, the wreck lay "on port side in sand on axis approx. 020-200 with list of 10-15 degrees. Stern opened up. Tank decks buckled in. Anchor windlass fallen through into hold. No trace of oil. Divers could see sand bottom through decks."

A formal report on the results of the survey noted that the wreck was "badly torn apart and in two large sections lying at slight angle to each other. Entire hull was completely overgrown. A section of rail and plate was recovered. No oil was found."

On August 21, 1967, the *Sweetgum* established a mooring over the *Varanger*, where the seabed was 140 feet deep. The next day, the commercial divers explored the wreck on tethers. According to the official report, they found the wreck "lying up-right in three parts: stern, bridge midsection and part of forebody to bow. All tankage sections open to sea with no oil present."

Then, with the Coast Guard's sanction, the divers indulged in a bit of scavenging: the kind that NOAA likes to blame on recreational divers. They recovered the ship's safe. With the lifting equipment onboard the *Sweetgum*, raising the heavy iron safe was a relatively minor task.

All hands gathered around as the safe was lowered to the deck. A photographer recorded the event. Excitement is evident on the faces of the men as they smashed open the iron door. If they hoped to find the gold of Midas inside, they were sorely disappointed, for the safe contained only two fish, assorted .38 caliber cartridges, approximately thirty coins of various Norwegian, British, and American denominations, and two Philadelphia subway tokens.

Additionally, the divers recovered a stanchion and a broken valve – supposedly as samples of metal corrosion – and "mud and water samples were taken." They found no oil: the black gold had long since seeped into the sea through pinholes in the hull, one drop at a time.

The death knell of the Sunken Tanker Project tolled on the *Coimbra*. At 180 feet, this was the deepest of the four initially-targeted shipwrecks. Divers examined the wreck between August 30 and September 5, 1967. The report put paid to all fears of pollution hazards: "After determining the hull thickness with ultrasonic gauging equipment, a stud gun and plug would be used to penetrate the hull and sample the cargo." Ultimately, "no oil was found in sufficient quantities for analysis."

But, "the *Coimbra's* tanks are in good condition and appeared to be closed to the sea and yet even her cargo has somehow been released over the years, leaving only the slightest traces of residual oil. Attempts to penetrate the hull of the *Coimbra* failed, and indicate that the corrosion has not occurred to an extent which would allow a mass release of entrapped petroleum. Best estimates are that the oil has escaped by rising through the tank ventilation systems. This would most likely have occurred gradually over an extended period of time, allowing the oil to be assimilated by the surrounding sea through bio-degradation of the persistent oils and evaporation of the volatiles to the atmosphere from the non-persistent oil cargoes."

In its conclusions, the Coast Guard found, "Evidence gathered from this project indicates that tankers sunk during World War II do not present a potential pollution threat to the American coastline." Against the weight of such intensive examinations, there was no need to inspect the remaining twenty-three tankers. The Project was discontinued.

Project Confirmation

The matter should have ended there, but several years later the issue of sunken tankers releasing oil was raised again, specifically with regard to the *Coimbra*. The primary alarmist and instigator was Henry Frey, associate professor at the Polytechnic Institute of New York. After making a single bounce dive on the wreck, he concluded that the Coast Guard investigation of 1967, involving forty-one surface supplied dives conducted by experienced commercial divers, was inadequate.

Frey claimed that as many as "ten tank compartments remain closed to the sea and may still contain oil." The basis for his viewpoint was an oil slick that was reputed to have been observed in the vicinity of the *Coimbra*. Frey began a campaign for a complete re-examination of all tankers that had been sunk off the American eastern seaboard during World War Two.

He lectured zealously on the subject, made proposals to government agencies, tried to get funding from private foundations and corporations, and sought publicity through the media. He claimed – or rather, reiterated – that each and every tanker on the bottom was a "sunken time bomb" waiting to explode and deluge public beaches with black, viscous sludge – this despite the fact that the *Coimbra* had not been loaded with crude oil, but had been carrying lubricating oil, which was lightweight and nearly transparent.

His hypothesis was based on the assumption that some of the wreck's tank compartments were intact and full of cargo, and that, instead of oil leaking out a drop at a time through valves, rivet holes, and cracks in the bulkheads, a massive quantity could gush out if a bulkhead collapsed suddenly.

Largely as a result of Frey's continued outspoken insistence, in 1975 the Coast Guard began dropping sealed drift cards over the wreck "at the rate of 20 a month for one year, to verify the institute's belief that the oil may reach Fire Island, Jones Beach and the Rockaways. The cards contain questions to be answered by those who find them, and should be returned to the school or the Coast Guard. They are designed to drift with the currents in patterns that are identical with the drift of oil slicks."

No positive evidence was ever obtained that a catastrophic release of oil from the *Coimbra*, if indeed significant quantities actually remained in the wreck's tanks, would reach New York beaches. Frey maintained his stance for several years, but eventually the threat of oil from the *Coimbra* contaminating Long Island's white sandy shores fizzled out.

Scare Tactic

The conclusions that the Coast Guard reached in its final report of the Sunken Tanker Project were convincing: "There is indication that a cargo will probably be lost from tanks thru ventilation or other fittings before plating and other structure corrodes away."

And, "Information received from fishermen and divers from various areas along the coast, including North Carolina and Florida, suggests that the condition of most known sunken vessels is comparable to conditions of those investigated by the Coast Guard. Therefore the Coast Guard has concluded that a continuation of the project at this time in other areas would not produce a substantially different determination."

I have personally dived on fifty-two shipwrecks that were sunk by Nazi U-boats (including the four that the Coast Guard examined). Of these fifty-two, twenty-two were tankers. Of the twenty-two tankers, eleven were located off the coast of North Carolina. Therefore, I am in a position to attest to the accuracy of the Coast Guard's findings.

Time and nature have taken their toll. The submerged tankers and freighters that lie off the Diamond Shoals are in worse condition than those that reside in more quiet waters. Nearly three-quarters of a century's worth of hurricanes and fierce northeasters have churned the seabed and pummeled the shipwrecks that rest on it. Raging currents and forceful ground swells have continuously punched the sunken hulls and interior bulkheads with the hard impact of battering rams.

Even the least experienced recreational diver knows that these torpedoed tankers contain no cargoes of oil. Most of the hulls appear to have been crushed flat, with their decks fallen straight down because the supporting beams and bulkheads buckled as a result of advanced corrosion; no interior spaces remain. Those that preserve a semblance of their original shape are nothing but empty shells that a diver can swim through with ease.

This information has not been kept secret. It is no exaggeration to state that *every recreational diver* knows these facts. Even armchair explorers accept the truth of the situation, because I did not simply dive on these wrecks; I *surveyed* them. And I published the results of my surveys. The information is available to anyone who takes the trouble to read the books in my Popular Dive Guide Series.

Why, then, did Alberg propose a fabulous scenario about an environmental threat that had been examined four decades earlier, and found to have been already eliminated by the natural processes of decay? Shipwrecks do not become more intact over time. Clearly, tankers that had lost their cargoes after twenty-five years of submersion would have collapsed even more after sixty-six years of submersion.

Was Alberg expressing an opinion in total ignorance of documented evidence? Was he clanging a false alarm in an era when "environmental threat" was a magic catchphrase that garnered loud public outcry that could result in government funding? Or was he hatching a feint whose purpose was to stampede Congress into allowing the expansion of the Monitor NMS so that NOAA could exercise absolute control over access to shipwrecks within the Sanctuary's newly expanded boundaries?

Only the Shadow knows what evil lurks in the hearts of men.

Immediate Aftermath

Such was the state of NOAA's affairs when I blew the whistle on the Strategic Plan of April 2005, in which expansion of the Monitor NMS was first articulated, along with the annexation of 1,200 shipwrecks.

NOAA was immediately deluged with phone calls about the expansion issue. NOAA representatives vehemently denied that any such plan for expansion was in the works. Thus NOAA continued to lie about the issue, perhaps oblivious to the fact that I had just commenced an awareness campaign about that very same issue.

NOAA held another SAC meeting four days after I published my newsletter. On the schedule for discussion at that out-of-state meeting – it was held in Virginia on February 14, 2009, conveniently distant from those North Carolina stakeholders who were most adversely affected by expansion – was the issue of expansion. Leading that discussion was the Expansion Committee, whose existence NOAA denied.

The head of the Expansion Committee was the superintendent of the Monitor NMS. According to the minutes of that meeting, "Dave Alberg reminded everyone that a subcommittee was formed last May to deal with any issues that might arise concerning expansion." This formation must have been done in secret because it was not mentioned in the minutes of the SAC meeting of May

16, 2008.

While NOAA representatives were denying to the public that a plan for expansion existed, the minutes recorded the following statement: "Dave explained that he will be making Hill visits in Washington DC to the new and incumbent Senators and Congressmen the first week of April." In those same minutes, Alberg reiterated his litany, "We have no formal position on expansion."

This begs the obvious question: If NOAA had no formal position on expansion of the Monitor NMS, why was expansion and the annexation of 1,200 shipwrecks annotated in the April 2005 Strategic Plan; why was there constant discussion of expansion behind closed doors; why had NOAA formed an Expansion Committee; why did the Expansion Committee continue to exist and discuss expansion; and why was Alberg promoting expansion to the people's representatives in the nation's capital, while all the time denying all these items to the public?

I turned up the heat on NOAA with my next newsletter, which I published on April 20, 2009. I entitled it appropriately, "The Rise of the Fourth Reich."

My previous newsletter created quite a stir among my North Carolina subscribers. Several of them contacted me about the NOAA expansion program. To recapitulate, I wrote that NOAA had conducted site surveys on offshore German U-boats with the express purpose of encompassing them – and every other shipwreck along the Outer Banks – in the Monitor National Marine Sanctuary. NOAA intends to do this by expanding the boundaries of the Sanctuary to include the entire Outer Banks and Diamond Shoals, and as far south as the *U-352* off Morehead City.

If NOAA does this, it will have autonomous control over practically every shipwreck off the coast of North Carolina.

Impossible, you say? Not in the least. Despite ardent local protest, in the Great Lakes, NOAA has already expanded the Thunder Bay NMS *eightfold!* [In this regard I was wrong. NOAA pronouncements led me to believe that the Thunder Bay expansion was a forgone conclusion. In the event, State government and public sentiments seethed with such intensity that NOAA backed down – temporarily.]

In Massachusetts, plans are in the works to expand the Stellwagen Bank NMS all the way to the beach – well, actually, to the 3-mile territorial border – westward to the mainland and southward to Cape Cod. NOAA kept these machinations such a closely guarded secret that, until recently, not even the head of the Massachusetts Board of Underwater Archaeological Resources knew about them. NOAA never notified him [Victor Mastone] of their expansion program. He had to learn the truth of NOAA's nefarious plans through the back door.

More than one subscriber has asked me for the source of my information about the expansion of the Monitor NMS, especially in light of denials given by NOAA representatives. I learned about NOAA's true intentions direct from a participant in the NOAA U-boat site survey trip. This participant prefers to remain anonymous. I recently spoke with this person again, and asked if I had misconstrued the facts. This person reconfirmed in no uncertain terms that NOAA's sole reason for surveying the U-boats was to lay the groundwork for the expansion program that was already underway.

NOAA's follow-up to the survey trip was a series of press releases in which agency representatives made ever-worsening and unsupported allegations that recreational divers are solely responsible for destroying the wrecks – notwithstanding the highly dynamic area in which these shipwrecks reside. NOAA will use this wrongful defamation of character to advance the claim that the wrecks need NOAA's "protection." ("Protection" is a NOAA euphemism for "control.")

Bobby and Renate Edwards have compiled a timeline that clearly shows where NOAA is going. For details, visit their website at:

www.atlantischarters.net/keepstatusquo.htm

The fact that NOAA is now (and for the first time since the Sanctuary was created, in 1975) holding "scoping" meetings about the Monitor NMS, demonstrates NOAA's true intention. The reason NOAA is holding public hearings when they have never done so before is because Congress has mandated that NOAA must hold such hearings in order to solicit public feedback before making changes to the status quo.

NOAA representatives bemoan the fact that divers do not appear at public hearings in order to voice their concerns and protest NOAA's aggrandizement. NOAA is not going to act upon divers' concerns, so what is the point of voicing them.

Although NOAA is mandated to *hold* public hearings and *listen* to public concerns, NOAA is under no obligation to *act* upon those concerns. NOAA holds hearings merely as lip service to satisfy its Congressional mandate, then goes ahead and does whatever the hell it wants. This is not a prediction, but a statement of past behavior – behavior that is entirely without exception.

Once NOAA gains control, it then has a blank check to do as it pleases. This means instituting a permit system which can be as restrictive as it wants to make it, along with stern reprisals for violating the system. Reprisals can take the form of huge fines and/or criminal prosecution ($50,000 and/or a one-year prison sentence). NOAA can also place shipwrecks off-limits forever.

A diver's request for a permit might be put on hold for years – or indefinitely. Again, this is not a prediction but recognition of past behavior.

This is what will happen should NOAA expand the Monitor NMS boundaries – an expansion that is many *thousands* of times larger than the current Sanctuary.

NOAA's first step will be to place the U-boats off-limits to all recreational divers. Other wrecks will follow. Wreck-diving off the North Carolina coast will cease to exist.

NOAA representatives, who deny that there are plans afoot to expand the Monitor NMS, are lying. In fact, NOAA already has a name for the expanded Sanctuary: the Graveyard of the Atlantic National Marine Sanctuary. This name tells it all: the expanded Sanctuary has nothing to do with preserving marine life; it has everything to do with controlling access to shipwrecks.

In this regard, it is ironic to note that the Marine Sanctuary Program is supposed to operate under the guidelines of the Marine Protection, Research, and Sanctuaries Act, which has nothing to do with shipwrecks but is concerned solely with the marine life environment.

BEWARE: the way the NOAA scam operates is like this: lower-echelon representatives make denials; then, after an unpopular change is made, the lower-echelon representatives claim that although they sided with public opinion, the decision was made by a "higher authority." By "higher authority" I do not mean God.

Adolf Hitler created the Third Reich in order to dominate the world. NOAA is creating a Fourth Reich in order to dominate the oceans: an area that is three times as large as the Earth's landmass. Don't let it happen.

Citizens who are concerned about the totalitarian takeover of North Carolina shipwrecks should write to their State and Federal representatives in order to voice their disapproval. NOAA is a juggernaut that has forever been out of control. If NOAA is not stopped, it will continue to expand its boundaries until it controls every bit of water on the planet. Perhaps even rainwater.

I apologize for my hyperbole but I am not ashamed of it. My intention was to inform a deliberately misled public, and to arouse that public to action with a likely extrapolation that was based on NOAA's documented history. To paraphrase one of the mankind's most ruthless conquerors: Today the *Monitor*, tomorrow the underwater world.

Radioactive Fallout

So fragmented was the diving community that many recreational divers continued to be unaware of NOAA's plans for expansion; some did not learn about it until several years later: even some who lived and dived in North Carolina. Nor did NOAA go out of its way to facilitate communication. Despite a self-avowed "outreach program," SAC members pledged allegiance to NOAA's flag by maintaining silence with regard to the diving community. But my newsletter prompted action among my subscribers, and among those to whom my newsletter was forwarded.

Bobby Edwards and his wife Renate continued to be the focal point in North Carolina. They maintained their timeline as events unfolded. One thing they noted was Alberg's complaint that his phone no longer rang. By this he meant that people were now relying on word-of-mouth information that he claimed was inaccurate, but no one called his office to hear NOAA's side of the story.

Could NOAA staff members possibly have been so obtuse as not to know that people did not call NOAA's representatives to be mollified by prevarications? No matter how many times Alberg claimed that NOAA did not have a position on expansion, concerned citizens quickly learned otherwise. They did not want to hear dishonest denials so they could go to bed feeling better;

they wanted to hear the hard-bitten truth. And NOAA did all it could to avoid confirming the verity of its expansion program. So people stopped calling Alberg.

Nor did people need to speculate about NOAA's plans for expansion. The facts existed in the form of the April 2005 Strategic Plan, the Monitor NMS Expansion Committee, and SAC minutes of meetings during which expansion was discussed and favored. The truth was out there no matter how much NOAA denied it.

According to the Edwards' Timeline of Events, "A 300+ member dive club in Pennsylvania has expressed concerns over the potential restriction of access to wrecks of the NC coast." The club addressed its letter to the Carteret County Economic Development Council. Located in Carteret County, North Carolina was Morehead City: an active port of departure for recreational divers who wanted to visit the *U-352* and nearby shipwrecks.

The club stated its intention to take its vacation trips elsewhere should NOAA restrict access to local shipwrecks. This potential loss of revenue caused a furor in the Council. In response to this letter, the Council invited Alberg to attend its next monthly meeting.

The Edwards' reported: "They wanted to know from Alberg what his plans were. He again was unwilling/unable to state that there were any plans for a sanctuary expansion. It is established that there will be an Expansion Committee formed to find out if a sanctuary is wanted/needed in this area."

"Will be?" The Expansion Committee had been formed a year earlier. And plans for expansion had been articulated three years before that. This was another one of NOAA's bold attempts to blindside local government.

Pointless Exercise

The next SAC meeting was held in Hatteras on May 19, 2009: three months after publication of my newsletter exposé. Twenty commercial anglers, dive shop owners, charter boat operators, and recreational divers attended. Despite the oppositional turnout, the so-called "public guests" were in the minority. They were out-gunned by twenty-four NOAA representatives, including one of NOAA's attorneys.

After the meeting came to order, the standard announcement was made for the benefit of the "public guests." According to the minutes, "The sanctuary does not have any formal position on expansion at this time."

This time the "public guests" had been forewarned and knew otherwise. No longer could NOAA rely on untruthful statements to obfuscate its territorial imperative. No matter how much NOAA denied its plans for expansion, the "public guests," as well as a growing number of non-attending citizens, were eminently aware of the awful truth that NOAA was trying to hide, in order to avoid a public outcry.

Despite Alberg's insistence that "the sanctuary does not have any formal position on expansion," he formed a "working group" to assist the Expansion Committee. The purpose of the working group was to "aid in the management plan review process."

This Expansion Committee working group was no more legitimate than the Sanctuary Advisory Council. All five members who volunteered to serve on it were SAC members. Now NOAA had a working group to advise the Expansion Committee to advise the Sanctuary Advisory Council who in turn advised NOAA to proceed toward the goals that the members had sworn to help achieve. This was a case of incest taken to the nth degree.

Under the Radar

Despite its best efforts to fly under the radar, NOAA was now under public scrutiny. The minutes recorded a few of the public comments and questions that went to the heart of the matter:

"Wrecks are falling to pieces, so not sure why you want to protect them."

"When will you answer the questions asked at the scoping meetings?"

"You have made your mind up, so isn't this pointless?"

"Has an economic impact statement been done?"

"I'm not seeing the environmental and economic benefit."

"Have you met with the Governor?" Alberg had not.

Due to windy weather, the ferry from Ocracoke to Cedar Island did not run on the day of the meeting, so Bobby and Renate Edwards were not able to attend. But they had previously submitted a letter which was read aloud in their absence. Their unspoken comments hit the proverbial nail on the head. Here is the body of their letter:

It is frustrating that:
1. MNMS meeting agendas are not posted on the website in advance of the meetings.
2. MNMS meeting minutes can take 10 weeks to post on the website.
3. NOAA/MNMS meetings are held on weekdays, often in remote locations. This leaves far too many interested parties unable to attend and be heard.
4. Comments from the public seem to be valid only when made at 'official' meetings.

For example:

-At the October 22, 2008 'informational' meeting: many people voiced strong opposition to any imposition of the government into recreational diving activities. Where was that strong opposition documented?

-Multiple direct individual comments (by phone) have been made supporting the status quo of NC diving. How have those comments been documented?

-Individual divers and dive operators who visit the NC wrecks (and who stand to be most affected by the idea of sanctuary expansion) are not being represented adequately at official NOAA meetings. The average citizen: who will never dive these wrecks and will never be directly affected by government regulations of dive sites is being over-represented, while it appears that local and regional diver opinions are minimized.

-NOAA evidenced a clear bias by releasing a series of press releases in 2008, which were unreasonably disparaging to the NC recreational diver. That method of influencing public opinion is neither impartial nor fair to all parties involved. Frankly, it reflects rather poorly on the tactics of a government entity. Even after repeated questions as to the intent or retraction of the published words, NOAA has yet to formally address their informal claim that their press releases were enhanced/altered by the media.

"There are tens of hundreds of recreational divers who are against any change to government involvement in their diving activities off the coast of NC. Those people would like to know how their voices could be heard. They do not wish to discuss the actions, plans, or lack of plans for NOAA to expand the MNMS boundaries. They simply wish for the Monitor Sanctuary to remain as-is, and for their tax dollars be spent on matters of greater importance to the future of the United States."

This letter clearly and succinctly articulated the true voice of the people. Yet, although the Edwards' letter was appended to the minutes of the meeting, it is not discoverable by means of the NOAA website search engine. It seems as if the letter was intentionally expunged from discovery, along with every other letter of opposition.

The NOAA website has been sanitized so that it displays only those comments from solicited government "partners" that favor expansion. This deceptive stratagem gives the false impression that everyone favors expansion, while no one opposes it.

New Boundaries
One of the "public guests" at this meeting was Aaron

Harmon. Harmon was a long-time recreational diver whose primary shipwreck interest was in Nazi U-boats. He also worked for a dive shop. In addition to diving on North Carolina's U-boats, he had done considerable primary research on them. Thus he was well acquainted with the Nazi U-boat campaign along the U.S. eastern seaboard.

Despite Alberg's disingenuous avowal that "the sanctuary does not have any formal position on expansion," he spoke about the Battle of the Atlantic and how it related to shipwrecks that NOAA wanted to "protect" (read "control"). Harmon was horrified when he recognized the chart that Alberg used to demonstrate the scope of the Battle, and, by insinuation, the ultimate boundaries of what NOAA was now touting as the Battle of the Atlantic NMS.

The visual aid was a chart of the Eastern Sea Frontier!

I wrote a comprehensive book about the Battle of the Atlantic, which raged from 1942 to 1945. It was entitled *The Fuhrer's U-boats in American Waters*. In it I described the theater of operations thus:

"Generally, the ESF covered the coast from Maine to Georgia, running offshore at first to about one hundred miles, then later extending halfway to Bermuda. The specific boundaries started at the southern coastal extreme of Duval County, Florida, just below the Georgia border at Jacksonville Beach. A southeasterly line was drawn from there to a point at $25°$ north, $72°$ west, which somewhat paralleled the Bahamas. The offshore limit was defined as then heading northerly to $40°$ north, $69°$ west; thence due north along the 69th meridian to the 43rd parallel; thence to Lucher Shoal Lightship; thence to land along the International Boundary Line between the U.S. and Canada. . . .

"On December 1, 1944, the boundaries were altered. Starting at the International Boundary, the line went south to $43°$ north, $67°$ west; thence southeasterly to $42°$ north, $65°$ west; thence southwesterly to the boundary of the Gulf Sea Frontier at $27°$ north, $75°$ $30'$ west;

thence back to the Jacksonville Beach area now defined as 30° 15' north, 81° 20' west."

By either boundary, it now became apparent that NOAA eventually expected to expand its Sanctuary boundaries to encompass the entire eastern seaboard!

The first step was to expand the Monitor NMS to include the so-called Graveyard of the Atlantic off the Diamond Shoals of North Carolina, while at the same time expanding the Stellwagen Bank NMS to include all the waters off the State of Massachusetts (see Subterfuge 301 for details). Afterward, the two sanctuaries would be joined as one massive sanctuary that would then be merged with the Gray's Reef NMS off the coast of Georgia. This conglomerate sanctuary would then extend from Canada to Florida, and perhaps later still, beyond.

This long-term hidden agenda brings to mind a couple of relevant quotes.

On September 4, 2004, NOAA released a 118-page document that was entitled "Proposed Northwestern Hawaiian Islands National Marine Sanctuary." As the title suggests, NOAA was proposing to establish a Hawaiian sanctuary that would encompass more than 135,000 square miles. To put the dimensions into perspective, the size of the proposed sanctuary would be larger than the State of New Mexico, slightly smaller than the State of California, and roughly half the size of the State of Texas.

(In aside, the document proposed to completely prohibit or severely restrict all forms of fishing, lobster catching, and coral collecting in most of the sanctuary. It even prohibited unannounced vessel passage *through* the sanctuary, subject to official approval that was based on three days prior notice.)

Daniel Basta, National Marine Sanctuary Program Director, indicated his hopes thus: "When the NWHI is designated, National Marine Sanctuary System will manage by far more real estate than all of the national parks and fish and wildlife refugees [sic] combined."

Talk about "creeping jurisdiction"!

Perhaps David Howe articulated NOAA's ultimate

goal better than Basta. (Howe was a member of the self-styled Institute of Maritime History.) He stated, "When I am king the entire territorial sea will be a NOAA sanctuary."

Enough said.

Fib or Fabrication

Meanwhile, Jim Bunch volunteered to take the SAC seat as "recreational diver representative." Bunch was a long-time recreational diver whose primary interest was the *U-85*: so much so that he wrote a book about it. He also used to own a dive shop on the Outer Banks, where I used to buy air fills.

After he took his oath of allegiance to NOAA, he sent emails to me and to other divers who had expressed opposition to expansion. Because he asked for input, I replied, "As always I advocate unconditional access to all wreck sites. But NOAA does not want to hear that thought, or permit it."

My invited input never made it into the SAC meeting minutes. By this I do not mean to imply that Bunch ignored my input, only that my input – and the input of others who opposed any and all NOAA involvement with the shipwrecks off North Carolina – went unrecorded.

Bunch announced SAC meeting dates and places in subsequent emails. But he also spread information that could be easily misinterpreted by recipients who were unaware of all the facts.

For example, on March 12, 2009, he wrote: "Recently there has been a lot of speculation both within our state and outside our state about the future of the [Monitor] Sanctuary with respect to possible Expansions in the future. At this time, to the best of my knowledge, there is nothing like this in the planning stages and certainly not in the works. Expansion is however a concept that has been talked about and will most likely be talked more about in the future."

This statement was true as far as it went, but it flew in the face of the facts: that NOAA's Strategic Plan of 2005 specifically called for hijacking 1,200 shipwrecks.

Since then NOAA had established an advisory council, an expansion committee, and a working group, all of which were geared toward filching ways and means to expand the sanctuary by fair means or foul.

Honesty is the best policy only when intentions are honest. When Bunch was sworn into the Sanctuary Advisory Council, he was kept in the dark about NOAA's four-year-old plan for shipwreck annexation.

Tell It Like It Is

On June 10, 2009, I published another newsletter update on NOAA's expansion plan. For obvious reasons I entitled it "Modern Day Pirate." After some introductory remarks, whose language I have utilized in the sections above, I wrote:

> You should also be aware that NOAA's Congressional mandate states absolutely nothing about controlling shipwrecks or monopolizing access to the sites. NOAA has taken this tack on its own; has, in fact, violated its Congressional mandate.
>
> The sole reason for creating the Marine Protection, Research, and Sanctuaries Act was, and I quote from the Act, "to protect valuable, unique, or endangered marine life, geological features, and oceanographic features." Nothing – I repeat, nothing – was ever mentioned about policing shipwrecks.
>
> By definition of the MPRSA, the Monitor NMS and Thunder Bay NMS are illegal. To add absurdity, Thunder Bay is not even a marine environment; it is a freshwater lake. The definition of "marine" is "of or relating to the sea." By no stretch of the imagination can Thunder Bay relate to the sea. In fact, the sole reason that NOAA created the Thunder Bay NMS was to control the shipwrecks that are located within its boundaries. The same is true of the Monitor NMS (which at least is located in the ocean).

In the old days, pirates were hanged for robbing ships – for taking even a single ship. Yet NOAA is getting away with wholesale piracy, and with complete impunity.

When will Congress wake up to the fact that the National Marine Sanctuary Program has been exceeding its authority ever since its inception thirty-five years ago? That although the MPRSA was mandated by Congress to "preserve, restore, or enhance areas for their conservational, recreational, ecological, research or esthetic values in coastal water," the program has never done anything to benefit the American people, and especially the "recreational" members of the public? That NOAA is hijacking shipwrecks under the guise of "preservation" for its own personal pleasure and use. That NOAA is getting more out of control with each passing moment?

One could hope that enlightenment might come as new blood is infused into the National Marine Sanctuary Program, as new people are hired to replace those whose views are outdated and dictatorial. Instead, new people are either infected by the diseased minds of their superiors in the hierarchy, or they are indoctrinated not just to maintain the status quo, but to further enforce aggrandizement of the Program.

There is only one logical manner in which to handle this situation. The National Marine Sanctuary Program must be abolished.

If you want to read the sad truth about NOAA's nefarious activities, read my book *Ironclad Legacy: Battles of the USS Monitor*. You can also read about NOAA's heinous handling of the Stellwagen Bank NMS in the chapter that is titled "The Stellwagen Bank Robbery," in my book *Shipwreck Heresies*.

Both accounts will make you cringe.

This newsletter is not just a well-deserved and vitriolic diatribe against NOAA. It is a wake-up call for all of you who are appalled by the government's excessive abuse of authority. Unless you want NOAA to continue to get away with cheating the public of its birthright, lodge complaints with your State and federal representatives.

Don't waste your time by attending NOAA scoping meetings or public hearings. NOAA representatives will only lie to you and misrepresent NOAA's intentions and future plans, in order to convince you that it has your best interests at heart, and that it will not alter the status quo without your full consent.

Nor will it do any good to air your views about how Sanctuaries should be managed. NOAA representatives will suffer through your dialogue, then kiss you off as soon as the meeting is over. NOAA doesn't give a wit about your opinions or suggestions. The scoping meetings and public hearings are merely window dressing, designed to lull you into believing that NOAA cares about your viewpoints. NOAA will do whatever it wants to do and can get away with.

I repeat: complain to your State and federal representatives. A congressional leader interceded in my *Monitor* case, and forced NOAA to rescind its ban against issuing permits to dive on the wreck. But Congress hasn't been keeping a tight leash on NOAA. A new generation of NOAA minions is continuing to take away freedoms that are supposedly guaranteed by the Constitution of the United States.

Thomas Jefferson once said, "The price of freedom is eternal vigilance."

That statement is just as true today as it was two hundred years ago. Perhaps more so.

Again I apologize for my acerbic rhetoric. Again I declare that I am not ashamed of it. I simply wrote the truth in hard-bitten terms without pulling any punches.

Besides, you can't punch NOAA below the belt because it wears its belt around its ankles.

The Perpetuation of Untruths

The next SAC meeting was supposedly held out-of-state on October 26, 2009, but NOAA has seen fit to suppress publication of the minutes. This leaves me to wonder what Machiavellian schemes NOAA is concealing from the public.

It should also be noted that the so-called "working group" either did not keep minutes of its meetings or withheld them from the public. This can be perceived as a clever deceit that was designed to keep its machinations out of the public eye. Nor were the working group's "advices" to the Council made available for public consumption.

From this point onward, NOAA, SAC, the Expansion Committee, and the working group went underground. No new information about NOAA's strategic plan for expansion was made public. On the contrary, NOAA continued its transparent denial that no such plan existed.

The next SAC meeting that NOAA acknowledged holding, was held out-of-state on February 17, 2010. According to the minutes, "Dave [Alberg] discussed his recent trip to the Richmond Dive Club where he presented to over 40 people. He described the members' responses as very positive for the need of protection for some shipwrecks."

According to James Young and James Dacey, president of the Richmond Dive Club, this was a departure from the truth. Some club members were taken in by Alberg's treacle and honey-coated statements because he misrepresented NOAA's actual goals. He claimed that NOAA wanted to "protect" less than a handful of shipwrecks, without describing what he meant by "protection." He failed to mention the other 1,195 shipwrecks that NOAA wanted to annex under its 2005 Strategic Plan. And he neglected to inform the audience that access to North Carolina shipwrecks could be either prohibited or severely restricted.

Subsequently, I gave a slide presentation to the Richmond Dive Club. At that time I polled the members about the expansion issue. Not only did no one favor expansion, they were all adamantly opposed to it.

Alberg also told the dive club, "NOAA has no position on expansion, but our sanctuary has had strong recommendations from our council to explore the possibility of expanding the boundaries of the sanctuary." This is the same council that swore an oath to assist NOAA in achieving the Sanctuary's goals for expansion.

Unprotected

I once wrote, "To preserve a flag one does not hang it on a pole during a full gale: it is folded and packed away safely. One does not store precious china on an exposed mountain ridge where it is subject to rock falls, summer sun, and winter snow: it is kept in a glass case under controlled conditions. An artifact must be preserved from the elements of nature, not consigned to its capriciousness; the longer it is constrained to these wild forces, the less likely it is to survive intact, to be found and appreciated by future generations."

Shipwrecks are time capsules that are rapidly disintegrating.

From the Edwards' Timeline of Events: "Mother nature yields a far heavier hand on our wrecks than any diver ever could. Concerns over damage at the hands of sport divers are overblown."

Worse than the obvious truth is the fact that NOAA keeps pretending to Congress, and to the non-diving public that does not know any better, that shipwrecks suffer more damage from recreational divers than they suffer from the devastating forces of nature. No matter how much NOAA bleats that its ultimate goal is to "protect" shipwrecks, the truth is that shipwrecks cannot be protected as long as they are left under water.

Foul Weather

Instead of expending its resources on restricting diver access, Edwards asked the question: "Why can't

NOAA maintain their weather buoys in the ocean off of our coast. There seems to be no time or money to provide the public with weather and ocean data that has been extremely useful to anyone venturing into the ocean off of the coast of NC." He also put it another way, "NOAA should spend more time and effort maintaining their dwindling system of Weather Buoys."

Pete Manchee posed the same question at the scoping meeting that was held on May 1, 2012. Manchee has a personal interest in offshore weather forecasting because he is a U.S. Coast Guard licensed captain, who operates dive boats on a weekly basis off both Carolinas. In a personal communication to me, Manchee wrote: "I suggested to Mr. Alberg that they spend their time and effort improving the navigational and weather buoy systems to make seafaring safer rather than grabbing more wrecks to control."

Alberg did not have an answer for him.

Edwards' and Manchee's complaints are as valid today as they were when they lodged them. As of this writing, the weather buoy in the vicinity of the *Monitor* (buoy #41025) has been out of service for more than a year. NOAA has made no prediction about when it might be repaired. Other forecasting devices are similarly deficient.

Yet in the January 2013 issue of *Sea Technology*, NOAA administrator Jane Lubchenco wrote: "Ocean observations are becoming increasingly important in this climate-changed world." And: "Challenges remain. Coverage remains an obvious one." And: "More reliable detection of extreme conditions is needed." She also stated the need for the "continuity of observations."

Despite Lubchenco's written observations, her true feelings are belied by her preoccupation on matters of sanctuary expansion and fraudulent violation penalties. (The latter subject is addressed in Subterfuges 401 and 501.)

Daft Management's Plan

In April 2012, NOAA released its massive 212-page

"Monitor National Marine Sanctuary Draft Revised Management Plan," complete with a 7-page justification for expansion despite nearly unanimous opposition from community stakeholders: anglers, divers, and businesses. I will begin discussion of this Plan by indicating items of misrepresentation, and end it with two short sentences which clearly and succinctly deduce its meaning.

Page IV: "Typically a management plan review is conducted at a sanctuary every five years. A sanctuary management plan is a site-specific planning and management document that describes the goals, objectives, policies, management strategies, and activities for a sanctuary." Yet, in the thirty-seven-year history of the Monitor NMS, this was only the second such plan review. (The Strategic Plan 2005 – 2015 was not site-specific, but included all National Marine Sanctuaries.)

Page XIII: "The wreck [of the *Monitor*] was in general good condition, although some structural damage and deterioration was apparent." This statement is belied by practically every other description of the wreck, including those that were made by NOAA.

Page XVI: "The wreck [of the Monitor] is extremely fragile." This statement directly contradicts the statement on page XIII. It seems as if NOAA's archaeologists and management personnel cannot make up their minds as to whether the wreck is "in general good condition" or "extremely fragile." Each description was used in support of a particular position that NOAA was advocating at the time.

Page XVI: "Diving in the sanctuary is done through a permitting system and MNMS works hard to promote access and minimize the time it takes to obtain a permit." There is no acknowledgment of the eight years and numerous federal lawsuits that it took me to obtain the first recreational diving permit, nor of Todd Baldi's six years in submitting permit applications that were ignored.

Page XVII: "Some fishing activities may negatively affect and threaten the fragile archaeological resources of

MNMS, but most pose no threat. The primary concern from fishing activities is the use of bottom gear and anchoring (which is prohibited within the sanctuary) and marine debris in the form of derelict fishing gear becoming entangled on the wreck." There is no mention of the fact that the sanctuary is not marked – that is, no buoys have been emplaced to warn mariners of the sanctuary's location. It is difficult if not impossible for the operators of fishing boats to know when they are crossing the sanctuary's invisible border.

Page XVII: "The discharge of untreated sewage from vessels is not allowed within or into the sanctuary." Again, NOAA's management decision to keep the sanctuary unmarked prevents transitory vessels from knowing when they are passing through sanctuary waters. Coastal freighters and supertankers traverse the wreck site all the time because the *Monitor* lies beneath the shipping lanes.

Page XVII: "NOAA has been working to make the wreck site more accessible to SCUBA divers through greater outreach efforts and by encouraging new permit applications." Documented history proves otherwise.

Page XX: "During the 2008 scoping meetings for the Monitor National Marine Sanctuary management plan, many of the commentors [sic] expressed an interest in expanding the sanctuary to include additional shipwrecks off the coast of North Carolina." In this sentence, not only is the word "many" not quantified, but the phrase "while the vast majority opposed expansion" is left out. This gross misstatement of the facts deliberately mischaracterized the true feelings of the constituency. The overwhelming majority of the "expressed interest" was expressed in opposition to expansion.

Page XX: "Further, the Monitor National Marine Sanctuary Advisory Council has recommended that NOAA start a formal process to consider expansion." This statement neglects to mention that the Sanctuary Advisory Council program was a scam. As noted numerous times above, SAC members were chosen on the basis of their allegiance to NOAA. The sole purpose of the

Council was to proffer the advice that NOAA ordered the Council to provide, in order to give NOAA's actions the appearance of legitimacy.

Page 16: "NOAA has prepared this current draft management plan in cooperation with the advisory council and with input from the public, state and federal agencies, and other stakeholders." This sentence gives the erroneous impression that NOAA *cooperated* with stakeholders and the general public, when in fact NOAA *ignored* them and proceeded with its agenda despite crushing opposition.

Page 17: "Working groups met numerous times in 2009 and developed suggestions and recommendations for action plans, strategies and activities, which were presented to the advisory council for consideration on October 27, 2009. The advisory council voted unanimously to accept these recommendations." Again, the working groups were nothing more than another scam that was created to add legitimacy to the SAC program. NOAA gives the false impression that the members of these groups and councils were unbiased, when in fact all members of all groups and councils were handpicked because of their favoritism toward NOAA, and all swore an oath of allegiance to promote NOAA's goals.

Page 31: It is imperative to understand that NOAA has expressed no intention of changing current sanctuary regulations. To wit: "Monitor National Marine Sanctuary regulations prohibit activities that could in any way alter the sanctuary's existing habitats or disturb or damage its natural resources. Activities such as anchoring . . . are highly restricted." And "Prohibition of commercial fishing and trawling in the sanctuary helps to eliminate the pressure of fishing gear on the living resources." Because these prohibitions will stay in effect in the proposed expanded sanctuary, all forms of fishing and recreational diving will be outlawed. (Boats must anchor in order to enable divers to descend safely to the bottom and ascend to the boat.)

Page 32: "The wreck has become covered in fishing line, monofilament, cables and other types of fishing gear and marine debris. Much of this debris was the direct result of fishing activities on the wreck." NOAA neglected to mention that its refusal to mark the site with a warning buoy effectively prevented the operators of pleasure craft from knowing that they were encroaching on sanctuary waters. Even so, the historical record contains only a single instance in which anglers were caught bottom fishing on the wreck: a wreck that they had been fishing on for years, because they did not know that it was the *Monitor*. NOAA also neglected to mention that it was common practice for people who were working under NOAA auspices to fish on the site from surface support vessels during NOAA's various survey and salvage operations, when the boat was moored over top of the wreck. As the saying goes, what's good for the goose . . .

Page 44: "In 1990, for the first time, NOAA issued research permits to private dive groups who dove to the *Monitor* using conventional scuba equipment." NOAA neglected to mention that the first so-called research permit was not issued voluntarily: it took six years of legal action to force the issuance of that permit. This deliberate omission gives the false impression that NOAA has always cooperated with the recreational diving community, when in fact it was staunchly opposed to the rights of the diving community. NOAA's acquiescence to the rights of the recreational diving community was forced upon it by courtroom judgment and Congressional intervention.

Pages 47-48: "The [Sanctuary Advisory] council serves as a forum for consultation and deliberation among its members and as a source of advice to the sanctuary superintendent regarding the management of MNMS." As long as NOAA keeps harping on the validity of SAC, I must keep refuting its legitimacy.

Page 80: "In proximity to the Monitor National Marine Sanctuary are wreck sites of vessels that were part of the Battle of the Atlantic during World War II. MNMS, in conjunction with the National Marine Sanctuary's Maritime Heritage Program, has incorporated the investigation of these wreck sites into a multi-year study of the Battle of the Atlantic. The goal of this study is to analyze the material remains from WWII vessels, determine their historical significance and identify degradation from environmental and human impact. In addition to studying each site individually, identifying how these sites are connected in a cohesive 'battlefield' is also being examined. Therefore, Allied, Axis, and merchant vessels have been and will continue to be vessels of interest."

NOAA was stating its intention to examine *every* World War Two shipwreck at the taxpayers' expense.

Page 152: This is the title page of a "PROGRAMMATIC AGREEMENT AMONG THE NATIONAL OCEANIC AND ATMOSPHERIC ADMINISTRATION AND THE MARINERS' MUSEUM AND THE VIRGINIA STATE HISTORIC PRESERVATION OFFICER AND THE ADVISORY COUNCIL ON HISTORIC PRESERVATION FOR PROTECTION AND MANAGEMENT OF THE MONITOR COLLECTION." The following nine pages consist of agreements and stipulations among the signatories. Under the clause for the resolution of disputes, NOAA asserts, "If NOAA determines that the disagreement cannot be resolved, NOAA shall request the comments of the Monitor SAC." Once again, because SAC members have sworn an oath of allegiance to assist NOAA in achieving its goals, thus making SAC nothing more than a NOAA puppet or instrument of trickery, this cleverly camouflaged clause means essentially that NOAA will act as sole judge, jury, and executioner if any of the other signatories disagree with NOAA's position.

NOAA constantly invokes SAC as if it were an honest, impartial, and disinterested referee, instead of a bogus in-house construct whose sole purpose is that of deception.

The Crux of the Matter

Worse yet is the most crucial item of all: not what is stated in this daft management plan, but what is unstated. Nowhere in the 2012 Draft Revised Management

Plan does NOAA propose to ease access regulations in the sanctuary, in either its present boundaries or in its yet-to-be-determined expanded boundaries. On the contrary, NOAA goes as far as to specify "Activities prohibited within the Sanctuary." Thus:

"Except as may be permitted by the Administrator, no person subject to the jurisdiction of the United States shall conduct, nor cause to be conducted, any of the following activities in the Sanctuary: (a) anchoring in any manner, stopping, remaining, or drifting without power at any time; (b) any type of subsurface salvage or recover [sic] operations; (c) any type of diving whether by an individual or by a submersible; (d) lowering below the surface of the water any grappling, suction, conveyor, dredging or wrecking device; (e) detonation below the surface of the water of any explosive or explosive mechanism; (f) seabed drilling or coring; (g) lowering, laying, positioning or raising any type of seabed cable or cable-laying device; (h) trawling; or (i) discharging waste material into the water in violation of any Federal statute or regulation."

In conclusion, no recreational diving or fishing of any kind will be permitted within the expanded boundaries without a permit. Only NOAA's officially designated Administrator is authorized to issue permits, at his or her discretion. No court of appeals exists or is planned. If this system sounds suspiciously like totalitarianism, so be it.

By deft sleight of hand, NOAA was ardently trying to conceal the fact that it wanted the old sanctuary regulations to apply to the newly expanded sanctuary: the size of which will be determined not by the voters but by NOAA's ambition for expansion of its territorial authority.

NOAA's Flimflam Plan

By this time, awareness of NOAA's intentions – of taking possession of all the shipwrecks off the coast of North Carolina as the next step in its bid for extension of its underwater sovereignty – had snowballed. Divers and anglers could no longer be caught off guard. When NOAA announced another series of scoping meetings, forum threads erupted on the Internet like flowers blossoming in springtime. The public attended these meetings in droves in order to voice fierce opposition to NOAA's plans for expansion.

Alberg duped attendees by making seemingly innocuous and unrelated statements at sporadic times during his oration, but which taken together – along with the knowledge of how NOAA premeditated its con game – reveal a brilliant subterfuge of hoodwinking the public while seeming to offer commiseration. At the risk of repeating myself, let me demonstrate his tactics from the May 4 scoping meeting (of which I have a recording).

First, Alberg mentioned in passing NOAA's reliance on advice from its Sanctuary Advisory Council. Ten minutes later, he stated flatly, "NOAA is not proposing expansion of the sanctuary. That is not in this plan. You can look through it all day long. You will not find it." A couple of minutes later, he said, "We were interested in hearing what people had to say about it [expansion]." Then, within seconds, he added, "It [the Plan] does not advocate for any closures. It does not advocate, um, for any expansion of the existing boundaries. And in fact this entire document has no regulatory changes in it whatsoever."

A minute or so later he repeated for emphasis, "This document does not suggest, or call, for any changes to the existing regulations, or any changes to the boundary."

Alberg's continued emphasis on *this* document tended to draw attention away from a previous NOAA document – "Our National Marine Sanctuaries Strategic Plan 2005-2015" – in which NOAA advanced its covert scheme to appropriate 1,200 shipwrecks.

As Alberg later clarified for the news media, "The need to discuss expansion was first raised during public scoping meetings in 2008, and ultimately was recommended by the sanctuary's advisory council."

When the elements are put together in their proper

order, and are viewed in light of NOAA's evident hostility toward the public in general and toward anglers and divers in particular, a different and more objective interpretation can be made, and NOAA's nefarious plot becomes overtly obvious.

The "need" to discuss expansion was raised by NOAA, not by the public; there was no "need" of expansion until NOAA created the concept. NOAA established a Sanctuary Advisory Council to offer advice about expansion. SAC meeting minutes were available to the public. SAC created a working group to make recommendations regarding the expansion issue. Working-group meetings either did not keep minutes or those minutes were withheld from the public. All members of SAC and the expansion working group were specially selected personnel who favored expansion, and who swore an oath of allegiance to assist NOAA in achieving the sanctuary's goals. The expansion working group recommended expansion. SAC voted unanimously to accept the recommendation of the expansion working group. SAC advised NOAA to consider expansion of the sanctuary; in reality, using SAC as a straw boss, NOAA advised *itself* to consider expansion of the sanctuary. The new plan calls for no regulatory changes. NOAA can adopt SAC's (NOAA's own) recommendations in whole or in part. NOAA will adopt the recommendations that suit its ultimate goal.

The end result will be precisely what NOAA wanted all along: NOAA can expand the boundaries of the sanctuary as far as it wants, and it can enforce regulations that prohibit or severely restrict access. All fishing and diving in the sanctuary can be banned; voters and stakeholders will have no say in the matter. Cumbersome access permits will be subject to administrative discretion; issuance of permits can be denied or placed in limbo for years.

NOAA can give the appearance that its hands were tied; that supposedly unprejudiced members of the Sanctuary Advisory Council agreed unanimously that expansion was necessary to "protect" shipwrecks. NOAA

comes out of the fray looking innocent, as if it did not
want to expand the sanctuary but was forced to accept
SAC's unanimous recommendation.

Alberg finally admitted that he had no decision-making authority; that the final decision would be made by
a higher authority. This "out" lets him don a false front
of sympathy, even though he has a history of expressing
contempt for divers and anglers: the very stakeholders
who have the most to lose from expansion and total regulatory control.

At the time of this writing, the "higher" authority is
NOAA's head administrator, Jane Lubchenco. She and
she alone will decide whether or not to expand the sanctuary, notwithstanding the overwhelming opposition of
the voters/stakeholders.

Lubchenco's administration of NOAA has been
fraught with controversy: running the gamut from gross
misconduct to outright fraud: all of which is in keeping
with NOAA's history of mismanagement. Under a storm
of protest, members of Congress have called for
Lubchenco's resignation, and it seems certain that she
will resign, if she has not done so already.

Unfortunately, Lubchenco's administration was not
much different from previous administrations: pretty
much in tune with NOAA's history of misconduct. There
is no reason to hope that her replacement will be any
better.

NOAA's scheme for passing laws is not democratic.
Whenever the wishes of a single individual supersede
the wishes of the majority of the voters, the system of
government is called a dictatorship.

Under NOAA's self-indulgent aegis, its cancerous
growth will only continue to expand. NOAA will maintain
sole discretionary power to decide how far to expand the
boundaries, and what regulations to enforce. Once expansion is accomplished in the Monitor NMS, NOAA can
indicate the need for additional expansion in order to
"protect" more shipwrecks; thus the first expansion will
set the precedent for expanding all the other sanctuaries, until the National Marine Sanctuary Program com-

pletely encircles the country and, eventually, the planet.

American voters have no say in the matter. World domination is complete.

The writing is on the wall for those who can read.

Opening Gambit

Of the five scoping meetings that NOAA held in May 2012, one was held out-of-state, in Virginia, on May 4. If this was an attempt to reduce attendance, the attempt failed. It may have excluded attendance of North Carolina residents who lived far away, but residents of northern States have a stake in North Carolina shipwrecks, too: recreational divers and weekend anglers who take holidays in the affected area.

Maryland resident Karen Flynn attended the final meeting. She was armed with a list of insightful questions. She also recorded the session for posterity.

Alberg opened the session with this statement: "The purpose of a management plan is that, we are required to periodically review how we do business, all facets, from, um, our regulations, our permitting, our access, go back, look at how we're doing, put that out for public comment, solicit input from the public, in terms of, uh, questions, suggestions, concerns, go back, revive the plan, and then put it out."

Note that Alberg did not state that NOAA had to *address* public concerns; it had only to *solicit* them. Afterward, it could determine at its own discretion what changes, if any, to implement. He spoke in such a halting and distracting fashion that this crucial point could easily have been misunderstood by the public in attendance.

Size Matters

Flynn pushed for an answer to the most serious question in the public mind: "No proposed boundaries of an expanded MNMS or specific shipwrecks are listed in this document. However, during the past several years, NOAA has surveyed many of the wreck sites near the Monitor National Marine Sanctuary ranging from the *U-701* site off Avon North Carolina to several sites off Morehead City, North Carolina. So it appears that NOAA has already been 'considering' expansion since approximately 2007/2008. While the boundaries of an expanded Monitor National Marine Sanctuary may not yet be determined, there is some thoughts and planning, and actual activity that has already taken place that would appear to indicate that NOAA has some thoughts regarding the scale of an expanded sanctuary.

"The current Monitor Sanctuary is nearly insignificantly tiny. It is a circular area only one mile in diameter and encompasses only .83 square miles. By being so tiny, it is easily avoided and its complete restriction of nearly all marine activities has a negligible impact on the public or regional marine interests. In contrast, the 'Graveyard of the Atlantic' off North Carolina is generally thought of as the entire North Carolina coast, which is huge – over three hundred miles in length and contains thousands of square miles.

"What is the general area of consideration of the proposed 'expanded' sanctuary area? Just how large will this 'expansion' be?"

Alberg deftly avoided answering this query by changing the subject to the *U-701*. Even after his uncalled-for digression, he never gave a forthright answer to Flynn's question. Nowhere, neither in the management plan, nor in SAC recommendations, nor in the published minutes of any NOAA meetings, nor in any of Alberg's comments, did NOAA specify – or even approximate – the overall dimensions of the newly proposed sanctuary. That issue still remains unknown to the public.

The U-boat Rationale

Alberg: "The work that has been done off the coast between, starting in the spring of 2008, was done, um, not, it was actually done in response to the German government's request, because of a planned expedition, a private expedition, out to *U-701*, to recover artifacts."

Once again Alberg's assertion deviated far from the

written record.

I was curious enough about this offhanded statement to seek the truth of the matter. On May 18, 2012, I submitted a request pursuant to the Freedom of Information Act, for "copies of all correspondence, documents, emails, notes, telephone transcripts, inter-office memos, and any other form of documentation to which Alberg referred: not only correspondence addressed *to* NOAA and other government agencies, but all replies, correspondence, documents, emails, notes, telephone transcripts, inter-office memos, and any other form of documentation *from* NOAA with regard to Nazi U-boats in American waters."

NOAA jerked me around for six months. Not until November 19, 2012, did I receive the full documentation that NOAA was willing to release to me. And this was only after nearly a dozen follow-up letters and phone calls. One NOAA agent told me on the phone that some documents had been put aside pending authorization for release. I argued that if a document existed, then it was discoverable.

Nonetheless, a number of documents were withheld – the number being unknown to me. I know this firsthand because a NOAA agent informed me so. But I also know from gaps in the documents that were eventually released to me. Some of them furnished answers for which I do not have the documents in which the questions were posed. Others ask questions for which I have no documents with answers. There is also a three-and-a-half-month hiatus – from February 20, 2008 to June 6, 2008 – during which span I have no dated documents.

Furthermore, numerous documents refer to phone calls that were either received or were to be made. I received no transcripts of phone calls, making it seem that phone calls were not recorded. The best way to keep information out of the public eye is not to create a discoverable document.

To start with the end of the matter, the German government did *not* ask for NOAA's assistance with regard to sunken U-boats. It was the other way around: NOAA contacted the German embassy in Washington, DC, claiming, "These vessels [*U-85, U-352,* and *U-701*] were discovered many years ago but unfortunately they appear to have been impacted by souvenir hunters and looters."

NOAA neglected to mention that its partner, the U.S. Navy, was the most responsible agent of negative impact: the recovery of a torpedo from the *U-85,* and the exhumation of 500 *tons* of sand, silt, cultural remains, and human bones from the *U-352.* These salvage operations were conducted *without* the approval of the German government. The Navy heisted these relics with impunity: behind the back of the German government. But let's go back a step, prior to NOAA's involvement.

In December 2007, Robert Gabriel sent a letter to John McCord, of the University of North Carolina Coastal Studies Institute. In part: "I propose that before the *U-701* is pillaged by man/time/and the elements with all information being lost, that a complete and professional program of research, on site mapping, photographing, filming, and recovery of artifacts, with special interest to the human aspect of the crew and equipment used be done as soon as possible with a full IMAX film of the work and history of the *U-701.*"

The opening salvo that led to contact with NOAA was dated December 18, 2007, from John McCord to Nathan Richards, at East Carolina University: "We have been contacted by a man named Bob Gabriel who is interested in a partnership with the Coastal Studies Institute on a project involving the sunken German U-boat U701. Bob is interested in a diving expedition in which the U701 would be mapped and filmed and certain artifacts of human interest would be recovered for display in the Graveyard of the Atlantic Museum located in Hatteras. He has also been in contact with the German government who are obviously interested in the recovery of any human remains that be still be [sic] on the German U boat."

Gabriel already had full funding for the project from

the German automobile manufacturer Mercedes-Benz, and clearance from the German Federal Ministry of Finance.

I do not have a copy of Richards' reply, but McCord wrote later: "I don't have a problem with you forwarding this on [presumably to NOAA], but I know he [Gabriel] is worried that someone would come in and sweep the project out from under him."

And that is where NOAA stepped in – to sweep the project out from under the person who formulated the idea. NOAA commenced to jump the gun on Gabriel sometime between December 18, 2007 and January 11, 2008 (the latter being the earliest date on documents that NOAA released to me). NOAA explored several options that would sabotage Gabriel's project.

One proposal was to nominate the U-boats to the National Register of Historic Places. This would effectively prevent disturbance of the sites. A great deal of correspondence (and presumably undocumented phone calls) involved discussion of this option, but ultimately NOAA ascertained that it did not have the authority to nominate property that was supposedly owned by a foreign government.

Another way to derail Gabriel was to convince the German government that his project would constitute "the disruption of these war graves." These were Alberg's words to NOAA attorney Ole Varmer, expressed on January 11, 2008. NOAA then asked the U.S. Navy to help put Gabriel in Dutch with Germany through the Navy's contacts: a strategy that NOAA pursued with a vengeance.

It appears from the historical record that the German government showed little if any interest in the wrecks of Nazi U-boats in American waters. The German government was probably unaware of the clandestine U.S. Navy salvage of the torpedo from the *U-85*. Nor had the German government made any formal protest about the highly publicized salvage operation on the *U-352*.

Documentary evidence shows that NOAA henpecked the German embassy in Washington, DC for the next five months, begging someone – any embassy employee – to take an interest in the North Carolina U-boats. Not until June 25, 2008 – only two weeks before NOAA's U-boat expedition was supposed to hit the water, did a single individual respond with a letter of acknowledgment. Apparently the new German government found contemporary matters of greater importance than the fate of sunken warships that belonged to a previous and infamous regime.

In the meantime, despite the lack of endorsement from the German embassy, NOAA proceeded to make detailed and expensive plans to conduct its own survey of the *U-701*, and of the other two U-boats as well.

At the May 4, 2012 scoping meeting, Alberg claimed, "We put together an expedition that was not funded with NOAA dollars, it was funded with actually at the time with what is now, was BOEM [Bureau of Ocean Energy Management], but it was Mineral Management Service at the time."

This statement is at variance with a letter that NOAA sent to the German embassy. Alberg should have known better because, not only did he lead the expedition, but he signed the letter of intent to the Germany embassy: the presumption being that he wrote it.

On June 6, 2008, Alberg wrote, "The expedition is being funded by the National Oceanic and Atmospheric Administration's (NOAA) Office of National Marine Sanctuaries (ONMS) as part of a larger Battle of the Atlantic archaeology study."

I don't know which of Alberg's declarations was false. Either he lied to the addressee in the German embassy, or he lied to Karen Flynn and the other "concerned" citizens at the meeting. Perhaps he lied to all. Perhaps none of what he said was true.

Once a person loses credibility, there is no way to distinguish his lies from his truths (if any).

The reality of the situation differed diametrically from Alberg's public presentation. The German government did *not* request NOAA's assistance; the German government – that is, the political body in Germany that represented the needs and requirements of the German people – took no sides on the Nazi U-boat issue. On the contrary, NOAA solicited – indeed, *begged* – an individual in the German embassy to quash Gabriel's expedition and to endorse its own, as a way of providing a rationale for its impromptu expedition.

Insertion 1 – the Potsdam Agreement

Before I continue with Flynn's request for elucidation, the reader must be made aware of World War Two unconditional surrender terms that relate to ownership of Nazi U-boats.

In accordance with the terms of the Potsdam Agreement, Germany was completely stripped of its army, navy, and air force. It was not allowed to produce either arms or munitions; indeed, Krupp (Germany's primary arms and armor manufacturer) was largely dismantled, and what remained of the company was converted to the manufacture of kitchen appliances. Germany's entire navy – its few remaining capital ships as well as hundreds of U-boats and even part of its merchant fleet – was seized by the Allies for reparations or disposal.

Each of the three major Allied powers (U.S., U.K. and U.S.S.R.) kept a number of U-boats "for technical assessment and experimental purposes." The others were scuttled at sea.

It was stipulated in the Potsdam Agreement that Germany was not allowed to possess instruments of war of any kind: tanks, cannons, artillery, rockets, surface warships, and particularly U-boats. Winston Churchill went as far as to specify that U-boats must be dismantled or destroyed.

What the Potsdam Agreement means in relation to the subject at hand is that Germany was not allowed to own U-boats: then or forever more. In turn, this means that the present-day German government does not and never has owned the Nazi U-boats that were sunk off the American eastern seaboard – or anywhere else in the world, for that matter.

Because the provisions of the Potsdam Agreement

specifically forbid Germany from ever again possessing U-boats, the German government has no claim to sunken U-boats.

I will mention only one instance that relates to this particular issue, although others abound. In 1993, Danish millionaire Karsten Lee funded the salvage of Nazi U-boat *U-534*. The hull was raised intact, and is now on public display in Birkenhead, England.

The German government neither protested the salvage nor had any say in how or where the hull should be exhibited.

The same legal rationale applies to U-boats off the coast of U.S. eastern seaboard.

Doubletalk or Newspeak?

To return to Flynn's question, after six minutes of misdirection and misinformation, Alberg said, "So, uh, in answer to your question, have, what have we been doing, have we been working on, where would it be, where would it not be, the truth is we haven't started it. That's why this is so important from our perspective, to begin that discussion. Nothing would make me happier than being able to hold, and, and, and the point was made last night, at, at uh, some of the other meetings, in terms of comments of the *Monitor*. It's fine. No one's really commenting about the *Monitor*. This is the, this is the issue. And nothing would make me happier than the ability to sit down with gentlemen like you, ladies like you, people that are, have a stake in this, and say, all is right, if we were ever to do this, provide me some feedback, because what's happened is that people, if you read the blogs, if you read the Internets, if you, in the postings that are out there, people unfortunately are responding to our lack of a position on the Internet: where it would be, what it would be. And the *Monitor* hasn't helped this. Because we've got forty year history on the *Monitor*, and it is the most regulated site, argument the most regulated ship other than the *Arizona* in U.S. waters, um, although the *Portland* is, er, is regulated up in the Stellwagen Bank, it is natural for somebody to assume that if there was ever an expansion to the Monitor sanctuary, what has happened in this column of water would naturally go to these other sites. That is not true. Any revisions to the, to the management plan, any of the, the, uh, the, the, the, federal registers, er, uh, CFR bullets that you've identified, in, in your letter, any of those regulations would be, would be, happy to be looked at. So do you permit? Do you not permit? Is it every wreck? Does every wreck off the coast of North Carolina have historical significance? No, absolutely not. Does every wreck out there, um, important to the dive community. No. Is every wreck out there important to the fishing community? It's certainly a concern to them because of what might happen, but, what this action plan does, in this document, what we're proposing, is the ability to sit down, and start hearing from you, about what it would mean and what it wouldn't mean. What – is there a model out there? Maybe, maybe the answer is no. Maybe from the dive community's perspective your perspective, um, there is no way to do this that would be a, a win-win for you. I'm not sure of that. I think that, that we've seen in places like Thunder Bay, um, that there is a way to do things that are a win-win. If you look at, when you talk to those folks up there, a community – and I, I throw Thunder Bay out there a lot, because it is in, uh, a good example. It's a community that was very much opposed to NOAA going up there. They passed resolutions, people not wanting NOAA out there, and the way we did it was we put a five-year moratorium on it, and said, you know, in five years, if this hasn't worked, and you don't, the citizens, this hasn't been a benefit, we're out. And what happened at the end of that five years? Just the opposite. The citizens of Alpena passed resolutions. The mayor went to Congress and said this in an area that has been struggling for economic relief for decades. It has been new life breathed into it. And these are, these are not my words. I can, I'm happy to provide you Carol Shafto, Mayor Shafto's words from their SAC, their dive seat, who was on this uh, the, a guy named Steve Kroll, who was adamantly opposed to the sanctuary program, read his testimony to Congress about what it's meant, as businesses have come in, as people have come in and, um, up there, you're not going to find somebody who's been prohibited from going to any the wrecks. You're going to find that it's, it's, it's free and open access. There are restrictions. You can't take anything off the wrecks. The intent is to leave it for, uh, the next diver that comes down. And, and I, and I, and I cannot fault anybody who is familiar with the *Monitor*, for having concerns about what anything new would, would uh, would entail, based on what's, on how we've run the *Monitor*. But what I can tell you is that the only way to get someplace with it would be good for all of us, if there, if in fact we go anywhere at all, would be through an open dialogue. And that is what this plan calls for. It doesn't for, for boundary changes. It calls for the ability to get around the table with people like you, and hear, is there a way to do this that would be a win-win. So, does that answer your – in terms of boundaries, and where it is, what's prohibited, none of that has happened."

Comparing the Monitor NMS to the Thunder Bay NMS was like comparing apples to oranges. The State of Michigan – which owns the bottomlands on which the Thunder Bay NMS was founded – did not allow NOAA to create the sanctuary on State-owned property until NOAA promised to guarantee unrestricted access to the shipwrecks, by divers and anglers alike.

Furthermore, what Alberg neglected to mention was that when NOAA tried to expand the Thunder Bay NMS eightfold, the plan was shot down – twice! The city of Alpena may have had a vested interest in the sanctuary, but otherwise community opposition to expansion was so enormous that two succeeding governors of the State of Michigan vetoed NOAA's plans for expansion because the majority of their constituents were set solidly against it.

Flynn was not satisfied with Alberg's longwinded gibberish because it did not answer her question. She persisted: "How can you actually ask the public to give you comments on an area of expansion that has yet to be identified?"

Alberg: "Right. And, and, and, which is an excellent question. We, we can't right now."

After another incomprehensible and irrelevant digression, he added, "Through public meetings, separate from this process entirely, um, and then start talking about, all right, now what, where's the impact, and there's cert, and one of the things that has been brought up a couple times, uh, and it is a very true statement by, even by The Mariners Museum, what's the cost to do this, too? Does NOAA have the ability to do this, um, at all? And that may be a, a game stopper right there. But, but until we get into these discussions, um, you can't, you can't, as you pointed out, respond to it. You can't make that, uh, have an opinion on it until there's something to respond to."

NOAA had created an intelligence vacuum that served is purpose perfectly.

When you sift through the grandiloquence and cut to the chase, although Alberg finally admitted that NOAA could not expect anyone to comment intelligently about a proposed expansion of unknown dimensions and undisclosed regulations, that is precisely what NOAA had been doing for the past four years. Furthermore, the issue that Alberg admitted to a roomful of "concerned" stakeholders who had been kept in the dark, was *never* addressed in the Draft Revised Management Plan. This begs the question: When *will* NOAA address this issue?

The short answer is: Not until NOAA obtains carte blanche authority to implement expansion and enforce regulations of its own devising.

NOAA's Ineptitude

After receiving no straightforward answer to her previous question – about the size of the proposed expanded sanctuary, in case you have forgotten – Flynn asked a question about access to the *Monitor*. "NOAA has not demonstrated an ability to effectively deal with ensuring public access to a single shipwreck site in 37 years, how will they deal with a nearly countless number of shipwrecks in an expansive, and as yet undefined area, known as the 'Graveyard of the Atlantic'?"

Alberg claimed that NOAA was continuing to work on a recreational permit for diving on the *Monitor*. This means that, in the quarter of a century since the first diving permit was issued to me in 1990, to the time of the meeting in 2012, NOAA had been unable to create a suitable recreational diving permit.

NOAA's inability to deal with one simple issue on a solitary shipwreck is an indication of how unfit it is to deal with twelve *hundred* shipwrecks, thousands of permits. and tens of thousands of recreational divers and anglers.

Shifting the Blame – Again

In NOAA's "Proposal for Battle of the Atlantic U-boat Surveys," it was written: "The *U-352* and *U-85* have undergone considerable alteration due to looting and illegal salvage operations and require documentation to preserve their remains in the archaeological record. This salvage activity has removed sediment from the U-boat's interior and the lack of internal support is causing their accelerated collapse."

By not explaining that the removal of sediment and nearly all the "looting and illegal salvage operations" were conducted by the U.S. Navy, NOAA implied that recreational divers were the culprits who were responsible for the collapse of the wrecks. Remember that the Navy sucked some 500 tons of sand, bones, and personal possessions out of the *U-352*, and spewed everything into the water column.

After NOAA's 2008 U-boat expedition was over, Alberg wrote to the German embassy with regard to the Sunken Military Craft Act: "I am hoping that we might be able to discuss the development of a cooperative agreement between [sic] the United States Navy, The [sic] German Government and NOAA to implement this law to properly protect these vessels [Nazi U-boats] from further damage and looting."

In my opinion, this goal could best be achieved by keeping the U.S. Navy off the U-boats.

Alberg then wrote an agenda for discussion in a follow-up meeting at the German embassy. One point that he wanted to stress was "In Situ Preservation Ethic." Apparently NOAA employs a double standard, as this ethic of preservation in place did not apply to the recovery of the *Hunley*, the salvage of the *Monitor*, the demolition of the *YMS-14*, or the U.S. Navy's salvage operations on the *U-85* and the *U-352*. NOAA wants it both ways: whichever way suits it best.

Insertion 2 – the Sunken Military Craft Act

It is important for the reader to understand that the Sunken Military Craft Act, to which Alberg referred in the previous section, is a U.S. law. This means that it applies only – I repeat, *only* – to U.S. military craft. It does not apply to military craft of foreign nations. And it certainly does not apply to sunken craft of the Nazi regime because of the terms of the Potsdam Agreement.

Alberg's invocation of this Act muddied the waters of reality.

Down to Brass Tacks

With regard to the section that preceded the one above, Flynn asked: "Wreck divers, sport and commercial fishing continue to be blamed as a source, or 'potential source' of accelerated deterioration of the USS *Monitor* wreck site. Yet the fact that NOAA and the Navy, between 1998 and 2002, have recovered almost 400 tons of material from the USS *Monitor*, including her revolving gun turret, engine, 11-inch Dahlgren guns and thousands of smaller artifacts (as cited in this draft plan) are NEVER attributed as a potential source for this 'accelerated deterioration'. Despite over 30 years of monitoring, there is NO evidence of any sport diver impact whatsoever.

"Yet I can tell you for a fact, having witnessed the wreck before NOAA's presence and what you show today, as the condition of the wreck, you have in fact contributed substantially to the deterioration of the wreck site. So, why is it that NOAA believes that their actions on the USS *Monitor* from 1998-2002 have not contributed to an accelerated deterioration of the wreck site, given that it was not mentioned as a concern in this plan?"

She was calling attention to the fact that, in the Draft Revised Management Plan, NOAA never referenced its own site disturbance as a contributing factor in the wreck's accelerated deterioration. NOAA was trying to make it seem that recreational divers, who had little or no access to the site, posed a greater threat to accelerating deterioration than NOAA's own destructive actions.

Understand that Flynn was eminently familiar with the condition of the *Monitor* prior to NOAA's disturbance of the site, because she had dived on the wreck on four different trips between 1994 and 1998. She missed only one year out of five.

Alberg: "That's an excellent question and it's, uh, it's a comment that probably should be addressed in the plan. You're right. NOAA's work did accelerate, there's, there's, it's very clear, you don't need to be an archaeologist to see accelerated detained parts of the wreck where we were operating."

A person who identified himself as Dave in the conservation lab, acknowledged: "The involvement of NOAA for an x year period made the wreck more unstable, and corrode more. That's a scientific fact."

Flynn found the management plan self-serving. She particularly objected to NOAA's 37-year history of blaming the *Monitor's* deterioration "on a dive community and a fishing community that has not impacted the wreck, anywhere near what NOAA has itself."

Alberg did not comment on this observation.

The revelations of these scoping meetings were transitory, existing only for those moments in time when the meetings were in session. Alberg's admission and apology in the present venue would not affect the derogatory perception that had been perpetrated intentionally in the management plan. NOAA could sweep under the carpet any disclosures that were made at the meeting, and work toward keeping those disclosures from the prying ears of Congress, the media, and the general public – just as NOAA had planned all along.

Although Alberg confessed that some changes should be made in the language of the management plan, it was too late for that. The management plan was a permanent document. Oral admissions of guilt were ephemeral.

Recovery versus In Situ Preservation

Flynn: "The Sanctuary realized in the 1990s that preservation of the major *Monitor* artifacts could only be effectively achieved by salvaging them from the bottom. A term used in this plan for wrecks in the expanded area is 'in situ preservation'. This appears to be a contradictory term given that time and tides will continue to erode these wrecks, as NOAA has already realized at the *Monitor* site. Exactly what does this mean when applied to shipwrecks in an open ocean, salt water environment?"

Alberg made another rambling digression that boiled down to: Do as I say, not as I do.

Sanitizing the Main Objection

Flynn objected strongly to the way the management plan sanitized the issue of expansion by stating that the vast majority of the comments were simply *about* expansion: a neutral statement that avoided the reality that the vast majority *opposed* expansion.

Alberg reluctantly admitted, "Yeah, I'd – I'd – so to answer your question, I'd say that the vast majority were concerned about expansion, opposed to it, um, or, or, uh, or, maybe a more fair statement would be that the vast majority of the comments were concerned because there was no information about it. Where would it be? We - what would it be? How can I – how can I say that I support this or don't support it when you provided no information. In the absence of that information I can't get behind it."

Alberg justified this oversight by claiming, "We haven't gotten into this. We haven't started talking about it." Then, "We don't know. Let's, let's start that discussion." And again: "We're not advocating for an expansion. NOAA is not saying we should do this."

As I have already shown, what Alberg claimed was true was not necessarily so. His verbal assessment of NOAA's desiderata contradicted the Strategic Plan of 2005.

Although he called the management plan the first faltering step, which was intended only to open the discussion of expansion, it was in fact the *last* step. This final scoping meeting of 2012 was the *end* of public debate. NOAA had no plans to schedule additional public meetings.

As a way to save face, NOAA *did* create a fake advisory council whose primary purpose was to recommend expansion, in which case NOAA could throw up its hands and claim, "We didn't want this, but our hands were tied because the council advised us to expand the sanctuary."

The Fat Lady Sings

Lest you think that I am painting too bleak a picture, let me provide some other Alberg quotes from the meeting that I am presently debriefing.

Flynn: "Can you describe the events that will lead to a final decision/recommendation regarding expansion and what the general timeline will be. What will be the means for continuing to engage the public in this process."

Alberg: "Yeah, yeah, um, I sound like I'm being evasive here. The intent of which, we're not going to be hold, this is the last public hearing on this, so NOAA will go back and, and look at all the comments, review them, they'll go before Paul Hugon go through a number of management plan processes, more than I have, but, but, typically we do, once, once we make final recommendations and they will be released. There will be no other, how do, how do I – "

After Alberg faltered on revealing the uncomfortable truth, an unidentified NOAA representative spoke up: "There are no other, um, public opportunities, but when this plan is revised as the final plan, it then must go through another review, through for instance [indecipherable due to a cough close to the microphone] parts of NOAA, the general council, to make sure there are no legal issues, but then it has to go through a political process to the top where if it's been acceptable and signed and then it becomes law."

Flynn was understandably confused: "I – I'm, but you mentioned several times in today's discussions, okay, that you wanted to create an environment of a dialogue within the diving community, okay, so the question is, is that separate from this process? Is it part of this process?"

Alberg now tried to weasel out of the corner with another diarrhea of words: "Yes, so, and so, so, at this point, and just, and we'll, try to get around to your question. We will respond to every, when we do the final, every comment, verbal, written, will be, will be, included in the final, and will respond to everyone. His points that he has outlined, that the gentleman who was here a moment ago, outlined in his, uh, uh, his letter, will all be addressed. In terms of discussion, um, separate, we can do that at any point. I'm, I'm happy to get together. In fact, uh, we've done that a couple times, um, did one in, in uh, I've tried to go out to dive clubs. We, we went out to Hatteras in 2009, and um, uh, I think it's a good thing to do. I want to do more of it. Sometimes it confuses things because even though it's just an informational exchange, here's what we're doing, here's who we are, that type of thing, sometimes those get interpreted as official meetings, as scoping meetings, in which case they're not. I've had, I've had dozens of meetings that, that, uh, the general topic comes up about expansion, um, you know, we try to be open and up front and they, they get interpreted as, well, that was, that was a public hearing, I didn't see that it was advertised, that type of thing. Um, so, in terms of official public hearings, no, but if at any point you got a group, you as an individual, let, let's get together. I, I'm, whether it's up in your neck of the woods or down in our, I'd be happy to get, although again, you can tell is outreach start to informally there, there is, just an exchange of ideas, um, until we formalize a, a, a the beginnings of a public hearing process on a potential expansion. If we do that at all, um, but, nothing prevents us from having a discussion now."

Alberg was now suggesting that he would like to work with the very same divers he had time and time again denigrated as looters and grave robbers.

You don't even have to read between the lines to see what Alberg was trying to do. After his cohort spilled the beans – that the public meeting process was over and done with: "in terms of public hearings, no" – he offered to have *un*official discussions with stakeholders. But the outcome of these unofficial discussions could be no more effective than the outcome of the public hearings, in having any impact on the final management plan.

In essence, the public would have no say in the passage of legislation for expansion. This was NOAA's way of saying, in its best imitation of W.C. Fields, "Go away kid, you bother me." NOAA would not poke its cigar into the stakeholders' balloon until it released the final management plan, which could call for expansion of the sanctuary with no regulatory changes.

Sucker Punch

Steve Gatto reminded Alberg that he (Alberg) had previous stated that not all the shipwrecks off the coast of North Carolina were historically significant. He asked, "Are you opposed to taking artifacts off of non-historical wrecks?"

Alberg's short answer was, "No," although he qualified his answer with a long-winded dialogue that was prefaced by, "I don't want to get, get myself caught while making a statement that I may regret some place down the road. But I think, I think, we don't think every wreck out there is, is a significant wreck."

Alberg then went on to describe how the Florida Keys NMS had a permitting system for treasure salvage. "So, again, is that a model that, that, might apply here. I don't know. But that, until we have a discussion on it, till, folks present that this is, this is one way, would you consider this, what do you think of this, I don't want to go on record as saying we're opposed to it, we're in support of it, because I don't have all the information, and we're not in a position to make any decisions unless people got all the information."

He was still promising discussion after he already admitted that the public comment period was over. And he did not stop there.

After Gatto raised other issues – such as anchoring or grappling into shipwrecks to enable safe diver access, and the donation of artifacts from recreational divers to museums – Alberg repeated his inappropriate promise: "What I would suggest is that, uh, you know, let's let today be the beginning of an opening discussion of these things."

This was not the beginning. It was the end. A dead end.

Everything that Alberg said was, quite frankly, BS.

The Façade Continues

The scoping meeting that I have been deciphering above was not only the last of the batch, it was the last public meeting forever; that is, with regard to expansion of the Monitor NMS. No additional meetings were planned; nor have any other meetings been scheduled.

Yet, according to Pete Manchee, a recreational diver who attended the May 1 meeting: "Mr. Alberg did apologize for not getting the word out effectively about the meeting and promised that they would hold additional meetings in the near future."

Manchee also noted another misrepresentation: "The questions indicated the general dissatisfaction with the proposed expansion. In reading the Expansion Action Plan one would think that everyone, veterans groups, historians, archaeologists, divers, the general public and preservation groups are all clamoring to have NOAA protect all the shipwrecks in the Graveyard of the Atlantic. Nothing could be further from the truth."

Manchee confirmed that attendees went to the meeting solely to register disapproval of any kind of NOAA intervention.

His comment to Alberg – "Past behavior is probably the best predictor of future behavior." – fell on deaf ears.

Catherine Kozak, a reporter for *Island Free Press*, wrote, "Alberg said that the need to discuss expansion was first raised during public scoping meetings in 2008." As always, the wording suggested that the *public* raised the issue of expansion. Once again I must counter this misleading impression: NOAA held the 2008 scoping meetings for the explicit purpose of raising the issue itself; it then downplayed the issue as a way of avoiding opposition.

Kozak also printed dive charter operator David Farrow's comment to Alberg: "Expand, expand, expand – you keep bringing it up. We don't want it. Nobody wants it."

Farrow's sentiment was representative of all the other comments.

Advocating Through Suppression

Jim Bunch attended the May 3, 2012 scoping meeting. He told me what occurred there and afterward.

The meeting place was crowded with "concerned" citizens: a few recreational divers but mostly irate anglers. Not a single concerned citizen in attendance favored expansion of the sanctuary. All were vehemently opposed. If there was ever any doubt about the feelings of the people, this united front put paid to that doubt.

Bunch stressed the fact that opposition was unanimous.

No one wanted NOAA interfering with their livelihoods. No one wanted NOAA to regulate fishing. No one wanted NOAA to have autonomous control over wreck sites.

These people were not even happy about the Monitor NMS, much less any kind of expanded sanctuary. Nor were they quiet about proclaiming their dissatisfaction. Everyone was dead-set against NOAA in every way, shape, or form.

After the meeting, SAC member Bunch had a private conversation with Alberg. Bunch was blunt. He told Alberg that NOAA had all the answers that it needed about sanctuary expansion. *No one wanted it.* NOAA had posed the question for discussion, received undisputed opposition, and that should be the end of the issue.

In shooting its bolt, NOAA received feedback that it did not want to pass on to Congress. NOAA's way of dealing with such an all-consuming negative response was to bury it. No oppositional viewpoints were made public. The criticisms of vocal dissenters were neither recorded for posterity nor transcribed in the form of minutes. Letters of opposition were not acknowledged or forwarded to Congress.

NOAA has not issued any press releases to inform Congress and the public about the results of the scoping meetings. NOAA has gone quiet on the subject of expansion. The submarine expression for this tactic is "silent running." It means to thwart your enemy – in this case, the public – by keeping a low profile so that no one will notice your presence in an area where you have no right to be.

Letter of Discontent

My response to this latest series of scoping meetings was immediate. On May 8, 2012, I submitted the following letter – not to NOAA, where it would undoubtedly be pigeonholed along with all the other comments that opposed NOAA's plans for expansion and overall control – but to the legislators who were in the greatest position of authority to put a stop NOAA's creeping territorial expansion, once they were apprised of the manner in which NOAA misrepresented the facts with cleverly concealed lies and deceits.

I sent hard-copies of my letter to the nine representatives that Karen Flynn suggested: Beverly Perdue (Governor of North Carolina), and Senators Phil Berger, Richard Burr, Kay Hagan, Kay Bailey Hutchison, Pat McElraft, Barbara Mikulski, Tom Tillis, and Stan White. These senators individually either represented the citizens of North Carolina, controlled NOAA's purse strings, or possessed other forms of influence with regard to NOAA and its activities.

I also sent my letter to Scott Brown: the senator from Massachusetts who was currently investigating NOAA's fraudulent practices with regard to commercial anglers in his State.

I wrote:

> I have been diving off the coast of North Carolina for more than thirty years. I continue to dive in North Carolina waters on an annual basis. I have many friends who dive and fish in North Carolina waters. We have all enjoyed the freedom of diving and fishing when and where we like without hindrance from the government.
>
> The National Oceanographic and Atmospheric Administration (NOAA) currently administers the Monitor National Marine Sanctuary (MNMS) off the Diamond Shoals, and has done so since that Sanctuary was established, in 1975. According to the Draft Revised Management Plan of April 2012, NOAA is now proposing to expand the MNMS to include every shipwreck off the coast of North Carolina (under the rubric "Graveyard of the Atlantic NMS"), and eventually every shipwreck off the entire eastern seaboard (under the rubric "Battle of the Atlantic NMS").
>
> I strongly oppose any proposed expansion on several grounds and for a variety of reasons:
>
> The expansion proposal is a blank check for NOAA to create a Sanctuary whose boundaries are unlimited.
>
> The expansion proposal allows NOAA to impose any and all restrictions without regard to

public input.

The denial of voter input contradicts the basic principle of a democratic government whose Constitution was ratified to guarantee freedom from oppression for its citizens.

Unfettered expansion will create an economic disaster for the State of North Carolina.

The proposal contains no language to guarantee free and uncontrolled access to all shipwreck sites. It has already taken four federal lawsuits for people to obtain permission to photograph the *Monitor*. Nonetheless, NOAA has subsequently either denied access, or has imposed a permitting process so cumbersome that it effectively prevents access by recreational divers who lack the means and resources to combat NOAA's expensive obstructionist tactics.

A condition of the permitting process is that recreational divers must perform work, free of charge, that NOAA arbitrarily and capriciously considers useful. Recreational divers are not permitted to simply look at the wreck because of its significance to their national and cultural heritage: the reason for which the MNMS was established.

The proposal is replete with misleading statements and outright prevarications. Here are only a few of the most egregious examples of subterfuge: NOAA claims that "many" shipwrecks in the area are military gravesites, when in fact only six of the thousands of North Carolina shipwrecks qualify for such a designation.

The proposal claims that in previous scoping meetings, "many" commenters favored expansion. In fact, attendees state categorically that there was universal opposition to the expansion program.

The proposal claims that NOAA's Advisory Committee favors expansion. This may be true, but only because committee members were selected on the basis of their favoritism. Volunteers who opposed expansion were excluded from membership.

The proposal advertises that in 1990, NOAA issued permits for recreational divers to photograph the *Monitor*. It neglects to mention that it required six years and three [sic] federal lawsuits to force the issuance of those permits; and that subsequent permits were issued only after another federal lawsuit was prosecuted, followed by direct Congressional intervention. NOAA's partial truth is contrived to put NOAA in a false light of benevolence.

The proposal states, "During the 2008 scoping meetings for the Monitor National Marine Sanctuary management plan, many of the commentors [sic] expressed an interest in expanding the sanctuary to include additional shipwrecks off the coast of North Carolina." This statement is deliberately misleading because *all* the expressed interest *opposed* such expansion. The sentence is cleverly worded so that readers who are ignorant of the truth are led to believe that the "interest" favored expansion; any hint of opposition was cunningly avoided.

Any proposal that is not based on honest reporting is not a good proposal.

Present regulations deny shipwreck access without a permit. Permits often require a lawsuit to obtain. If the Sanctuary is expanded, access to every shipwreck that the Sanctuary encompasses will be automatically denied.

Present regulations in the NMMS prohibit anchoring or grappling. This prohibition makes it unsafe, difficult, or impossible to access shipwrecks. The proposal contains no language for deleting this prohibition which, by default, will still stand. Thus shipwreck access will be denied without an affirmative assertion of denial.

The proposal fails to explain how expansion

will benefit the public that will be asked to fund the Sanctuary, but will not be allowed to visit its assets.

The proposal states, "These shipwrecks offer a unique opportunity to study and better understand our maritime history." This is equivalent to stating that the study of rusting cars in a junk yard can yield important information about twentieth-century traffic patterns. Even if the statement about shipwrecks were true, shipwrecks can be studied without being located within a Sanctuary. Furthermore, thousands of books and articles have already been written about this maritime history; the proposal neglects to state what expansion can add to the understanding that is readily available. Additional study is largely redundant.

The proposal neglects to describe how expansion will protect shipwrecks from natural deterioration in a corrosive environment. In fact, the proposal avoids the issue altogether. Never once does it mention how this so-called "protection" is to be provided. The word "protection" is left undefined.

The control of shipwrecks is not part of the charter of the Marine Protection Research and Sanctuaries Act, under which the MNMS was established. The MPRSA was passed by Congress solely as a measure to protect endangered marine life. Thus the MNMS was established and is operated under illegal sanction.

NOAA has misallocated much of its funding by using taxpayers' money to send their employees on all-expenses-paid shipwreck extravaganza vacations that they euphemistically call "surveys," when in fact the wrecks that they claim to have "surveyed" were surveyed years ago, and the results of those surveys are a matter of public record.

NOAA wants to increase the number of so-

called "surveys" by re-examining shipwrecks under the guise of the "Wreck Oil Removal Program," the putative purpose of which is to examine tankers that were torpedoed by Nazi U-boats
during World War Two, and to assess their oil-
leakage potential. A thorough examination in
this regard was conducted in 1967. Called the
"Sunken Tanker Project," Coast Guard investigators found that World War Two tankers presented no current or future risk to the environment because their hulls had already collapsed,
their tanks were open to the sea, and the cargo
had long since leaked away.

The economic impact of the proposed expansion will be catastrophic for the State of North
Carolina because tourism will drop dramatically.
If divers are not permitted to dive on shipwrecks,
and if anglers are not permitted to fish on shipwrecks, diving and fishing in North Carolina waters will practically cease to exist. Charter operations will either fold or move elsewhere; dive
shops will close; bait and tackle stores will go out
of business; restaurants, motels, and local ven-
dors will see a sharp decrease in income.

The only beneficiary to NOAA's expansion
proposal is NOAA. NOAA funding would be better
spent on forecasting weather, maintaining neglected aids to navigation, and engaging in other
functions that benefit the public.

The Name of NOAA's Game is Duplicity

In order to give the illusion that everyone NOAA
polled favored expansion of the Monitor NMS, NOAA declined to publish the vast volume of letters from people
who opposed expansion. The false allegations in the
management plan stand alone in the eyes of Congress
and the public because the NOAA website is silent in
this regard. Not that this contrivance is anything new
for NOAA.

As I have shown at length, NOAA's stock in trade is

to repeatedly misconstrue the facts in order to create a mistaken perception of reality. NOAA plays with the truth as if it were a toy in the hands of a child.

The truths that NOAA declines to publish are those that contravene the image that it wants to present to the world. As a case in point . . .

McCarthyism is Alive and Well

After all the negative feedback that NOAA received at the 2012 scoping meetings, and in the letters of opposition that followed those meetings, NOAA conducted a sting operation that was designed to put recreational divers in a bad light.

The idea was to nab divers for retrieving souvenirs from the *U-352*. You might think that there was not much left to retrieve from the Nazi U-boat, after the U.S. Navy callously removed more than 500 tons of sand, silt, and cultural debris from the interior of the pressure hull – and you would be right. Everything that the Navy expelled into the sea was lost to history forever, and little of historical value remained to be seen and studied. But NOAA believed – or wanted the world to believe – otherwise.

It was easy to determine when recreational dive trips were scheduled to visit the U-boat. Dive shops and charter operators promoted such trips by advertising them in brochures, in mailed circulars, and on websites. Just as NOAA employed shills who subscribed to my newsletter, NOAA used decoys to ascertain the dates and times of departure of recreational dive trips to the Graveyard of the Atlantic.

NOAA relies heavily on the Coast Guard to enforce the law in marine sanctuaries. On July 12, 2012, the Coast Guard cutter *Vigorous* lingered in the vicinity of the *U-352*, lying in wait to ambush dive boats after they left the site of the U-boat. One after another the *Vigorous* stopped four dive boats: *Diver Down*, *Midnight Express*, *Sea Quest II*, and *Tortuga*. Not all had visited the *U-352*; some had gone to the nearby *Schurz*.

Armed Coasties boarded each boat. They performed

a gratuitous safety inspection to justify their presence, but readily admitted that their actual purpose was to search for contraband artifacts.

The result of these Gestapo tactics was nil. No mementoes were found onboard. No vessels were cited. As is most often the case, the divers had merely been sightseeing; some divers speared fish, while underwater photographers captured lasting images of broken-down hulls and attendant marine life.

The witch-hunt was a bust for NOAA. No divers were nabbed for violation of any laws. As one pundit paraphrased, "The best laid schemes of mice and NOAA go often awry."

Had the Coast Guard found any keepsakes among the divers' personal possessions, the information would have been leaked to the media in order to draw attention to NOAA's libelous accusations.

But because the divers were innocent of all wrongdoing, NOAA said and wrote nothing about it. NOAA issued no press releases that exonerated divers from its previous castigations. NOAA did not announce the innocence of the divers. NOAA published no reports to confer blamelessness upon putative "looters."

NOAA simply slunk away in silence, without giving credit where it was due.

The Desperate Depth of Disparagement

Another attempt to discredit recreational divers involved what I call the Billy Mitchell wrecks. In 1921, eight German warships were scuttled off the coast of Virginia during a series of explosives tests. The centerpiece of this underwater fleet was the battleship *Ostfriesland*. This historic anomaly measured 546 feet in length, and grossed 24,500 tons.

The *Ostfriesland* was protected by 12 inches of armor plate. The hull had four skins for defense against mines and torpedoes. The interior was divided into so many watertight compartments that the ship was thought to be impregnable. At the Battle of Jutland, the *Ostfriesland* survived a mine explosion and hits from 18 large shells.

General Mitchell wanted to prove that battleships could be sunk by means of aerial bombardment. The test commenced by dropping a host of 250-pound bombs on the German warship. After U.S. Navy examiners studied the extent of the damage, Mitchell's aircraft dropped a number of 1,000-pound bombs on the *Ostfriesland*. Two of them scored direct hits.

The *Ostfriesland* was so badly torn up that examiners were unable to go below the third deck. They peered through gaping bomb holes at the water seeping into the hull from below.

Finally, the *Ostfriesland* was bombed with seven 2,000-pounders. The concussion from two intentional near misses visibly lifted the battleship out of the ocean. Thousands of tons of seawater descended upon the *Ostfriesland's* deck. The third bomb scored a direct hit on the forecastle; it tore a frightful hole in the steel deck, and created a raging fire. Another near miss lifted the hull again. Bomb number five fell near the stern, and the *Ostfriesland* began to settle aft. When the sixth bomb struck, the after two turrets were already submerged. The battleship's bow nosed upward, the ship rolled over onto its port side and disappeared from view. A Handley Page delivered the final stroke by dropping the last bomb on the huge vortex of escaping air.

The other German warships were sunk by either aerial bombardment or naval gunnery, within a mile or so of the *Ostfriesland*.

The *Ostfriesland* lies at a depth of 380 feet: 150 *deeper* than the *Monitor*. The wreck was discovered by recreational divers in 1990. Diving to that depth requires exotic breathing mixes such as heliox or trimix, tanks of nitrox and oxygen for decompression, plus a vast amount of training and expertise. For a bottom time of ten minutes, a diver must decompress for two full hours in the open ocean. Only an astonishingly few recreational divers in the entire country are qualified to dive to that depth. In the two decades since the wreck was first discovered, the *Ostfriesland* has been seen by no more than a couple dozen recreational divers.

Yet, after a NOAA-funded examination by means of a camera that was mounted on a remotely operated vehicle, NOAA had the gall to make the absurd claim, "We have evidence that divers have damaged some of them."

NOAA published this unsupported allegation on the Internet. NOAA offered no proof, no pictures, no videotape footage – only an unjustified condemnation of recreational divers in general.

One has to wonder how NOAA could possibly distinguish between the extensive destruction that was caused by some 25,000 pounds of bombs, plus nearly a century of natural deterioration and collapse, and damage that a diver could have caused during ten minutes on the bottom.

NOAA's unconscionable accusation demonstrates to what depths it is willing to go in order to stigmatize recreational divers in the eyes of the public, and in the eyes of Congress: to which august body NOAA is trying to lay the claim that *all* shipwrecks need to be "protected" from the effects of recreational divers.

Deception as an Art Form

It needs to be stressed how NOAA, when not lying outright, has raised the art of deception to new heights. Time and again NOAA has issued cleverly phrased statements in which the string of words was true in a literal sense, but in which the sentence was constructed so as to intentionally mislead the reader: in other words, the statement gave a false impression of candor by concealing underlying information that would shed different light on the subject.

For example, take this line from the Draft Revised Management Plan that I noted above: "In 1990, for the first time, NOAA issued research permits to private dive groups who dove to the *Monitor* using conventional scuba equipment."

I have already noted above (in my Congressional letter) how this sentence is true as far as it goes, and how it hides the fact that it took six years and two federal lawsuits to force NOAA to issue that first permit, and that it took another two years, two more lawsuits, and Congressional intervention, to assure continued issuance of such permits.

By specifying "research permits," the sentence further declines to mention the photographic permit that was issued to the Cousteau Society.

Similar sophistries and one-sided assessments are embedded in practically every sentence that NOAA publishes. The Draft Revised Management Plan is rife with statements which, when parsed in full knowledge of the facts, reveal ruses, dodges, and stratagems in numerous forms.

Let me cite a few examples.

Bold-Faced Lies

In relation to expansion of the Monitor NMS, consider this patently false statement in the Draft Revised Management Plan: "Many of the WWII shipwrecks are protected under the 2005 Sunken Military Craft Act."

NOAA's definition of "many" differs from that of Webster. According to the dictionary, "many" is defined as "being one of a large, indefinite number; numerous."

Yet, as previously noted, of the *thousands* of shipwrecks that lie off the coast of North Carolina, only six are covered by the Act: much less than one-tenth of one percent of the aggregate.

NOAA's statement is designed to fool people who do not know any better: people such as Congressional representatives who are not conversant with local history, and who are inclined to accept NOAA's written word as gospel.

Consider this statement in the Plan: ""During the 2008 scoping meetings for the Monitor National Marine Sanctuary management plan, many [there is that word again] of the commentors [sic] expressed an interest in expanding the sanctuary to include additional shipwrecks off the coast of North Carolina."

In fact, *every* commenter expressed *horror* over expansion.

But once NOAA casts a lie in ink, the lie assumes the perception of truth in the eyes of the public and their Congressional representatives.

Propaganda

Another example of such obvious chicanery – a deception rather than a patent falsehood – is Alberg's digression to one of Karen Flynn's questions, in which he laid great emphasis on the fact that one single solitary recreational diver who was initially opposed to the formation of the Thunder Bay NMS, later changed his mind. NOAA later wrote several paragraphs that stressed this individual instance of reversed viewpoint in its self-laudatory house organ *Sanctuary Watch* for Fall 2012.

NOAA avoided all mention of the fact that literally *thousands* of other recreational divers who initially opposed formation of the sanctuary *still* opposed it; and furthermore, they adamantly opposed expansion of the sanctuary that they did not want in the first place. NOAA's slanted artifice does not qualify as honesty in reporting.

NOAA presented its side of the story, and hid the other side.

Grand Deception

Perhaps the worst case of deception involves the oft-repeated and seemingly innocuous statement that the possibility of expansion of the Monitor NMS was raised at the scoping meetings in 2008. Once again the statement is true, but its validity is spurious because of what is *not* stated.

The statement is phrased in such a way that it conceals the key underlying truth.

The possibility of expansion did not simply pop out of thin air. "Concerned" citizens who attended the meetings did not raise the issue.

NOAA itself raised the issue. In fact, the only reason that NOAA held public meetings in 2008 was so that it could raise the issue. NOAA even specified that fact in small print when it announced the initial scoping meetings in tiny back-page notices in local newspapers.

After NOAA raised the issue of expansion, it then deleted its own involvement in raising the issue, and proceeded with a whitewash campaign that implied (without actually stating) that "concerned" citizens raised the issue, perhaps because those citizens wanted NOAA to "protect" shipwrecks that might otherwise go unprotected (uncontrolled).

Phrasing the sentence in the passive voice was a subtle but effective way of misleading readers to infer something other than what was actually stated. For example, "NOAA raised the issue of expansion" states an absolute and incontrovertible fact. But "the issue of expansion was raised" avoids naming NOAA as the culprit. By then stating in the same sentence that the issue was raised at a public meeting, the statement gives the impression that the public raised the issue.

NOAA representatives continued to phrase the expansion issue in this manner, both in press releases and in speaking venues. This made it seem as if NOAA had been accosted against its will with the issue of expansion, and was forced by public demand to make plans for it.

Once this groundwork was laid, NOAA then stated blatantly in its Draft Revised Management Plan: "During the 2008 scoping meetings, held as part of the management plan review, and in the subsequent comments received, the issue of possible expansion of the MNMS boundary was raised repeatedly."

NOAA avoided mentioning that NOAA itself raised the issue repeatedly. Unstated was the fact that everyone else opposed expansion repeatedly.

This kind of deceptive practice is NOAA's bread and butter. Nearly everything that NOAA prints or states has a hidden meaning. If I were to give a line-by-line clarification of the real meaning behind every sentence in the Draft Revised Management Plan, as I have done with the few examples above, I would have a document many times the length of the one that NOAA contrived to deceive the public.

NOAA's pronouncements seldom have any relationship with fundamental facts.

Fairy Tale Vows

In February 2013, NOAA released its "Monitor National Marine Sanctuary Final Management Plan and Environmental Assessment." For the most part it apes the lies and deceptions in the Draft Management Plan. I won't bother to parse the entire Plan; most of its 272 pages is fatuous: a sop to the sordid masses.

Consider this ambiguous and disingenuous passage that was contrived to placate the public (page 238): "If expansion is considered, NOAA will ensure that the dive community, fishing community, and all relevant stakeholders are fully involved in the public scoping and review process, and that continued, unimpeded access to wreck sites will be one of the priority criteria considered for achieving the primary objective of resource protection."

If you decipher the gobbledygook by not skimming over it quickly and by reading it slowly and carefully, you'll find that the sentence does not actually state what it appears to pledge. NOAA will *listen* to the grievances of divers, anglers, and stakeholders, but it does not promise to *satisfy* those grievances. Access to shipwrecks is not guaranteed; it is an activity that NOAA will only *consider.*

If the public and their State and federal representatives fall for this claptrap, and allow NOAA to have unfettered dominion over offshore shipwrecks, NOAA will then have a blank check to do whatever it wants to do, without any further consideration given to divers, anglers, and stakeholders.

In other words, NOAA will listen to or "consider" grievances only until it achieves the authority to ignore those grievances, after which all bets of fair treatment are off.

To the question on page 238, "If the Monitor NMS is expanded, will there be the same type of restrictions in regards to drilling, anchoring and fishing which exist now at the *Monitor* wreck site?" the most that NOAA acknowledges is, "Not necessarily."

NOAA then suggested that regulations for the expanded sanctuary "*may* vary distinctly from the current regulations." I placed emphasis on the word "may" in order to stress the point that NOAA is holding regulatory changes in reserve. NOAA "may" change the regulations; then again, it may not. And if NOAA does change the regulations, it may make them more restrictive than they already are.

NOAA does not have to deny access to diving by denying access. It can deny access to diving by disallowing grappling into or anchoring near shipwrecks. The effect is the same because divers cannot reach most shipwrecks without descending an anchor line to the site.

Consider this statement on page 239: "The current perception is that the permitting process [for diving on the *Monitor*] is onerous, costly, and prohibitive." The permitting process is perceived to be onerous, costly, and prohibitive because it *is* onerous, costly, and prohibitive. NOAA wants it that way as a deterrent to access.

Page 243: "At this time, NOAA is not proposing any new regulations or changes to the MNMS terms of designation. However, some regulatory initiatives that derive from the strategies presented in the draft management plan ultimately could be considered for action prior to the next management plan review."

This is highfalutin sophistry for stating that NOAA can and will change the regulations as it sees fit, despite any adverse effects that these changes may have on diving and fishing in the expanded sanctuary.

I could go on but my argument is clear: the plan is riddled with passages that are intended to deceive the reader – and the reader's congressional representatives – into believing that NOAA has the best interests of the community at heart, when in fact the plan is an illusion that is calculated to placate the public, and to convince Congress to legislate expansion, so that NOAA can dictate terms over more underwater territory.

158   Subterfuge 201

Deceit by Omission and Misdirection
The reader may recall from a few pages back that at the May 4, 2012 scoping meeting, Karen Flynn asked David Alberg why NOAA persistently blamed divers and anglers for the *Monitor's* accelerated deterioration, instead of citing its own recovery of 400 tons of material (including the guns, turret, and engine).

Alberg replied: "It's a comment that probably should be addressed in the plan. You're right. NOAA's work did accelerate, there's, there's, it's very clear, you don't need to be an archaeologist to see accelerated detained parts of the wreck where we were operating."

Here is how NOAA addressed this issue in the Final Management Plan (page 21): "NOAA's initial site characterization research and recent monitoring and research activities by NOAA and private researchers, resulted in the detection of a significant increase in the rate of deterioration of the *Monitor*. The rapid degradation of the hull, as described later in this document, may have been precipitated by an incident in 1991, when a private fishing boat was cited by the U.S. Coast Guard for anchoring illegally in the wreck."

Small print in a table on page 32 allows that accelerated deterioration might result from a "combination of natural deterioration and site alterations due to archaeological activities from 1998-2002."

Yet the large print emphasis is placed on an anchor snag, thus shifting the blame from NOAA to anglers.

This obvious misdirection accentuates a single instance of fishing boat damage, while distracting the reader's attention from the far greater destruction that was caused by NOAA's massive recovery operations during a five-year period.

On page 35, the Final Management Plan bemoans the fact that "the site also displayed observable natural collapse of bottom hull plating." By claiming that this collapse resulted from purely natural processes, NOAA disclaimed responsibility for contributing to this collapse. Yet the record clearly shows that in 1979, NOAA conducted extensive excavations in its search for artifacts in the forward compartments: excavations that severely undermined the plates of the inverted lower hull above the tunneling site.

The hull collapsed on top of this burrowing area because NOAA removed the sand and silt that were supporting the overhead hull plates. The only part that nature played in NOAA's fictitious collapse scenario was enactment of the law of gravity after NOAA removed the hull's underpinnings.

NOAA's Ministry of Truth

The most crucial bold-faced lie was printed on page XX: "During the 2008 scoping meetings for the Monitor National Marine Sanctuary management plan, many of the participants expressed an interest in expanding the sanctuary to include additional shipwrecks off the North Carolina coast."

The truth of the matter was that the only participants who expressed any interest in expanding the sanctuary were NOAA employees. Non-NOAA participants unanimously opposed expansion.

Deceptions abound. Consider this instance on page 103: "During the 2008 scoping meetings, held as part of the management plan review process, and in the subsequent comments received, the issue of possible expansion of MNMS boundary was raised repeatedly." This is essentially the same deceptive language that I quoted in a previous section.

Rendered truthfully this sentence should read: "In 2008, NOAA held scoping meetings for the explicit purpose of raising the issue of expansion. Every comment that NOAA received energetically opposed any and all plans for expansion."

On the same page: "In 2009, the sanctuary advisory council considered this topic and voted unanimously to establish a working group to examine the benefits and implications of possible future expansion of MNMS."

Rendered truthfully: "In 2009, NOAA established a charade to legitimize the seizure of shipwrecks that lie beyond the jurisdiction of the United States."

Also on the same page: "That working group studied the issues and concerns regarding possible expansion and submitted to the full advisory council a recommendation that NOAA should explore expansion formally."

Rendered truthfully: "In 2012, NOAA conducted a study of the expansion issue by holding a series scoping meetings in which public comment was solicited. The result of that study amply demonstrated that opposition to expansion was overwhelming if not unanimous."

In short, NOAA suggested expansion at its sole discretion, and the public has consistently opposed the suggestion. Case closed.

There is no further need to discuss the issue of expansion: it has been discussed and dismissed by universal opposition. But that is not what is stated in the Final Management Plan, in which NOAA has cunningly concealed the true facts by means of concoction and grammatical legerdemain to present a doctored distortion of the truth.

Newsmanship (the art of conveying a false impression without actually lying)

Another way in which NOAA knowingly misrepresented the facts was by appending a handful of letters from its academic partners which supported expansion. The ethics of this kind of solicited support is dubious because the university factions are either already on the NOAA payroll by dint of NOAA grants and employment, or they have been promised grants and employment once the sanctuary is expanded, and the need for local support facilities and services becomes necessary: all of which puts them in the position of being paid voters, a practice that has been outlawed for decades.

Yet the *hundreds* of letters of protest from individuals and organizations who opposed expansion were *not* published in the Final Management Plan. Worse yet, the Plan does not even acknowledge that NOAA *received* letters in opposition to expansion.

NOAA does not heed the courtroom promise to "tell

the truth, the whole truth, and nothing but the truth."
When NOAA does not lie outright, it tells only that portion of the truth that will help to promote its agenda

This one-sided manipulation of oral and written
comments suggests to the reader – and to Congress –
that everyone favors expansion and no one opposes it,
when the true state of affairs is quite the opposite.

NOAA's Wicked, Wicked Ways

The Final Management Plan is a Trojan horse that
NOAA has given to Congress. It purports to present the
true state of affairs of the Monitor NMS, especially with
regard to the issue of expansion; but it presents nothing
of the sort. The Final Management Plan is a bogus report
which NOAA prepared consciously and with malice
aforethought to withhold the truth from Congress, in order to trick the people's representatives into authorizing
expansion against the universal will of the people.

The truth is that only NOAA wants expansion; the
American public does not.

NOAA's submission of this Final Management Plan
to Congress constitutes premeditated fraud. The majority of its 272 pages is ornamental: pretentious disinfor-
mation and conjured concepts that sound impressive to
the uninitiated but which in fact are meaningless.

The Plan is intended to convince Congress that the
citizens who attended the scoping meetings in droves,
and who submitted manifold letters of protest (which
NOAA euphemistically calls "comments"), endorsed
NOAA's plans for expansion of the Monitor NMS, when
in fact those citizens vehemently disapproved of any and
all NOAA presence off the State of North Carolina.

The misinformation in the Final Management Plan
is deliberately designed to convince Congress that no opposition exists, when in fact opposition is nearly unanimous. I know – or suspect with conviction – that the
same situation holds true for all the other sanctuaries
that NOAA wants to expand.

If Congress hears only NOAA's side of the story – the
abomination that NOAA has fabricated – then it will be

led to believe that NOAA's falsification is factual instead of a veil of lies and deceptively worded declarations.

Say No to NOAA

There is little left to write about the expansion issue that I have not already written. I did not strive for a climactic denouement after all the clues were presented, but instead provided enlightenment in dribbles as I peeled off the onion skins of NOAA's many-layered scheme for absolute control of the underwater world.

NOAA's self-serving image is a concoction of chicanery and legerdemain that is wholly without substance. It's all smoke and mirrors with but one object in mind: to enhance NOAA's power and dominion over an unsuspecting populace.

The only people to be deceived by NOAA's clever concoctions are those who have seen only one side of NOAA's double-headed coin; that is to say, either side: both heads of which depict the evil face of Janus unlocking the same transparent door to territorial expansion.

After this revelation of truth, it is abundantly clear that America needs new management rather than a new management plan.

Subterfuge 301
The Stellwagen Bank Robbery

If you have read this far in the present volume, then you know that I have a passion for justice, and that I am not afraid to fight for it. My passion indeed goes deep (pardon the pun).

The following polemic was published in Shipwrecks of Massachusetts: North. *I wrote it as a warning to unsuspecting local recreational diving victims who were at risk of having their shipwrecks annexed by NOAA as a result of its planned expansion of the Stellwagen Bank NMS.*

Small bits and pieces of the text are slightly repetitive, in that I refer to issues that are covered elsewhere in NOAA's Ark. *I have deliberately not deleted these sentences because the voids that such deletions would leave would detract from the cohesive theme of my argument. For the purpose of temporal relevance, note that the year of publication was 2008. I have appended additional material to the end of the published version. Here goes . . .*

> "This is my last territorial demand."
> - Adolf Hitler

On October 11, 2006, I attended a meeting that was sponsored by the Metro West Dive Club, at which a representative of the Stellwagen Bank National Marine Sanctuary was scheduled to address the members and other interested attendees. The Sanctuary sent Matthew Lawrence as its spokesperson. To him fell the task of delivering carefully phrased claptrap that disguised the Sanctuary's true motives of territorial conquest and expansionism. He gave a spiel in which he touted the goals of the National Oceanic and Atmospheric Association to preserve the marine environment through its Marine Sanctuaries Program.

The insincerity that was obvious to me was not so obvious to those who did not have my long and dreadful experience with NOAA. I will digress for the moment in order to provide some background to NOAA's continuing saga of illegitimacy. The depth of NOAA's depravity is exemplified in this chapter. Read it and weep.

"Government of the people, by the people, for the people."
- Abraham Lincoln

In 1972, Congress passed the Marine Protection, Research, and Sanctuaries Act, the avowed purpose of which was to create marine sanctuaries in order to "preserve, restore, or enhance areas for their conservational, recreational, ecological, research or esthetic values in coastal waters." Areas deserving of such a designation were those that were "necessary to protect valuable, unique, or endangered marine life, geological features, and oceanographic features. Areas to complement and enhance public areas such as parks, national seashores and national or state monuments and other preserved areas. Areas important to the survival and preservation of the nation's fisheries and other ocean resources. Areas to advance and promote research which will lead to a more thorough understanding of the marine ecosystem and the impact of man's activities."

The MPRSA made no mention of shipwrecks.

The primary goals of the MPRSA were, among others, "to enhance public awareness, understanding, appreciation and wise use of the marine environment" and "to facilitate to the extent compatible with the primary objective of resource protection, all public and private uses of the resources of such areas."

On November 4, 1992, Congress designated the Stellwagen Bank as the twelfth National Marine Sanctuary since the inception of the program twenty years earlier. A National Marine Sanctuary is the underwater equivalent of a National Park. The focal point of this latest addition to the National Marine Sanctuary Program was the Stellwagen Bank: a shallow area that was a rich source of cold water marine life, and that was a major source of food for large marine mammals, particularly the humpback whale. The boundaries of the Sanctuary encompassed a number of shipwrecks.

The National Oceanic and Atmospheric Association administers the National Marine Sanctuary Program. Historically, NOAA and NMSP have been antagonistic toward recreational divers in the pursuit of their hobby. This antagonism was manifested largely in overly restrictive access to wreck sites, or in outright denial of access. Self-serving bureaucrats who were mandated by law to encourage research and to enhance public awareness have instead taken the opposite stance: they have tried to the best of their power and ability, and by exceeding their authority, to prohibit public access to wreck sites.

> "I will either find a way, or make one."
> - Hannibal

I learned this firsthand in 1984. Nine years earlier, NOAA created the first National Marine Sanctuary for the explicit purpose of encompassing the Civil War ironclad *Monitor*, which sank in a gale in 1862 off the Diamond Shoals of North Carolina. It goes without saying that this shipwreck met none of the avowed sanctuary criteria for sanctuary status, as stated in the MPRSA.

When I requested permission to photograph the *Monitor*, NOAA denied my right of access to the site. This was tantamount to creating a National Park, but not permitting people to enter and see the sights that had been expressly set aside for them.

I objected to NOAA's self-serving attitude. I initiated a series of lawsuits whose cost to me personally was extravagant: it took eight years, four federal lawsuits, and tens of thousands of dollars in legal expenses to force NOAA to grant permission for me to conduct a photore-connaissance expedition to the wreck site. Finally I prevailed. I won the right for all Americans to visit the wreckage of the *Monitor*, and to see for themselves an historic piece of their national heritage. Previous, only NOAA personnel were granted the privilege of observing the *Monitor* firsthand, through the medium of videotape footage that was shot by means of remotely operated vehicles.

Even after my first successful *Monitor* expedition, NOAA continued to play hardball by denying my next diving application. NOAA's denial was overturned only by Congressional intervention. Thereafter, NOAA was forced to concede to Congressional mandates.

The landmark decision of the court was well worth the cost and effort, because it established two important precedents: it forever opened public access to the *Monitor*, and it forbade NOAA from using depth of water or safety considerations as excuses to prevent access. In the latter regard, although NOAA divers were prohibited by NOAA regulations from diving deeper than 130 feet on scuba, non-NOAA citizens did not have to abide by NOAA regulations. And many non-NOAA divers have far greater training and underwater competence than NOAA divers.

NOAA's attitude has not changed over the years. If anything, administrative conceit has worsened. In their bid for bureaucratic territoriality, NOAA's minions are serving themselves instead of serving the public. They continue to ignore the tide of public sentiment in order to expand their ill-gotten authority. Like Adolf Hitler, they keep saying that the next spree of territorial expansion will be the last. In fact, NOAA is administered by a host of control freaks who are insinuating themselves insidiously into the public domain much like a deadly cancer invading and destroying the human body. NOAA is a bureaucratic metastasis.

The minions in charge of the Stellwagen Bank National Marine Sanctuary have taken the same uncooperative tack as those who claimed access to the *Monitor* only for themselves. They have steadfastly refused to release public information that they hold in the public trust: among other data, the locations of the wreck sites. They have done this despite their avowed Action Plan whose language states specifically that the Stellwagen Sanctuary "is designed to protect these non-renewable resource sites and *promote responsible public access* for generations to come." (Italics added for emphasis.)

What NOAA wrote for public consumption was contradicted by NOAA's actions. According to law, NOAA does not have discretionary authority to either deny public access to wreck sites or to keep public information from the public.

"The great enemy of the truth is very often not the lie – deliberate, contrived, and dishonest – but the myth – persistent, persuasive, and unrealistic."
- John F. Kennedy

I discussed these issues at length with Dennis St. Germain. We decided to test NOAA's honesty and integrity by submitting a request pursuant to the Freedom of Information Act for the locations of the wrecks that lay within the borders of the Stellwagen sanctuary. Even after all these years, mention of my name still raises hackles among NOAA personnel because of NOAA's utter defeat in the case of the *Monitor*. So Dennis submitted the request under his name.

FOIA mandates the disclosure of information that is held by the government in trust for the people. "The basic purpose of FOIA is to ensure an informed citizenry, vital to the functioning of a democratic society, needed to check against corruption and to hold the governors accountable to the governed." FOIA provides that "every agency shall, upon request for identifiable records . . ., make such records promptly available to any person." Note that the law does not apply only to American voters and taxpayers, but to "any person," which by definition includes foreign nationals.

FOIA has been tested and upheld in federal court. For example, Judge David Alan Ezra ruled, "The Congressional message behind FOIA is unequivocal. The government must make available documents it possesses to anyone who requests disclosure. Congress explicitly listed the only possible exceptions in the Act. . . . The spirit and purpose of FOIA mandate a strong presumption in favor of disclosure."

NOAA responded predictably, as it did in my *Monitor* case. Assistant Administrator John Dunnigan's justification for denial was threefold: that the disclosure of such information might "cause a significant invasion of privacy," that it might cause "risk or harm to the historic resource," or that it might "impede the use of a traditional religious site by practitioners."

Dennis's appeal was a masterpiece of logic. "The public knowledge of the location of the shipwrecks within the confines of the Stellwagen Bank National Marine Sanctuary would not result in the occurrence of any of the three listed reasons for withholding the disclosure of said information. It is from this position that I base my argument that my FOIA request was wrongly denied.

"How can the knowledge of the location of shipwrecks which are tens, and in some cases, hundreds of years old cause a *significant* invasion of privacy? Can the known location of the wrecks impede the use of a traditional religious site by practitioners? Clearly reasons number one and three in no way apply. The only reason that the Department of the Interior could possibly remotely consider is number two: the risk of harm to the historic resource.

"I submit to you that it is an implausible idea to think that the public knowledge of shipwrecks submerged 200 to 400 feet deep, 20 to 60 miles or more from the nearest landfall would 'risk harm to the historic resource.' The location of the wreck of the *Monitor*, which lies at the shallow end of the depth range which we are discussing, was known to the public and no harm was done to that 'historic resource.' Quite the contrary, a case can be made that the expeditions embarked upon by Mr. Gentile and others to document the wreck fueled the public's curiosity and garnered support for the subsequent raising of sections of the ironclad vessel. The locations of the wrecks in the marine reserves of the Great Lakes are public knowledge, and they are situated in far shallower waters, and much nearer to land, yet no harm is coming to those historic resources. The invoking of 16 U.S.C. 470w-3(a) for not releasing the information is at best specious, and at worst absurd.

"It is with much surprise and great dismay that, as a tax paying American, my government is withholding information that I and others like me paid for."

The fallacy in St. Germain's argument was its discursive reasoning. Logic and reason work only with people who are logical and reasonable, or who do not have a personal agenda; or, in NOAA's case, with people who are not self-indulgent controllers. One might just as well argue with a charging lion that it should give the matter a little thought before ripping off your head. Nonetheless, our purpose was to ascertain to what lengths NOAA would go to justify its unlawful position.

By no stretch of the imagination can any of the wrecks in Stellwagen be perceived as religious sites. By the exclusion relating to invasion of privacy, Congress meant invasion of a *person's* privacy, not a shipwreck's. Exclusions refer to a person's vital statistics, contact data, criminal convictions, and so on.

The three-page denial of St. Germain's appeal must have taken hundreds of hours to research and write by a Stellwagen bank of meticulous NOAA attorneys. In grandiose language, the denial simply reiterated NOAA's position that the "Disclosure of the Shipwreck Sites Creates a Risk of Harm." NOAA cited previous cases that were clearly irrelevant, but that proved two points: that NOAA attorneys had expended an inordinate amount of time in researching case law and prior suits, and that the denial was written as a pre-emptive rebuttal should the appeal ever go to trial.

Barbara Fredericks, Assistant General Counsel for

Administration, ended her letter of appeal denial by stating, "This is the final decision of the Department of Commerce. You have the right to obtain judicial review of this denial." In other words, her thinly veiled threat was: go ahead and sue. NOAA was fully prepared to spend its enormous resources to fund expensive and protracted litigation.

Few people have the means to litigate against the government, while the government has unlimited funds with which to mount a defense. In fact, the government's most effective defense – especially when it is in the wrong – is to prolong a suit with delaying tactics that continually increase the cost to the litigant. Instead of fighting a case on its merits, the government often tries to win a case by means of wealth and stealth: by making the case so costly that the litigant is brought to financial ruin. To add insult to injury, the government utilizes taxpayers' money to fund its wrongful defense against its citizens: a clear case of government gone awry like metastasizing cancer. Witness my *Monitor* case.

A rational person might wonder how a shipwreck could be harmed by divers looking at it, or by taking pictures of it. This pretext smacks of the primitive belief that a person's soul can be captured on film. Again, the application of intellectual thought has nothing to do with the true motives that underlie NOAA's illegitimate scam: bureaucratic territoriality. All too often, so-called "public servants" perceive themselves as owners instead of administrators. They view the public as trespassers upon the bureaucrats' private preserves. I call this misanthropic attitude the "junkyard dog complex."

A junkyard dog is an aggressive pet whose purpose is to protect a junkyard from thieves and trespassers when the premises are closed for business. At first, the dog barks at only those interlopers who attempt to enter the junkyard after hours or at places along the fence that are remote from the gate. After a while, the dog barks at all passers-by on the other side of the fence. Then the dog barks at bona fide customers who enter the gate in the normal manner. Finally, the dog barks at everyone but the junkyard owner. It may even attack people. The dog has lost sight of its original purpose. It now presumes that the junkyard belongs to *it* and not to the owner, and that every visitor is trespassing on its domain.

I wanted to determine how far NOAA would go to protect its junkyard of sunken shipwrecks from public access. I figured that at the very least NOAA would co-operate with local government. Victor Mastone, head of the Massachusetts Board of Underwater Archeological Resources, told me that NOAA had not even shared the locations with *him* – without even suggesting that it might share the information subject to a nondisclosure agreement. Even though the Sanctuary lay in international waters and not in State waters, one would think that one government agency would cooperate with another government agency – especially with one whose primary responsibility was archaeological resources in adjacent State waters.

"There is a gap between one's real and one's declared aims."
- George Orwell

As a means to draw attention to the value of the Sanctuary, NOAA nominated the *Portland* for eligibility as an historic site with the National Register of Historical Places. This so-called American trust was designed primarily to protect old buildings from demolition, to prevent reconstruction that would change their original characteristics, and to enforce their maintenance in their present state. Since the NRHP was authorized by Congress in 1966, it has become a clearing house for "protecting" self-styled historic properties from destruction and modern alteration.

In the past four decades, the NRHP has granted historic status to more than 85,000 properties nationwide. In fact, NRHP personnel admitted that they never – *never* – turned down an application as long as the forms were filled out correctly.

The NRHP conducts no investigations to determine the historic quality of a site. It merely processes applications. There are no standards or guidelines for eligibility. The merits for eligibility are left entirely to the nominators to research and document. Once the NRHP determines that an application conforms to its guidelines for applicability – that is, that all the t's are crossed and the i's are dotted – it rubberstamps the nomination, and the rest is history (or historic preservation).

You could nominate your neighbor's eyesore garage as an historic building, and the NRHP would grant it protective status as long as you described the structure with sufficient academic pomposity and infused the text with enough bombastic phrases and buzz words – and they would never know the truth. This process begs the question: What is the value of acceptance as an historic site if no qualifications are required for granting such a status other than a nominator's knack for composing highfalutin language?

If the nomination process is merely a giveaway, then it follows that a site whose address is listed on the National Register of Historic Places is no more significant than that of a person whose address is published in the telephone directory, because no one ever gets turned down.

The listing of shipwrecks on the National Register of Historic Places seems to be one of NOAA's ways of bringing attention to itself, and to obtain funding and grant money in order to care for its so-called historic holdings. NOAA must believe that by calling a shipwreck a cultural resource – the political buzzwords that bureaucrats commonly overuse and abuse – the administration can maintain a firm grip on those wrecks for administration employees to explore and enjoy. Most people will swallow NOAA's song and dance routine because their only knowledge of the Sanctuary stems from Sanctuary propaganda.

Nomination applications that are submitted to the NRHP constitute public information. In order to test the honesty of the NRHP, Marcie Bilinski and I devised a two-stage probe to obtain a copy of the *Portland's* application form, which of necessity must provide its precise location. Buildings and other properties have street addresses; a shipwreck has GPS coordinates.

For the first stage, we drafted a letter in which we asked for a copy of the *Portland's* nomination. So as not to draw attention to the *Portland* per se, we also asked for the nomination of the USS *Arizona* (in Hawaii). Bilinski then asked her nephew, Andrew Arnold, to submit the letter in his name. Because he was a high school student, which was mentioned in the letter, we hoped that the NRHP would look upon the letter as an innocent request for historical information.

In due course, Andrew received a package that included both nominations. Although the GPS coordinates were included in the *Portland's* original nomination, the numbers were redacted in the photocopy: that is, a NRHP employee used indelible ink to black out the numbers so that they were illegible. By this means we ascertained that the NRHP was in cahoots with NOAA to withhold public information from the public.

For the second stage, Bilinski made an appointment to visit the headquarters of the NRHP in Washington, DC. In her introductory letter, she represented herself with her actual affiliations: she was a member of the Massachusetts Board of Underwater Archaeological Resources, and she was a member of Stellwagen's Maritime Heritage Resources Working Group. Thus she possessed an official status that should have provided her with VIP treatment.

Again, to draw attention away from the *Portland*, she asked to see several other nominations of Chesapeake Bay shipwrecks in which I was interested for a future book. The NRHP office and records were so disorganized that staff members were unable to locate any of the Chesapeake Bay shipwreck nominations. When they pulled the *Portland* file, there was a large red cardboard warning in the file that stated "address restricted." Bilinski was not allowed to look at the original application. Instead, a staff member made a photocopy of the appli-

cation, and redacted the GPS coordinates before giving
the copy to her.

"Only two things are infinite, the universe and human
stupidity, and I'm not so sure about the former."
- Albert Einstein

Despite these conspiratorial efforts to keep the GPS
coordinates to themselves, NOAA was so inattentive as
to air the location on public television and broadcast it
to the world. In order to promote the Sanctuary, NOAA
provided underwater footage that was shot from a remotely operated vehicle, or ROV. They also provided
footage of the control room aboard the surface support
vessel from which the ROV was deployed and operated.
This topside footage focused on the ROV pilot who was
watching the monitor that showed what the ROV camera
was seeing on the wreck. Because a GPS unit was interfaced with the ROV, to enable the pilot to plot his course,
the GPS coordinates were displayed on the screen and
were duly recorded by the topside camera.

This informative scene was deleted from later broad-
casts, but the damage was already done. NOAA's later
attempts to cover up its stupidity, and its continued refusal to release the coordinates, came to naught. NOAA
was pre-empted by its own inattention. NOAA's only saving grace was that most of those who noticed the errors
of its televised ways did not write down the numbers, or
think in advance to record the broadcast.

Others took a different tack. Bob Foster correlated
published survey information with the historical record.
This enabled him to pinpoint the locations of several
wrecks that lie within Sanctuary boundaries. The GPS
coordinates that have so far been ascertained – by Foster and others – are published in the present volume,
both at the end of this chapter and in the GPS/Loran
list at the back of the book. As other wreck sites are discovered (or uncovered), they will be published on my
website and printed in future editions.

"The smaller the mind, the greater the conceit."
- Aesop

Now to return to the meeting that was noted at the beginning of this chapter.

After Lawrence's introductory poppycock, divers in the audience posed queries about access to shipwrecks within the Sanctuary. Lawrence danced around the issues with true political abandon by never directly answering the questions. Instead, he went off on tangents, during the course of which he expressed NOAA's avowed intent to consider the interests of the people by holding a public hearing.

I was well aware of how NOAA had conducted similar hearings with respect to other Sanctuaries. I was also well aware of their outcomes. Attendees were getting frustrated because they could not get a straight answer to a simple and straightforward question. Finally, I decided to provide what Lawrence refused to give them.

I announced, "NOAA is a totalitarian government agency that doesn't care what you want." I went on to explain that the only reason that NOAA promised to hold a public hearing was because it was forced to do so by Congressional mandate. But, although Congress demanded that NOAA had to *listen* to the concerns of the citizens, NOAA did not have to *act* upon those concerns – and never in its more than thirty-year history had it done so.

The public hearing was a smokescreen: a mere pretense so that NOAA could show Congress that the people had a say in the matter of Sanctuary regulations. NOAA was going to do whatever it damn well pleased.

Lawrence's appearance was a façade – nothing but window-dressing to convince the dive community that they were bound to be part of the decision-making process when in fact they were not. In effect, NOAA was trying to lull recreational divers into a false sense of security, so that it could pass restrictions unopposed – restrictions that were not in the best interests of the public, and that were contrary to the wishes of the people who had the greatest stake in them. That was the way NOAA operated, and had always operated.

The proof of the pudding is NOAA's steadfast refusal to divulge the coordinates of shipwrecks that lie within Sanctuary boundaries. At a subsequent meeting (of the Bay State Council of Divers) on September 26, 2007, Lawrence reiterated NOAA's publicly avowed stance. It was no more believable to me then than it had been the year before.

When I told Lawrence that I had just surveyed the *Pentagoet* – a site whose location NOAA had refused to divulge – he asked me to submit a survey report. I told him that he could read it in the book (which you now hold in your hands). He added further insult by requesting reports of any other wrecks that I might survey in the Sanctuary. Bilinski then asked him for GPS coordinates for sites that he wanted us to survey. With a smirk on his face, Lawrence refused to give them to us.

I turned to Bilinski, and said, "NOAA doesn't believe in give and take. NOAA only takes."

Lawrence made no comment.

Even though Lawrence appears to enjoy his position of withholding information from the public, I do not mean to single him out from a large group of culprits. Despite the fact that NOAA has designated him as the spokesperson of its dictatorial doctrine, he is but a cog in an imperious wheel of chicanery that goes all the way to the head of NOAA in the person of Dan Basta. On October 27, 2007, as part of NOAA's endless stream of self-promotion, Basta wrote that one of NOAA's accomplishments over the past thirty-five years was that it "involved people in its decision making, through the 14 advisory councils that provide a critical link to communities adjacent to national marine sanctuaries."

What Basta neglected to mention was that the advisory councils were stacked decks: their members were carefully chosen from among those who agreed with NOAA's policies. Most of the *real* people – those who actually lived near sanctuaries and who earned their livings in sanctuary waters – opposed further aggrandizement, but their voices were either stifled or ignored. Opponents had no say in the decision-making processes. NOAA listened only to proponents of its power-hungry policies and territorial expansion.

Nor is there any end of NOAA's territorial expansion in sight. NOAA is now in the process of expanding the Thunder Bay National Marine Sanctuary *eightfold* in size. The absurdity of this situation is that Thunder Bay is not even a marine environment: it is a freshwater bay in Lake Huron. Like Hitler annexing neighboring countries, I doubt that NOAA will ever be satisfied until it controls the entire underwater world.

Fiefdom is alive and living in the NOAA hierarchy.

Millions of dollars have been spent on side-scan surveys and videotape reconnaissance from remotely operated vehicles. Yet when a member of the Massachusetts Board of Underwater Archaeological Resources asked for a side-scan image of the *Pentagoet*, Lawrence refused to provide it. NOAA has consistently declined to provide *all* other shipwreck information – photographs, footage, and side-scan imagery – that is not published gratuitously on the Sanctuary website.

> "Repetition does not transform a lie into truth."
> - Franklin D. Roosevelt

Listed at the end of this chapter are the locations of those shipwrecks that I have been able to obtain from non-NOAA sources: recreational divers who have spent their own time, effort, and resources to rediscover what NOAA maliciously withheld from them; and recreational divers who are willing the share with the public the information that was so costly for them to procure.

Now that the publication of the present volume has let the cat out of the bag, NOAA will no longer have a reason to keep these locations secret. Yet full disclosure has never been part of NOAA's protocol. I doubt that publicizing NOAA's long history of dishonesty will force its administrators to change their tune. Based upon their past behavior, I suspect that they will continue to promote the Sanctuary program as if it is in the best interests of the public.

Consider this: NOAA's literature contains no mention of my victorious court battle against the Monitor National Marine Sanctuary. Both my name and my successful court battle have been expunged from NOAA's published history. NOAA has made no endeavors to inform the public that a legal confrontation occurred in which NOAA was found at fault. As far as NOAA's publications are concerned, the case never existed, and diving permits were always available to American citizens.

Despite my legal victory, the *Monitor* permitting process has again become a façade. Over the past three years, Todd Baldi has submitted five applications to dive on the *Monitor* – and has never been favored with an acknowledgment of receipt, much less the courtesy of a reply. His requests to see copies of existing applications, on which to model his own, have met with the identical treatment: no response. NOAA simply ignores him as if he does not exist, or like W.C. Fields saying, "Go away, kid. You bother me." Todd wrote to keep me updated on his lack of progress: "I spoke to Jeff Johnson once over the phone. He guided me through the process and basically gave me the complete runaround."

It is the same story all over again. NOAA is doing to Todd what it did to me.

I suspect that NOAA's cover-up will in large measure continue. NOAA may eventually publicize shipwreck locations after the fact of their publication in this volume – doing damage control for a fait accompli – but I doubt that NOAA will acknowledge the true reason for its grudging release of information. Instead, they will word the disclosure in such a way as to make it appear that they had *always* provided locations.

Nor will NOAA praise the achievements of those who were the first to dive on the *Frank A. Palmer* and *Louise B. Crary*: unless it is to belittle my predictions. I suspect that NOAA will write this book out of its history the way they wrote me out of the *Monitor's* history.

NOAA's blatant agency hype and self-delusion are ingrained in its policy and in the attitude of its administrators. I think that NOAA will continue to provide partial truths while refusing to admit to all the facts.

I also suspect that if NOAA ever releases the locations of Stellwagen shipwrecks, it will not mention that it did so because it was pre-empted by *Shipwrecks of Massachusetts: North*. Now that I have made the locations public knowledge, I suspect that NOAA might try to save face by making them available without acknowledging my priority: as if NOAA had never kept them secret. These suspicions are based upon NOAA's past actions. In actuality, these suspicions are more in the way of extrapolations rather than forecasts of future behavior.

Worst of all, I suspect that NOAA will endeavor to place at least some of the Sanctuary shipwrecks off limits. They are already laying the basis for this action by claiming that the *Frank A. Palmer*, *Louise B. Crary*, and *Portland* are "very fragile." These are the most intact historic shipwrecks so far discovered in the Sanctuary. Yet they do not describe other wrecks as fragile – those that are almost completely collapsed, such as the *Paul Palmer* and the false *Pentagoet*. It is oxymoronic – or perhaps just moronic – to claim that nearly intact wrecks are fragile, while nearly collapsed wrecks are not. But no one ever accused NOAA of sound reasoning.

> "Big Brother is watching you."
> - George Orwell

Other groundwork that NOAA is laying to preclude public access is water movement. NOAA claims that strong currents and tides pass through the Sanctuary. I would not dispute this claim, because strong currents and tides occur in every ocean, even in Boston Harbor. NOAA's current and tidal sophistry may sound plausible to a naïve citizen or his ingenuous representative, but it is no more meaningful than stating that the Moon revolves around the Earth. The truth that NOAA ignores is that divers do not dive during those times when the water is moving strongly.

NOAA also claims that dive boats utilize a seven to one scope for anchoring, implying that long mooring cables might sweep across and damage a wreck. While this ratio of anchor-chain length to water depth is true for large ocean-going vessels, it is not true for small boats. Small boats do not use a scope that approaches even two to one. By means of comparison, a large ocean-going vessel would use 700 feet of hard iron chain to anchor in 100 feet of water, whereas a dive boat would use no more than 150 feet of soft nylon line to anchor in the same depth. NOAA's imagery insinuates a false impression that is clearly deceptive.

Furthermore, many dives are conducted without anchoring at all. Live-boat diving is commonplace. In this technique, a weighted line is lowered next to a wreck, and is held aloft by means of a buoy, float, or tuna ball. Divers are dropped off and descend the line while the boat drifts or maneuvers in the vicinity.

NOAA commonly ignores well-established diving practices in order to justify its restrictions. If NOAA truly wanted to facilitate access, it would establish mooring buoys next to the wreck sites. I doubt that this will ever happen. NOAA's attitude is antagonistic and dishonest toward the public that provides its funding.

Sanctuary superintendent Craig MacDonald has laid the groundwork for a "switch and bait" scam. He professed to have the interests of divers at heart, but in aside admitted that the final decision for shipwreck management and control will be made at a higher level in NOAA. His disingenuous posture allows him to present himself as a supporter of the wants of the recreational diving community, but lets him off the hook when high-level administrators overrule his putative recommendations in order to close the wrecks to the public. The situation is nothing more than a conspiracy that is designed to deceive gullible believers.

NOAA can prevent diver access by means other than

direct prohibition. For example, one ploy is to claim that a wreck will be kept off-limits only until staff members complete a survey or examination of the site: a process which they can extend indefinitely while divers grow old and die. If site studies are never completed, the wreck is never opened to the public.

Another way is to claim that a wreck is too "fragile" for divers to explore. It goes without saying that a wreck cannot be damaged by ocular observation or exposure to photographic processes. Yet the government has used this smelly red herring numerous times in the past, and continues to get away with it.

In the past, NOAA's most effective means of denying public access is abuse of the permit process. NOAA has already announced the likelihood of requiring recreational divers to obtain a permit in order to dive on Sanctuary shipwrecks. This system sounds innocent at first blush. After all, the National Park Service requires backpackers to obtain a permit before entering the backcountry. But there is a substantial difference between the NPS permit process and the NOAA permit process.

When I backpack in a National Park, I either fill out a permit form at the self-service kiosk at the trailhead, or I stop at the visitor center and fill out the form under the guidance of a Park ranger, who advises me on conditions and the availability of water and camping facilities. On the one-page form I write my name, address, telephone number, make and model of my vehicle, my planned route, and the anticipated length of my stay. The permit enables Park personnel to determine trail usage. The permit benefits the backpacker by alerting Park personnel of his location and his anticipated date of return. If the vehicle is spotted at the trailhead after his anticipated return date, Park personnel possess information that is necessary to enable them to initiate search and rescue operations along the backpacker's projected route.

Now consider NOAA's history and proven track record: the process that I encountered when I submitted an application for a permit to dive on the USS *Monitor*.

The first NOAA ploy was to ignore my written requests: about a dozen of them over the course of a year. After my persistence paid off by forcing a response to an avowedly hostile letter, Sanctuary manager Edward Miller sent me a multiple page outline of the information that I was required to furnish. He wanted lengthy essays on every aspect of the conduct of my proposed dive plan, backup procedures, and photographic objectives: the name and full background resume of every diver on the expedition; a complete Research Design to include the "scientific questions to be addressed;" a detailed budget "with sources of funding and amounts" and the "reliability and commitment of funding;" and a totally irrelevant Letter of Transmittal.

After I submitted a permit application that was eleven single-spaced typewritten pages in length, another year passed during which I received no answers to my written requests for a status report, and noncommittal answers to my telephone calls. When I finally received a response, it was only to notify me that my application failed to satisfy a new criterion. Long after I furnished the information to satisfy *that* demand, I received a notification that NOAA had found another part of my application that was unsatisfactory. Whenever I satisfied a new requirement, NOAA created another.

NOAA then pigeonholed my permit application for more than a year. This bureaucratic legerdemain continued through eleven applications over a period of several years, and would have gone on forever if I had not retained an attorney to take the case to federal court. NOAA knows that most people do not have the time, money, or energy to take it to court, while NOAA has unlimited funding (which is paid by the taxpayer) to prolong the case, to wear down the plaintiff, to drain his financial resources, and to prevail without ever adjudicating the case on its merits.

It took me six years and two federal court cases to obtain my permit. Then NOAA denied my next permit, and it took another two years, two more lawsuits, and Congressional intervention to achieve a permanent per-

mitting process that subsequent divers could utilize
without having to take NOAA to court in order to dive
on the *Monitor*. NOAA may very well employ these same
tactics in the Stellwagen Sanctuary. The proof of the
pudding is what NOAA is presently doing to Todd Baldi
with respect to the *Monitor*. NOAA's shenanigans never
cease.

There is no end to what a pack of creative autocrats
can devise to hoodwink the public.

> "War is peace. Freedom is slavery.
> Ignorance is strength."
> - George Orwell

The NOAA thought police are keeping wreck locations and survey data to themselves. It is only through
the efforts of private individuals that the locations of
some of the wrecks in Stellwagen Bank have been made
available to the public. Here are the locations that I have
been able to obtain so far:

Fishing Vessel 1 (100 feet deep)
                        42-18.737   70-17.824
Fishing Vessel 2 (425 feet deep)
                        42-31.679   70-14.780
Frank A. Palmer (bow) (360 feet deep)
                        42-29.030   70-16.000
Frank A. Palmer (stern) (360 feet deep)
                        42-29.942   70-16.146
Granite Wreck (370 feet deep)
                        42-29.140   70-16.260
Josephine Marie (80 feet deep)
                        42-10.925   70-13.466
Louise B. Crary (bow) (360 feet deep)
                        42-29.030   70-16.000
Mystery Collier (405 feet deep)
                        42-34.722   70-15.672
Paul Palmer (unconfirmed)
                        42-11.206   70-16.682
Paul Palmer (unconfirmed)

	42-10.206	70-16.682
Portland (450 feet deep)		
	42-28.348	70-17.238
Pentagoet (false) (165 feet deep)		
	42-13.840	70-09.067
Unidentified (110 feet deep)		
	42-11.119	70-12.062
Unidentified (100 feet deep)		
	42-22.340	70-22.220

There is a good reason for my predilection for quoting George Orwell's famous dystopian novel, 1984. It is the only book that I ever read that truly scared me. I read it as a teenager; I read it again as a young adult; and memories of the book still terrify me today.

I can conceive of nothing more horrible than a totalitarian government that rules its citizens as if they were slaves or, worse, livestock. The loss of freedom, the loss of identity, and the loss of reality are very real threats that I experienced firsthand when I was drafted into the U.S. Army and sent to Vietnam. (I was given a choice of two years in the Army or five years in a federal penitentiary. I made the wrong choice.) It is the height of absurdity to take away one person's freedom in order to make that person fight for someone else's freedom.

As Thomas Jefferson wrote, "The cost of freedom is eternal vigilance." In relation to today's world, that means vigilance against aggression both foreign and domestic. The most insidious attacks are those that originate within the political system in which the citizens hold their trust.

When I wrote Ironclad Legacy, *I harbored the mistaken notion that, once trounced and placed under Congressional scrutiny, the National Marine Sanctuary Program would toe the line. How wrong I was. Congress has not been vigilant, so Program administrators have again gone astray. Like runners in a relay race, each power hungry Program bureaucrat has passed his obsessive abuse of authority to his successor.*

The NMSP is so consumed by control and territorial

expansion that I don't believe that it can ever be brought back into the fold – even by firing every administrator, staff member, and employee in any capacity, and restarting the Program from scratch. I am afraid that the infection is so entrenched in the system that it can never be eradicated.

There is only one solution to the problem. The National Marine Sanctuary Program must be abolished.

As an ironic side note, in the Introduction to The Technical Diving Handbook *I wrote about an incident that occurred on May 18, 1991. While diving on the freighter* John Morgan *off Virginia Beach, the anchor line broke free from the wreck. I did a drift decompression.*

On the boat were several NOAA employees who were making recreational dives. After twenty-six minutes of decompression, I surfaced in five-foot seas about a mile astern of the boat. I waved slowly to attract attention. One of the NOAA employees spotted me. He alerted the skipper, who raced the boat to my rescue.

Safely onboard, I jokingly suggested to the NOAA employee that he not inform his superiors that he was responsible for saving my life, or they would certainly fire him for stupidity. I was a thorn in the side of NOAA that its administrators wouldn't mind having plucked.

Apparently that NOAA employee did as I suggested, and kept his mouth shut. He rose through the ranks from a lowly underling to the highest position in the Administration. His name is Dan Basta. I wonder if he has any regrets about that day on the John Morgan.

I would be remiss if I did not mention some other buffooneries and stupidities that NOAA has perpetrated in the Stellwagen Bank NMS.

With regard to the *Portland*, NOAA literature proclaims, "This significant shipwreck will now be managed and protected by the National Marine Sanctuary Program." In order to attract attention to the Stellwagen sanctuary, NOAA has begun touting the *Portland* as the "*Titanic* of New England."

This hype panders to the hope that Sanctuary personnel can inveigle more money out of Congress in order to promote their personal agendas: another grim example of NOAA corruption.

While I am on the subject of the *Portland*, I should mention that shortly after publication of *Shipwrecks of Massachusetts: North*, recreational divers became the first people to actually visit the wreck in person. These audacious divers were Paul Blanchette, Dave Faye, Bob Foster, Slav Mlch, and Don Morse.

NOAA still has not released the GPS coordinates of the wreck. Thus casual visitors to NOAA's website are led to believe that the location has not been published elsewhere.

With regard to the *Paul Palmer*, hardly any of the hull remains. Nonetheless, NOAA nominated the wreck for inclusion on the list of the National Register of Historic Places. On the application form, NOAA described the wreck as "substantially intact" in one place, and "moderately intact" in another. These descriptions are not just stretches of the imagination; they are outright lies. Not only did the ship burn to the waterline, but the wreck was demolished by means of explosives. Practically none of the wreck is exposed. The largest chunk of wreckage is the windlass on the bow.

NOAA's nomination descriptions contradict NOAA's previous description of the *Paul Palmer*, which was given in the nomination of the *Frank A. Palmer* and *Louise B. Crary*. In that application, NOAA wrote, "Stellwagen Bank National Marine Sanctuary has located a number of archaeological sites associated with the New England coal trade. These sites represent a variety of vessels ranging from smaller two and three-masted schooners to another five-masted coal schooner, *Paul Palmer*. None of these sites have the structural integrity of *Frank A. Palmer* and *Louise B. Crary*, and in some cases all that remains are pieces of the lower hull protruding from a large pile of coal."

In Sanctuary literature, NOAA described the *Paul Palmer* as "typical." If it is typical, then it is not unique or outstanding. Much of the Statement of Significance in the application form was copied verbatim from the application of the *Frank A. Palmer* and *Louise B. Crary*. Furthermore, NOAA claimed that the wreck was an archaeological resource because it offered "archaeologists the chance to examine a representative example of a New England coal schooner operated during the climax of coastwise transportation of bulk commodities by pure sail. The site can reveal information about hull and rigging design, construction, use, and condition as well as the state of affairs onboard at the time of its loss."

I do not know what NOAA means by "chance," but archaeologists had plenty of *opportunity* to examine the *Hesper* and the *Luther Little*: two prime representative examples of New England coal schooners that were docked in Wiscasset, Maine from 1932 until 1998, when they were demolished as eyesores. What can archaeologists hope to learn from the *Paul Palmer* that they did not learn during the sixty-six years that the *Hesper* and *Luther Little* sat high and dry?

Furthermore, the five-masted schooner *Cora F. Cressy* was built in the same year as the *Paul Palmer*. The *Cora F. Cressy* is presently in use as a breakwater in Bremen, Maine. Any archaeologist who wanted to study hull construction could do so better by examining the *Cora F. Cressy* than by examining the *Paul Palmer*, which is almost entirely buried in deeper water and farther away from shore resources. But then, my arguments bear logic, and logic has nothing to do with NOAA protocol.

The case of the *Pentagoet* is even more outrageous. Stellwagen Bank National Marine Sanctuary archaeologists believe that a wreck that lies at the southern end of the Sanctuary is the *Pentagoet*. According to Sanctuary literature, "several anonymous sport diving sources" call this site the Toy Wreck, or the Christmas Wreck, "due to its cargo of toys." True to form, Stellwagen refused to divulge the coordinates of this site. Fortunately, the Massachusetts Board of Underwater Archaeological Resources had the coordinates on file, so I was able to survey the site.

Lying at a depth of 165 feet, I found the wreck of a wooden-hulled coal barge. It measures approximately 150 to 175 feet in length, with a 40 feet abeam. The outline of the hull is discernible, as the turn of the bilge on either side is sporadically exposed. The keelson is exposed for nearly its entire length. Otherwise, the interior of the wreck is completely filled with sand. A few small chunks of coal – about 2 inches across – litter the seabed in the stern.

Maximum rise of the keelson and the outer timbers is about 6 inches.

The primary (and practically the only) features are two chain lockers in the bow. Each locker measures approximately three to four feet in width, and five to six feet in length. They are spaced about ten apart. These lockers are filled with anchor chain. The rise of the chain and lockers is about one to one and a half feet.

At the opposite end of the wreck, the sternpost stands thirteen feet high. Ironically, a length of anchor chain extends along the starboard stern, past and adjacent to the sternpost, and off the wreck to port for about thirty feet.

A deadeye lies on the keelson about twenty feet forward of the sternpost.

There are no signs of machinery of any kind, not even a donkey boiler (or a windlass). There is no engine, there is no boiler, there are no bedplates, there is no piping – in short, there is nothing that would lead one to conclude that this was the wreck of a steamship. The keelson is clearly exposed at the place where the engine and boiler should be located. No toys or any kind of merchandise other than coal is anywhere in evidence.

I have named this wreck the Stellwagen Coal Barge.

I have no idea why recreational divers would believe this site to be the *Pentagoet*. Far worse, I cannot understand why Stellwagen archaeologists would concur with such a belief. In a personal communication among witnesses, Stellwagen archaeologist Matthew Lawrence told me that Stellwagen deployed a remotely operated vehicle on the site and conducted an extensive video survey of the wreckage. Although he refused to let me see the videotape footage, he told me that the lens depicted the same images that I saw with my own eyes. Yet Stellwagen persists in its notion that this wreck is the *Pentagoet*. Not only that, but the Sanctuary is contemplating nominating the site for inclusion on the National Register of Historic Places, because "it could possess potential historical importance." This is patently absurd, but strongly in keeping with NOAA's policy of aggrandizement.

The true resting place of the *Pentagoet* is unknown. I predicted that eventually, after publication of *Shipwrecks of Massachusetts: North*, NOAA would abandon its presumption that the Stellwagen Coal Barge is the *Pentagoet*. I also predicted that, as NOAA did with the *Monitor*, it would not mention why its belief changed. Instead, I thought that NOAA would take the course that was taken by the totalitarian government that continually rewrote history in the George Orwell classic *1984*: it would change its promotional literature to reflect the new information, but would not bother to inform the populace that any changes had been made, leading people to believe that such had always been the case.

So far, five years after publication, none of my predictions has come to pass. NOAA archaeologists persist in calling the wreck the *Pentagoet*, despite the fact that there is absolutely nothing on the site that resembles a steamship.

Expansion

Despite its bungling and blind mishandling of shipwrecks in the Stellwagen Bank NMS, NOAA wants to increase the size of the sanctuary as far as it can go toward land: their reach stopping at the three mile territorial border, inside of which the waters belong to the State of Massachusetts. If NOAA has its way, every bit of ocean off the Massachusetts coast farther than three miles from the beach, would be under NOAA's control and dominion.

So secret did NOAA keep its expansion plot that even Victor Mastone, head of the Massachusetts Board of Underwater Archaeological Resources, was kept out of the loop. He learned of the expansion plot tangentially from non-NOAA sources.

But that is not the only ruckus that NOAA has been causing for the public in general and for Massachusetts residents in particular. Read the next chapter (Subterfuge 401) to learn about more NOAA chicanery.

Subterfuge 401
The Magic Money Game

Now You See It, Now You Don't

On May 1, 2012, NOAA posted an advertisement in which it proposed to hire a magician to entertain NOAA employees who were slated to attend a management-training session in Silver Spring, Maryland. Among the topics that the stage mage was required to address were "magic tricks, puzzles, brain teasers, word games, humor."

To anyone who was the least bit familiar with NOAA's history of prestidigitation, the contracting of a spirit-caller would seem to be a total waste of time. NOAA was a master trickster when it came to sleight-of-hand. After all, NOAA managers could make permit applications disappear for years at a time.

I would venture to bet that there are no wiles that a well-versed conjuror could teach an up-and-coming NOAA manager that NOAA did not already know how to do better. In fact, I would venture to bet even more that NOAA had so many ruses up its proverbial sleeve that it could well be the instructor.

In this case it did not need the likes of me to blow the whistle on NOAA's obvious splurge of the taxpayers' hard-earned money. Numbered among the people who held no illusions about the extravagance of NOAA's enchanted scheme were Congressional representatives who were looking out for their constituents.

"Frivolous" and "ridiculous" were words that Congressional leaders used to describe NOAA's consumption of government resources. House Science Committee Chairman Ralph Hall "gave NOAA Administrator Jane Lubchenco a week to provide a detailed explanation about past spending on magicians and comedians." She never did.

Senator Scott Brown of Massachusetts went one farther: he demanded Lubchenco's resignation.

The eight-page flyer specified the performer's required attributes with such detailed precision that it appeared to have been written with a pre-designated individual in mind: that is, only one person in the world
possessed the exact qualifications to match the job description. In other words, the flyer looked like a political
favor that was designed to use the government coffer to
enrich a single person for doing very little work. The en-
comium – the munificent sum $3,500 for a one-day gig
with but a single performance – implied that a kickback
was part of the deal.

The flyer gave Patricia McBride-Finneran as NOAA's
point of contact. NOAA did not report the names of any
entertainers who applied for the job. (Natch.) To Congressional inquiries, McBride-Finneran replied, "Somebody from communications [is] coming up to talk to me
about what I should be saying."

Her statement about NOAA's standard protocol was
more telling than it appears at first blush. *It never occurred to her to tell the truth.* Instead, she essentially told
callers that she was waiting for NOAA's attorneys to create a cover story.

Senator Brown was blunt about NOAA's subversive
tactics. He said, "This is a low point even by Washington's standards." He also said, "The best magic that
NOAA could perform would be to make this wasteful
spending disappear."

The ad itself must have had inherent magic qualities
because, presto-changeo, it did exactly as Brown recommended: it vanished before anyone could say abra-
cadabra.

But not until the news media had a field day.

Catch of the Day

Senator Brown kept his political finger on NOAA's
racing pulse because his constituents had a personal ax
to grind with administrative mishandling of fisheries
regulations.

NOAA's adjunct – the National Marine Fisheries Service – regulated the deep-sea catch with what has often been described as "overzealous law enforcement practices." Senator Brown's investigations recently discovered the reason for these fanatical practices. But let's lay the groundwork before cutting to the chase by citing a few of the most egregious examples of unwarranted enforcement.

In order to put angling into perspective, however, I first need to set the stage by relating some first-person accounts with marine fisheries officers and local anglers.

Late one night I was taking my scuba gear off a boat in Cape May when I noticed a Marine Fisheries officer strolling along the quayside. He was asking returning boaters about their catch for the day – species, quantity, and size – and making entries in a statistical log for later analysis. When he reached the *Big Mac*, he asked me and my fellow divers what we had caught. Harold Moyers, the skipper, told him that we had been diving, not fishing (or spearfishing).

The officer asked, "Did you catch any lobsters?"

His question was appropriate because the majority of New Jersey recreational divers went diving for that purpose only. We had been exploring a deep-water shipwreck, not lobster diving, so Harold said, "No."

The officer nodded and turned to walk away. I stopped him with a question. Historically, the minimum size of a lobster that a person was allowed to keep was 3-1/4 inches, measured from the rear of the eye socket to the end of the carapace. Most lobster divers carried an aluminum gauge in the water with them, so they could measure a questionable lobster on the bottom instead of bringing it to the surface, and then having to return it to the water if it was not a keeper. New Jersey was in the process of increasing the minimum size by 1/16-inch increments over the course of several years.

I did not engage much in lobstering. I knew that a change in the works, but I did not know its current status. So I asked the officer for the present minimum size in case I caught a lobster on my next dive trip.

He thought for a moment, then said, "I don't know."

"What do you mean, you don't know? You're the one who issues violations for shorts."

He shrugged. It was his job to know the rule book inside out. If he caught a diver with a lobster that was shorter than the minimum size, he would fine the diver. If he caught an angler bringing in catch that was either out of season or not within the legal size limits, he would fine the angler. How could he know whether to fine someone if he didn't know the rules and did not carry a rule book? The fisheries offices were closed, so he could not call anyone for elucidation.

He had no explanation. He simply shrugged and walked away, to continue gathering statistics, ostensibly for someone who *did* know.

Toeing the Fish Line

On another occasion I was chatting with an off-duty Marine Fisheries officer who offered some interesting insights. He was in charge of a local fisheries office in North Carolina. He enforced regulations by inspecting commercial fishing boats and examining their catch. He issued violations to anglers who, as noted in the previous section, either brought in fish that were not in season, or were either too small or too large.

The problem that he normally encountered with fishing regulations was that they were subject to change without prior warning. It was common for commercial anglers to visit his office in order to obtain the latest regulatory updates, so that they could avoid breaking the rules and getting fined for doing so. These anglers were law-abiding citizens who earned an honest living by fishing, and not by poaching. The officer duly disseminated copies of the current regulations.

However, late in the afternoon he might receive a fax from a higher authority, the subject of which encompassed revisions in the fishing regulations. The season might then be closed on certain species, or the minimum size might be elongated. When he did his rounds of the docks on the following day, he might then issue violations to the very same anglers he had advised the previous morning. The following dialogue approximates our subsequent conversation.

"How could you do that?" I exclaimed. "You were the one who told them what was legal."

He shrugged. "I know, but I had to do it. My job was to cite everyone who broke the rules."

"Why didn't you just give them a warning about the change instead of fining them?"

"I'm not authorized to issue warnings. I can only issue violations."

I was appalled by the absurdity of the situation. The officer allowed that if the angler protested the violation, and pleaded extenuating circumstances, a judge might eliminate the fine. But the angler had to miss a day's work in order to appear in court, so he lost money no matter what course he took.

Common sense along with sensible delegation of authority would have achieved the legislative goal without penalizing innocent anglers who were struggling to earn a living. All too often, the implementation and enforcement of laws work against the common good because they are blind to the short-term effects of those laws.

What possible difference could there be in a short delay in enforcement, until the new laws could be disseminated to the fishing community? Instead, anglers were blindsided by overnight vagaries that allowed for no leeway in communication. No species of fish could be depopulated by a 24-hour postponement of enforcement.

Due to deliberate lack of good will, valuable court time was wasted, anglers lost money (or time that equated to money), and no justice was served in the process.

A Seahorse of a Different Color

While I was recreational diving off a boat in South Carolina, both boat skippers were fishing by means of rod and reel. During decompression, I watched in astonishment as they reeled in fish after fish but usually landed only the heads. More often than not, barracuda charged up from the bottom at phenomenal speed, sideswiped the wiggling catch on the hook, and absconded with three-quarters of the body.

After the dive, I listened as the skippers discussed the fish that they managed to land through the barrage of barracudas. They were packed in ice in coolers. Most of the fish they caught were snappers. There are about 100 species of snapper. The most common one in the area was the red snapper. Red snappers are not colored bright red; they have a slight reddish tinge whose intensity differs with sex, age, geographical location, and time of year.

Other varieties of snapper resemble the red snapper in shape and coloration, again depending upon sex, age, geographical location, and time of year. The big discussion between the skippers was whether the snappers they had caught were red snappers or some closely related subspecies.

The similarity in appearance was bewildering. They all looked the same to me. Some were less red than others; some were more red than others. No two were exactly the same color.

Each skipper had been fishing commercially for thirty-some years. Between them they had more than sixty years of experience. In my opinion, this qualified them as experts. Yet these two experts could not agree on which fish were red snappers and which were one of several related subspecies. Each one could not even agree with himself. He might examine one fish and decide that it was a red snapper, then a minute later say that he wasn't sure that it wasn't a subspecies. Both skippers studied the fish and changed their minds several times.

The difference was important because some of the subspecies were not in season.

Neither skipper was certain of identification. They did not release any of them for the very simple reason that they might release a legal fish, and by misidentification bring in one that was illegal at the moment.

If these two experts could not distinguish one snapper from another, how could a snot-nose Marine Fisheries officer who was fresh out of college make such a distinction? His expertise – or lack of same, as I demonstrated in the previous section – lay only in enforcing laws that were defined only in published regulations. Only a trained ichthyologist could make a bona fide determination, and then only by dissecting all the fish in a laboratory.

Fisheries officers issued violations, not ichthyologists.

Tracking Tactics

Van Strickler is a commercial angler who told me how the Marine Fisheries guarded his fishing trawler, which was docked in Virginia Beach, Virginia. In accordance with federal regulations, he was permitted to operate his vessel only at certain times of the year, and then for only a specified number of days. This was the way his catch (and profit) was limited.

The Marine Fisheries monitored vessel movements by installing a tracking system on his and other commercial fishing vessels. A transponder transmitted a signal that was intercepted by a satellite receiver, then telemetered to a land-based tracking station. The transponder signal was interfaced with the Global Positioning System (GPS) so that the Marine Fisheries office knew precisely where his boat was located every minute of the day. This is the maritime equivalent of LoJack.

The commercial fishing fleet was constantly tracked. If Strickler's boat was located someplace where it was not supposed to be, the Marine Fisheries knew about it and cited him with a violation. Now that I think about it, this is more like an inmate wristband identifier than LoJack; and the boats are more like prisoners than commercial fishing vessels.

The fishing fleet was so strictly regulated that each vessel was permitted to be in its assigned fishing territory on preordained days only. If a boat had a mechanical malfunction that prevented it from reaching its territory on the day when it was allowed to fish, it lost that day of fishing forever. There were no make-up days.

The One Fish Case

Keep the previous absurdities in mind as we now return to Senator Brown's investigations. For the first volley we will study NOAA's eleven-year harassment of the Gloucester Seafood Display Auction, which is located in Gloucester, Massachusetts.

It all started in 2000, when NOAA accused the auction house of selling cod that was alleged to have been caught illegally. Understand that the auction house did not catch fish; it purchased catch from commercial fishing boats and then sold the fish on the block to the marketplace.

Cod live near the bottom of the ocean. Cod are caught by rod and reel by means of ground tackle, either by commercial anglers or by sport-fishing enthusiasts on charter boats. The harvest is regulated by littoral States and the National Marine Fisheries Service (under NOAA). The cod fishing season lasts from April through October. Regulations change from year to year, and within the year. Regulations vary in accordance with geography.

Saltwater fishing permits may or may not be required, depending upon location. The permit is issued not by NOAA but by an adjacent State. For example, a permit is required in Massachusetts but not in New Hampshire. The incongruity here is that cod are seldom if ever caught in State waters; they are hooked mostly in international waters. The need for a permit is not based upon the locality of the catch, but upon the registration of the vessel. A boat whose anchorage is in Massachusetts requires a permit from that State, whereas a boat whose anchorage is in New Hampshire does not require a permit.

Jurisprudence is uncertain. It is not clear which State has jurisdiction if a boat from Massachusetts lands its catch in New Hampshire.

Be that as it may, other restrictions may also apply. For example, in international waters south and east of Cape Cod, the permissible catch on a Massachusetts boat is limited in a number of ways. Each person onboard is allowed to catch two cod per day. However, this catch limit is subservient to the boat limit of either ten cod per day or seventy-five pounds of cod per day, whichever limit is reached first. This convoluted system incurs a number of permutations.

Let us use a standard party boat as an illustration. If five anglers catch two cod each, no one else on the boat is allowed to fish. If one angler catches a seventy-five-pound cod (Atlantic cod can attain a weight of two hundred pounds), no one else on the boat is allowed to fish. In either case, paying customers come home empty-handed.

Furthermore, we are talking about the regulations for only one area of the ocean, and only with regard to boats from Massachusetts. Other catch limits apply to adjacent areas and to boats from other States in the Union.

Worse yet, these regulations are subject to change at a moment's notice. And, as I have already demonstrated, a Marine Fisheries officer may be clueless about the regulations that *do* apply – at that particular moment, at that particular place, to that particular species.

Worst of all, none of this has anything to do with the auction house in question. As I have already pointed out, the auction house did not catch fish; it bought fish from the local fleet. Therefore it cannot violate ever-changing fishing regulations. This state of affairs begs the question: Why did NOAA cite the auction house instead of the commercial anglers who allegedly caught cod illegally?

It has been suggested that the auction house refused to pay bribes to fisheries officers, and that NOAA's decade-long persecution was a form of retribution.

It would seem that NOAA should have gone after the anglers who allegedly caught the cod illegally. But that course would have entailed a lot more work. Charter boats are legion, especially six-packs: small boats that carry no more than half a dozen paying customers. Unlike commercial draggers and trawlers, they come and go as they please, and without tracking devices attached to their hulls. Marine Fisheries officers would have to catch violators on the spot: either in the act of landing fish illegally on the high seas where the crimes were allegedly committed, or in the marinas when and where the boats docked after returning from a charter in order to count and weigh their catch.

Another disadvantage with citing individual boat owners is their limited resources. Most small charter boats are heavily mortgaged, their owners possess few if any other assets, and they have hardly any savings or sustainable cash flow. The boat is a capital investment from which the owner earns a living, like small business people who work out of an office.

Rather than going after alleged violators, it was simpler and more financially rewarding to attack an established large-scale business. The Gloucester Seafood Display Auction was a family-owned concern that had been in business for decades. The auction house had permanence, money, and a vested interested in continuing commerce with its customers so that its competitors did not move into its territory.

In other words, NOAA could make more money by fining a wealthy innocent bystander instead of the poor guilty violators. There was strong precedence for this shift in accountability.

Zero Tolerance

Zero tolerance laws were designed to prevent judges from exercising leniency in certain types of offenses and criminal activity. The laws imposed minimum sentences that a judge could neither reduce nor suspend. These laws were most often used (and abused) in the war on drugs. Marijuana users who were caught with as little as a single joint received mandatory jail sentences.

During the days of Prohibition, Coast Guard cutters employed small arms and deck-mounted guns as forceful means to stop rum runners from entering U.S. territory with their cargoes of illegal hooch. Now, with a new prohibition against the importation of "controlled substances," the Coast Guard was again called upon to stop suspected drug runners, and to seize all vessels that were transporting illicit freight into U.S. territorial waters.

It did not take long for the Coast Guard to realize how profitable it was to confiscate the boats that it seized, and to auction them to the highest bidder. Whereas foreign drug lords and South American cartels were trafficking in proscribed narcotics, the Coast Guard began trafficking in domestic vessels.

It soon stepped up its search and seizure operations, not only against high-powered speed boats that habitually carried hard dope, but against ordinary party boats that were running fishing charters and dance cruises.

The latter two classes of vessel were not importing drugs. They were taking American citizens to sea for recreational activity and bringing them back. Some of those citizens carried non-alcoholic stimulants in minute quantities, strictly for personal use. The Coast Guard saw these individual users as bait to land larger and more prosperous fish (so to speak). The Coast Guard invoked the zero tolerance law not only to arrest the casual user, but to confiscate multi-million dollar head boats and posh cruise ships.

The take was fantastic. And the Coast Guard got to keep the proceeds.

The Coast Guard scheme of exploiting the letter of the law was clearly not the Presidential intent of the law. No matter: the Coast Guard possessed its own legal system that was beyond the pale of due process. It corresponded with NOAA's administrative law system in that it ignored the most sacrosanct of Constitutional rights: it did not allow alleged offenders to be judged by a jury of their peers.

Like NOAA, the Coast Guard acted as judge, jury, and executioner, all rolled up into one biased ball. By interpreting zero tolerance to its financial advantage, the Coast Guard raised abuse of the law to new heights.

If, in the goodness of its heart, the Coast Guard decided not to keep a confiscated vessel for auction, it cited the owner with a fantastically high fine: a fine which had to be paid before the vessel was released to the owner. Meanwhile, the vessel was quarantined, costing the owner a fortune in lost business income.

Perspectives

Let me put the Coast Guard's zero tolerance money-making scam into perspective. Let us say that a skipper owns a million-dollar charter boat that he uses to take half a dozen anglers on a fishing trip; or a corporation owns a multi-million dollar cruise ship for taking passengers to sea. A Coast Guard cutter stops the vessel. A Coast Guard boarding party conducts an inspection. A passenger with unsmoked marijuana in his pocket drops the weed into the head. Coast Guard personnel find the offending joint – perhaps only a roach – and on that basis confiscate the vessel.

The Coast Guard either sells the vessel at auction, or holds it for ransom until the owner – not the offender – pays an amount that is determined not by law but by the Coast Guard: which has the most to gain by jacking up the fine.

All this begs the most crucial question of all: Why is an innocent boat owner forced to pay for a crime that he did not commit; that the Coast Guard knows was committed by someone else? The answer is obvious: because the boat owner has major assets that the Coast Guard can attach. The real culprit has only the clothes on his back and perhaps a fishing pole. The perpetrator can be sent to jail, but that does not fill the Coast Guard's coffers with revenue.

A vessel owner is not allowed to inspect his customers' possessions (tackle boxes, coolers, suitcases, and the like). A vessel owner is not allowed to frisk his customers or stick his hands into their pockets or pocketbooks. A vessel owner has no way of controlling what his customers bring aboard his vessel. Yet the vessel owner is the one who is held responsible for crimes that are committed by another.

Let us try some other perspectives. If metropolitan police had the Coast Guard's authority, they could confiscate a taxicab because a customer in the back seat was found to have a joint in his pocket . . .

. . . and they could confiscate an intercity bus as soon as a drug-toting passenger boarded . . .

. . . and a subway car . . .

. . . and a commuter train . . .

. . . and a commercial jet aircraft . . .

. . . and your home, if a visitor (even a solicitor) had drugs on his person.

The way the Coast Guard implemented zero tolerance laws may have been advantageous to itself, but it was legally absurd. No rational system of law allows an innocent bystander to be held liable for the actions of someone who happens to be nearby. That constitutes guilt by proximity.

Administrative Abuse

I do not know if Coast Guard piracy and profiteering from existing laws prompted NOAA to adopt a similar policy. All I can say is that NOAA's abuse of fishing regulations followed the Coast Guard's exploitation of a Congressional mandate.

NOAA was holding the auction house accountable for regulatory violations that were committed by others. Worse yet, the violations of those others were only *alleged*; they were never proven.

The violations that NOAA lodged against the Gloucester Seafood Display Auction resulted in fines that far exceeded the severity of the crime – which I have already shown the auction house did not commit. NOAA contended that the auction house *knew* that the fish they purchased had been caught illegally: perhaps by net instead of by rod and reel, or perhaps on a boat whose legal limit was exceeded, or perhaps in an area where cod was either prohibited or not in season.

Under similar circumstances, most people simply fold their cards and pay the fine. They may grumble about lack of fairness, but they figure that they will never prevail in a case in which an Administrative Law Judge takes the place of a jury.

Not so the auction house. The house claimed that it was guilty of no wrongdoing, and hired an attorney to defend its position. This put NOAA on the defensive. And so began the protracted courtroom contest. In one corner was the auction house that was fighting to stay in business as its legal fees mounted; in the other corner was NOAA with a cornucopia of funds.

NOAA found itself in a battle in which the only way it could save face was to force the auction house to shut down for a specified period of time, and to pay an excessive fine: options which the auction house had no intention of doing in light of its professed innocence. The saga of courtroom thrusts and counterthrusts would fill a book, and the amount of paper that was consumed by legal process would level a forest.

One of the charges that NOAA levied was that the auction had handled an extra 75 pounds of fish: an amount that exceeded the legal limit. It was this allegation that tarred the whole debacle as the "one fish case."

Against NOAA's self-serving finding of guilt, the auction house appealed to the Coast Guard, whose administrative law system conceded to "sweeping aside the case."

Yet still NOAA persisted. Its own administrative law judge reversed the Coast Guard's opinion, and Jane Lubchenco, NOAA's chief administrator, sided with her subordinate. NOAA wanted the auction house to pay a fine of $300,000, and – in retaliation for having the temerity to defend itself – to shut down its operations for four months.

The inshore waters were muddied by NOAA law enforcement officers who charged regulatory violations against local anglers, but who promised to quash their cases if they would "rat out" the auction house. Solidarity struck a pose as not one was willing to do so.

Outraged State representatives and officials got involved in the case: Senator John Kerry, Senator Edward Kennedy, Attorney General Martha Coakley, Congressman John Tierney, and, as noted above, Senator Scott Brown. Brown's investigations opened a can of worms.

Money Laundering

Massachusetts anglers complained bitterly to their representatives that the penalties that NOAA levied were not only exorbitant, but were based on unproven violations.

NOAA operated on a presumption of guilt: a cited angler was guilty until he proved his innocence beyond all shadow of doubt. No jury ever heard the case; it was resolved by an Administrative Law Judge who was paid to find defendants guilty in order to ensure payment of the fine.

Not only that, but a comparison with penalties that were levied in other areas of the country revealed that Massachusetts anglers were fined *five times* more than non-Massachusetts anglers for identical violations. This 500% surcharge against Massachusetts anglers had no legitimate basis; it was purely arbitrary.

And there is the crux of the scandal that Brown's investigations unearthed.

After NOAA's judge and prosecuting attorneys found the auction house guilty as charged, and levied the fine, they all went on a junket to Kuala Lumpur, Malaysia, supposedly to attend a conference that NOAA funded with ill-gotten gains. This was the incentive that NOAA gave its employees for victimizing commercial anglers.

The swindle conspiracy went deeper than that. Much deeper. Free vacations to foreign countries constituted only the tip of the illegitimate iceberg.

There is no need for me to tell the story. Congress already told it when it began the process of framing laws to prevent NOAA's abusive and fraudulent practices from continuing.

The Fraud is Exposed

After Brown uncovered NOAA's unethical and illegal practices, North Carolina Congressional representative Walter B. Jones jumped on the bandwagon. On December 2, 2010, he sent a letter of disgruntlement to Jane Lubchenco, in which he made the following statement with regard to the introduction of new legislation that sought to curtail NOAA's underhanded tactics:

"As you know, a recent Inspector-General-commissioned audit of the NOAA Fisheries Asset Forfeiture Fund (AFF) found extensive waste, fraud and abuse by the agency. It also proved what fishermen have long suspected: allowing NOAA Fisheries to retain the proceeds from forfeitures, seizures, fines and penalties against fishermen gives the agency a perverse incentive to continue its abusive enforcement practices against fishermen. This conflict of interest must be eliminated. While the draft policy includes encouraging elements, it unfortunately falls short of that goal.

"It is important to reiterate just how badly NOAA Fisheries mismanaged the Asset Forfeiture Fund. The audit found that NOAA Fisheries administered the AFF in a manner that is neither transparent nor conductive to accountability, thus rendering it susceptible to both error and abuse. It also found that NOAA Fisheries used the AFF extensively to cover a variety of expenses which do not appear to be directly related to investigations and civil or criminal enforcement proceedings, which they are required to be by law. Such expenditures include over $500,000 spent on international travel in the past four and a half years. Other expenditures include $4.6 million for the purchase of 200 vehicles for only 172 enforcement personnel; $2.7 million for the purchase of vessels, including $300,000 for an undercover vessel that the manufacturer's website described as 'luxurious' with a 'beautifully appointed cabin': and dozens of purchase card transactions that were either improper, fraudulent or duplicative.

"The agency's draft policy wisely includes proposals to curb some of these abuses, including prohibitions on the use of AFF funds for:

  funding for NOAA employee labor, benefits, or
     awards;
  funding for vehicle or vessel purchases or leases;
  funding for travel not related to specific investi-
     gations or enforcement proceedings; and
  funding for equipment such as computers,

blackberries, cell phones and furniture.

"These prohibitions are necessary to help realign NOAA policy with the statutory language in the Magnuson-Stevens Fisheries Management Act that authorizes the AFF. However, they are not sufficient in that regard.

"On that note, it is extremely troubling that the agency's draft policy would allow proceeds from fines, penalties and forfeitures from fishermen to be used to pay the salaries of the Administrative Law Judges (ALJ) deciding cases brought against fishermen. Not only is this use of funds not authorized by the Magnuson-Stevens (Fisheries Management Act that authorized NOAA's AFF), it is terrible policy. The right to a trial before an unbiased, impartial judge is a bedrock principle of our democracy. If fisheries law judges are compensated with money from judgments against fishermen, the appearance, if not the practice, of impartiality is fundamentally compromised."

Not to Beat a Dead Horse, But . . .

Jones based his apprehensions on a July 1, 2010 report that was authorized by Department of Commerce Inspector General Todd Zinser, who had hired KPMG (an international corporation that provided audit, tax, and advisory services worldwide) to compile the report. That exhaustive report of misappropriation of funds was 72 pages in length. In submitting the report to Lubchenco, Zinser added an 11-page summary that distilled the most salient features of KPMG's findings.

It is important to note that NOAA refused to furnish a large number of documents that KPMG requested. For example, when KPMG requested supporting documentation that pertained to purchase activity and travel expenses, NOAA claimed "this document request would be unduly burdensome." Therefore, KPMG was unable to trace all of NOAA expenditures, or to substantiate that those expenditures were authorized.

With regard to purchase cards (called pcards, which are credit cards issued to NOAA employees for official use only), "the Northeast division destroyed all 2005 pcard records in October 2008." How convenient.

These examples demonstrate that I am not the only one whose request for discoverable documents was denied.

Time and again, KPMG noted that "many transactions had no supporting documentation or were missing approvals." The implication is obvious: NOAA employees were using government credit cards to make untraceable personal purchases.

In addition, KPMG encountered numerous instances "where a larger-than-$3,000 transaction was split into smaller transactions, presumably to fit under this threshold amount."

KPMG "identified duplicate pcard transactions involving the same employee, amount, and date, but a different vendor." Not just one instance, but 93 instances.

Due to the complexities and graphical analyses that formed a large part of the KPMG report, I will quote a few of Zinser's summations to Lubchenco instead of quoting from the actual report.

The Dead Horse Brays

Zinser prefaced the findings by noting "concerns" (there is that NOAA euphemism again) that "NOAA's fines were excessive, constituting a form of bounty, partly because of NOAA's ability to retain and use proceeds from its enforcement cases. . . . We found that despite OLE [Office of Law Enforcement] reporting a balance of $8.4 million as of December 31, 2009, OLE officials could not provide evidence that the AFF had ever been audited. We found that . . . internal controls over the fund were weak. . . .

"KPMG was unable to discern the current balance of the AFF because it found that NOAA did not have a consistent definition of the AFF, and indicated that the AFF was more of an abstract concept than a tangible entity within NOAA. This is attributable to KPMG's assessment that no unit or individual with NOAA has a clear understanding of the AFF and how it functions from start to finish. As a result, KPMG was unable to verify the $8.4 million balance provided by OLE and NOAA's Office of Finance, as cited in our January 2010 report. KPMG's analysis suggests that the AFF's current balance likely falls within a broader range. Based on complicated definitional, data analysis, and reconciliation efforts, KPMG found that during the period of its forensic review (January 1, 2005, through June 30, 2009), the AFF received approximately $96 million (including interest on prior balances), while expending about $49 million through over 82,000 transactions. This analysis suggests that the balance could be much higher than $8.4 million. . . .

"The results of KPMG's review evidence a history of inattention within NOAA to a substantial and highly sensitive monetary function of the agency. KPMG's findings show that NOAA has administered the AFF in a manner that is neither transparent nor conductive to accountability, thus rendering it susceptible to both error and abuse. . . .

"As KPMG found, the AFF has operated through poorly defined, disjointed, and inconsistent processes that lack effective internal controls, and for which no single NOAA office appears to be in charge or accountable because it is so decentralized. . . .

"OLE policy authorizes AFF expenditures for vehicle leasing and rentals, but does not include authorization of AFF expenditures for vehicle purchases. OLE's vehicle inventory as of June 1, 2010, lists 202 vehicles, only two of which are leased. According to OLE, the other 200 were purchased at a cost of about $4.6 million, predominantly with AFF monies. OLE's 202 vehicles exceed by a substantial margin its staffing of approximately 172 enforcement personnel.

"Further, OLE lacks policy for take-home vehicles, which are assigned on a full-time basis to nearly its entire enforcement workforce of 172 personnel – including the Director, Deputy Director, Assistant Directors, and Special Agents-in-Charge."

In other words, by citing anglers with exorbitant fines, enforcement personnel were feathering their own beds: each one was given permanent use of a company vehicle, with 28 vehicles leftover in case an assigned vehicle had to be sent to the auto shop for repairs or maintenance. Thus NOAA employees did not have to buy a vehicle of their own. Quite a perk.

In addition to the illegal purchase of a fleet of vehicles, "OLE policy does not include authorization of AFF expenditures for vessel purchases, yet OLE has used the AFF to acquire vessels. OLE's vessel inventory as of June 1, 2010, lists 22 vessels, purchased at a cost of nearly $2.7 million. These include, for instance, the 2008 acquisition of a $300,000 undercover vessel that the manufacturer's website describes as 'luxurious' with a 'beautifully appointed cabin,' which was the most costly operational vessel OLE had purchased up to that time. We found the acquisition of this specific vessel bypassed an internal review process instituted by OLE headquarters and was approved by the then-Director prior to competitive procurement procedures being applied."

Although I noted both vehicle and vessel purchases in the previous section, these fraudulent acquisitions are so egregious that they are worth repeating.

"Between January 2005 and June 2009, OLE and GCEL [General Counsel for Enforcement and Litigation] charged nearly $580,000 to the AFF for international travel to over 40 destinations. However, only about 17 percent of the cost for this travel was directly related to specific investigations or enforcement proceedings, accord to NOAA records. . . .

"Between collection and disbursement, there are a significant number of 'hand-offs' from one NOAA organization to another, without a consistent method of tracking the funds. . . .

"KPMG found that 62 percent of 604 transactions it selected for further analysis (i.e., document review) did not have required supporting documentation, and 27 percent did not have required approvals. . . .

"KPMG identified approximately 4,000 OLE and GCEL purchase card transactions that appeared to be split into two or more transactions to circumvent single purchase limits and/or avoid competitive procedures – in violation of Federal Acquisition Regulation requirements that protect against improper or fraudulent purchases. Of that population, KPMG selected a sample of about 400 transactions for further review, finding 10 percent to be improperly split. KPMG further reported that over 50 percent of the transactions selected for further review lacked supporting documentation, and 34 percent had incomplete or missing approvals. . . .

"KPMG identified nearly 1,200 potential duplicate purchase card transactions, of which 290 were selected for further review. While 15 were confirmed to be duplicate transactions, KPMG was unable to asses over half of those selected for review as they lacked supporting documentation. . . .

"Regarding purchase cards issued to nearly all OLE special agents and enforcement officers, KPMG tested all purchase card transactions where the monthly total value purchased from any single vendor had a value above $3,000. KPMG selected 394 for further review, of which 54 percent (totaling approximately $204,000 did not have required supporting documentation. . . .

"As monies pass through different NOAA Finance accounting funds, they are labeled with serveral different Finance accounting program and project codes. Revenues comprising the AFF are co-mingled with other funds in various finance funds, making it nearly impossible to delineate, track, and oversee the receipt and expenditure of only those monies which comprise the AFF.

"For example, KPMG found that of the relevant 99,251 records examined, there were 20,589 Accounts Payable records with organization codes that did not correspond with the 11 OLE or GCEL organization codes applicable to the AFF. Similarly, while the MSA [Magnuson-Stevens Fishery Conservation and Management Act] requires that fines and penalties imposed for violations of the Northeast Multispecies Fishery Management Plan are to be specifically used to enforce that Plan, NOAA has not tracked the use of these funds."

In other words, by muddying the financial waters, there was no way to determine which individuals had their hands in the till.

I will take it upon myself to repeat the following paragraph from Zinser's highlights to Lubchenco: "KPMG was unable to verify the $8.4 million balance provided by OLE and NOAA's Office of Finance, as cited in our January 2010 report. KPMG's analysis suggests that the AFF's current balance likely falls within a broader range. Based on complicated, definitional, data analysis, and reconciliation efforts, KPMG found that during the period of its forensic review (January 1, 2005, through June 30, 2009), the AFF received approximately $96 million (including interest on prior balances), while expending about $49 million through over 82,000 trans-actions. This analysis suggests that the balance could be much higher than $8.4 million."

By inference, $47 million is unaccounted for. It seems as if unidentified persons were skimming the AFF for millions of dollars.

Full discovery of the facts was impossible to obtain because NOAA employed a massive shredding operation: emptying its files of falsified records, and destroying in-criminating evidence that would substantiate its impro-prieties and unjust persecution practices.

Gag Me With a Spoon

Although Zinser's submission of the KPMG report, along with his clearly explained summary, gives the ap-pearance of cooperation with the fundamental precepts of open and honest inquiry, Zinser himself was under investigation by the Office of Special Counsel (OSC).

OSC investigators were hampered in the conduct of their duty by the actions of Zinser and three other high-ranking cohorts in preventing (excuse me: *allegedly* pre-venting) four federal employees from testifying in the OSC's investigation. The names of the four "affected in-dividuals" were held in anonymity in order to safeguard them against retaliation.

In this case, I will quote from Petitioners v. Department of Commerce, Docket Number CB-1208-13-0011-U-1, dated November 29, 2012, with citations deleted:

The allegations involved "(1) a significant change in working conditions imposed by allegedly unlawful nondisclosure agreements, and (2) threats to send failing performance appraisals to the four affected individuals should they either fail to sign or revoke the allegedly unlawful nondisclosure agreements. OSC contends that the nondisclosure agreements are interfering with an ongoing investigation of an independent prohibited personnel practice complaint (hereinafter "Ongoing Investigation"). . . .

"In its November 26, 2012 stay request, OSC alleges that the four affected individuals (hereinafter "Former Employees") previously worked in the agency's Office of Inspector General (OIG). . . . OSC asserts that three of the Former Employees are current federal employees. . . . As alleged by OSC, the three highest officials in OIG, consisting of the Inspector General [Zinser], the Deputy IG [Wade Green] and Counsel to the IG (Deputy IG), and the Principal Assistant IG for Investigations (PAIGI) [Rick Beitel], coerced the Former Employees to sign nondisclosure agreements in an effort to chill the Former Employees from whistleblowing, cooperating with OSC, and reporting wrongdoing to the United States Congress. . . . Specifically, OSC alleges that, from 2010 to 2011, the IG, Deputy IG, and/or the PAIGI issued a failing performance appraisal to each of the Former Employees. . . . Based on the timing and the content of the performance appraisals, OSC asserts that the appraisals did not reflect an honest assessment of each employee's performance. . . . OSC asserts that each of the Former Employees had worked in OIG for several years but was actively seeking employment elsewhere, as was known by the IG, Deputy IG, and/or the PAIGI. . . . In addition, OSC alleges that each of the Former Employees had received superior performance evaluations in previous years and had recently received at least a satisfactory appraisal. . . .

"According to OSC, immediately after the IG, Deputy

IG, and/or the PAIGI issued the failing performance appraisals to each of the Former Employees, the IG, Deputy IG, and/or the PAIGI presented each employee with the allegedly unlawful nondisclosure agreement and stated that, if the employee signed the agreement, the failing performance appraisal would not go into the employee's Official Personnel Folder (OPF) and the agency would provide prospective employees with a neutral job reference. . . . OSC further asserts that, if the employee did not sign the agreement, however, the IG, Deputy IG, and/or the PAIGI threatened to put the failing performance appraisal into the employee's OPF and notify the employee's new employer about the failing performance appraisal. . . .

"[Employee] further agrees . . . not to disparage the Agency in any communications to any person or entity, including but not limited to Members of Congress, the Office of Special Counsel, and the media. . . .

"OSC alleges that the nondisclosure agreements are chilling the Former Employees from whistleblowing, filing complaints with OSC, cooperating in an OSC investigation, and exercising their right to petition Congress."

After reviewing the evidence – which included "nondisclosure agreements of at least two employees" – the court found "that there are reasonable grounds to believe that the agency took or threatened to take these actions against the Former Employees because of their perceived whistleblowing."

The court ruled: "(1)All agency actions issuing or threatening to issue any performance appraisals based on an alleged violation of the nondisclosure agreement for any of the Former Employees employed in an 'agency' are hereby stayed; (2) All agency actions taking or threatening to take any other personnel action that may adversely affect the Former Employees employed in an 'agency' based on an alleged violation of the nondisclosure agreement are hereby stayed."

Wipe-out with Smoke and Mirrors
Working under a dark cloud of scrutiny was nothing

new for NOAA. Motivated by evil greed, it continued to employ decidedly underhanded tactics in its clash with the Gloucester Seafood Display Auction.

In response to hundreds of complaints "from fishermen, dealers, and various other representatives about action they believed represented unfair treatment or overzealous enforcement by OLE or GCEL employees," Secretary of Commerce Gary Locke was forced to upend the fish cart by completely revamping the leadership at OLE and GCEL.

Supposedly he fired and hired, but in reality he merely reassigned personnel like pieces on a chess board. No one – not a single person – was indicted for committing any criminal offenses or prosecuted for exercising what he called "overzealous and abusive conduct."

Locke also appointed a Special Master "to review and evaluate the cases identified by the IG in his September 2010 Report as warranting further review of the enforcement act and to recommend appropriate action to me."

In other words, Locke promised to apply "an independent process for equitable relief or resolution of past enforcement cases meeting appropriate eligibility criteria." This highfalutin lingo translates in lay terms to "pay back people NOAA has screwed."

He also promised to "identify those instances in which clear and convincing evidence establishes that NOAA enforcement personnel engaged in conduct that overstepped the bounds of propriety and fairness expected of them, and had a material impact on the outcome of the case. Examples of such conduct may include:

"(a) Abuse of process, including vindictive prosecution or other prosecution in bad faith, and unreasonable delay that prejudices the defense of the case;

"(b) Abusive conduct that amounts to coercion, intimidation, or outrageous behavior; and

"(c) Presenting false or misleading evidence or other conduct that impacts the truth of the case presented."

Again in lay terms, this boils down to reopening cases in which people were screwed by NOAA.

Again, although a number of maliciously maligned anglers received rightful restitution, no NOAA employees were indicted or prosecuted.

In the aftermath of Locke's promulgations, the Gloucester Seafood Display Auction was first in line for re-evaluation. But NOAA's on-the-spot enforcement officers continued to harass the auction house by upholding violations that had already been dismissed, and by inventing new ones.

Congressional Investigation

Counts against the auction house continued to increase with no settlement in sight. Despite Locke's new policy, local agents were still striving to enmesh the auction house with expensive hanky-panky and legal gymnastics.

However, before I can resume the auction house saga and present the climax – along with numerous red herrings and several premature ejaculations – I must make yet another diversion. The following testimony will enable the reader to fully comprehend the complexities of the situation, as well as to understand how viciously, arbitrarily, and capriciously NOAA attacked not only the auction house but commercial anglers in general.

Condemnations – that NOAA's scorched-earth enforcement procedures were pungent with corruption – resulted in a special session of the Oversight and Government Reform Committee, which was held on March 2, 2010 in the most appropriate of places: Gloucester, Massachusetts. The testimony of maritime attorney Stephen Ouellette – who for fifteen years had specialized in representing commercial fishing interests – was so clear and concise that I am doing him a great disservice by not quoting his 22-page testament verbatim and in full. Not a single word of Ouellette's ardent disapproval is irrelevant or duplicative. Nonetheless, in order to save space, I will pluck only a few of his perfectly worded phrases from his descriptive narrative.

"Higher level managers" in NOAA are "highly antagonistic to the fishing industry. . .

"Many on OLE and GCLE are completely disconnected from the fishery, having little understanding of the purpose of regulations, the nature of the industry they are regulating, the difficulty in compliance, financial strains, economic hardship of running a small business, economic condition of the fishery and the overall impact of regulations on fishermen. As a result, enforcement becomes unusually harsh and fines become unrealistically high for minor violations, and are multiplied where innocuous violations are repeated due to ignorance, misunderstanding or inadvertence. In some cases, it is almost as if enforcers are making sport of how large a fine they can impose or how complicated they can make a simple case appear. . . .

"The rules are horribly complicated and fill volumes. Reportedly the only agency producing more regulations is the Internal Revenue Service." Parenthetically, IRS tax law books total more than 60,000 pages in length.

"Rules change frequently and dramatically, with fishermen and boat owners in the Northeast receiving on average 500 pages of permit holder letters each year from the Northeast NOAA Region of NOAA alone. Many receive duplicates and multiple vessel or permit holders receive sets for each vessel they own, often in multiples. . . .

"We too often receive calls from fishermen who, due to weather or mechanical issues, need to return to port, but have too much fish for their time at sea. We advise them to discard, as NOAA makes NO allowances for even life threatening emergencies. In one case, NOAA Office of the General Counsel did, too late, allow one of my client's vessels to bring in a Bluefin tuna that belonged to a vessel that had foundered (whose crew was rescued by the Coast Guard). After waiting an hour for a response, with conditions deteriorating, I instructed the crew, by phone, to cut the fish loose and return to port. When the NOAA attorney finally called me, I advised him that safety considerations forced us to make a decision. He seemed incensed and the crew was met by NOAA agents who reportedly questioned them for over three hours. . . .

"Vessels are limited as to when, where and how long they can fish. Their gear is strictly regulated and their catch limited, often on a daily basis. Most vessels must notify NOAA before they leave the dock, wait for a sailing confirmation number and report again when they land. Vessels' positions are electronically monitored. Catches are reported to NMFS on vessel trip reports submitted monthly, in some cases electronically on a daily basis, and receiving dealers submit electronic reporting on a weekly basis. There is actually little opportunity to cheat, but great opportunity to make an honest mistake. . . .

"Fishermen . . . are treated like criminals . . .

"While NOAA agents will respond to questions, they are not always correct – in one case I was involved in 20 years ago, fishermen landed an extra bluefin tuna after they were told by OLE they could take if off the following year's quota, only to have it seized when they landed. . . .

"In other cases, fishermen have arrived at dock and found their estimate of catch exceeds their allowed limits. Action to bring an unintentional overage to the attention of enforcement through self reporting often results in seizure of catch and hefty fines. . . .

"NOAA has been given authority to fine up to $140,000 per violation, with each day being a separate violation. We frequently see fines of $50,000-250,000 for reporting violations, minor overages, common misunderstandings of rules . . .

"Fines regularly start at $30-100,000 and paperwork violations can result in million dollar fines. . . .

"Often, fishermen end up in violation because NMFS issues confusing or obscure regulations . . . A number of violations occur because NOAA is unable to timely do such tasks as calculate a vessel's available days at sea. Fishermen can no longer do this with new rules on differential counting and the fact that their annual allocation can [not] be determined until NOAA figures 'carry-over' DAS [days at sea], which may not be done until 3/4 of the way through a fishing year. . . .

"GCLE attorneys actually have stated . . . that when faced with an overage, the dealer should accept the legal limit and turn the balance back to the boat, rather than accept it . . . In one typical episode, one NOAA attorney was citing fishermen for estimating his catch and not waiting for dealer weights before filling in his logbook, and another was citing fishermen for not estimating and waiting for his dealer's weights – these two attorneys worked out of the same building. . . .

"Fishermen feel victimized by the process, with fines for innocent violations routinely exceeding a fisherman's year's pay . . .

"If any fish is believed to have been harvested illegally, e.g. from a closed area or in excess of limits, the catch is seized. Until the investigation is completed a vessel may be prevented from leasing days at sea or other rights, which can result in the vessel being prevented from fishing.

"Hearing before an ALJ offers limited opportunities for discovery. NOAA attorneys frequently fail to disclose documents they believe are 'not relevant.' (Shades of my first lawsuit against NOAA, which is still practicing the same ploy after 25 years!)

"The hearing process takes months, and provides no ability for interim rulings on individual counts, absent consent from the Agency. With costs for briefs, etc, the process may cost $5-10,000 for a small case, and significantly more in complex cases. . . .

"One case . . . has now extended over the course of 13 years, and has just reached the US District Court for the second time. (Frontier Fishing Corp)." (Not the Gloucester Seafood Display Auction, as the reader might presume.)

"Capt. Lee tried his best to follow the rules, but violated a rule when he entered port too early with 200 pounds of excess fish. Legally caught, he simply had to discard this dead fish at sea, or stay at sea for an additional sixteen hours. . . .

"Capt. Lee also lacked the so-called yellowtail letter (LOA)." (LOA stands for "letter of authority" to catch yellowtail tuna.) "At least 25 other boats landing at the Gloucester Seafood Display Auction similarly lacked the LOA. This fact came to light after the LOA was eliminated. NOAA won't tell how many of the 500 or so active groundfish vessels lacked them – two other vessels were given warnings, not fines, for LOAs violations. The difference between them and Capt. Lee – they didn't land at the Gloucester Auction. . . .

"The agency's position on the LOA . . . is yet another 'gotcha' for NOAA to further vilify fishermen. . . .

"Capt. Richard Burgess . . . apparently misjudged his available Days at Sea . . . on his vessel, a 42-foot gill-netter fishing from the port of Gloucester, but not without NOAA's help. This occurred, in part, because at various times NMFS has been unable to timely provide him with DAS usage calculations for months at a time, due to computer issues and problems calculating DAS usage based on differential counting. NMFS also continued to issue sailing numbers to the vessel, despite the apparent overage. Mr. Burgess had literally hundreds of available DAS that he could transfer from permits on skiffs he holds for that purpose. The NOAA attorney advised that if the Capt. Burgess agreed to forfeit $25,000 of the total of approximately $27,000 in catch, in addition to the DAS that would have been used, NOAA would seek no further penalty. In the interim, the boat would not be permitted to lease days to the boat and fish until he agreed to settle the case, or until the vessel received its next year's allocations in May. As a lawyer for the fishing industry, the complete lack of judicial remedy placed me in an impossible position, other than to advise him to accept what NOAA so 'generously' offered. . . .

"Mr. Burgess also lacked a yellowtail LOA for one of his boats in one year. Although NMFS says they didn't issue him one for the 2005 fishing season, we located a duplicate they issued, inexplicably for the 2004 year, indicating that because he renewed his permit early, NMFS may have been unable to issue a new letter for the 2005 year, and just issued him a duplicate for the 2004 year. In any event, all of his fish was reported, by his boat and by the GSDA. The violation was de minimis and a common mistake, made by as many as 50% of the active vessels in the Northeast Region. The tenor of his interview by agents and offer of leniency in exchange for getting him to make a statement against the Gloucester Seafood Display Auction made it clear that the charges against him were only a pretext to seek information on the Auction. . . .

"A number of vessels fell out of compliance with NMFS Interactive Voice reporting systems. In most cases the vessels were reporting their catches monthly through Vessel Trip Reports and dealers were reporting purchases and attributing them to vessels weekly. IVRs had been completed by personnel at the Maine State Division of Marine Resources. When the individual gave notice that she would stop doing it, some fishermen believed, incorrectly, they would be contacted by someone at NMFS. A number of vessels fell out of compliance. Although NMFS claims they need the vessels' IVRs on a weekly basis to avoid precipitous shutdowns of the fishery due to quota concerns, NMFS personnel were fully aware that these vessels were landing herring – and of the quantities through dealers – but did nothing for months and then notified NOAA law enforcement. When notified, vessels came into compliance. NOAA then issued fines of up to $520,000, $10,000 per violation, despite the fact NMFS personnel allowed the violations to occur. . . . NOAA should not be permitted to impose repetitive fines where it is aware that fishermen are unwittingly out of compliance, but they do, and they do it frequently, at great cost to the industry.

"It is quite common for fishermen to begin to fish, adjacent to a closed area, alongside a Coast Guard cutter, only to have the cutter's crew wait and watch until an offense has been unwittingly committed, and then stop the vessel – law enforcement never seems interested in stopping a fisherman from making a mistake that turns into a violation, where it can seize a catch or assess a fine."

The reader must appreciate that there are no fences in the ocean. No physical barrier separates an area in which fishing is permitted from one in which it is prohibited. No line of demarcation is drawn on a navigational chart. The boundaries of a prohibited area are buried in hundreds of pages of legal documents, where they are delineated by GPS coordinates.

When a fishing vessel is adrift and anglers are hauling in pots or nets, they are too busy working to watch a display monitor in the wheelhouse. Coast Guard cutters lurk along electronic boundary lines and keep radar tabs on approaching fishing vessels, waiting for them to cross the invisible border.

The Coast Guard *could* warn anglers when the current is drifting their boat into a prohibited area, either by calling them on the radio or by using the loud speakers on the cutter's public address system. The reason they do not take preventative action is that there is no money to be made by deterring a regulatory violation.

"In other cases, scallop vessels landing under 18,000 pound trip limits have had trips seized for variances as small as 2.5%, despite the impossibility of accurate weights on board and scientific evidence showing how scallop weights change based on water absorption in the vessel's hold. . . .

"One dealer, during a change in NMFS permit structure where he was told that his permits would all be issued by the Northeast Region, failed to note that his shark permit issued from the Southeast Region. When the permit was not renewed the first time, he fell off the notification list. Eventually, as reporting requirements changed, he was not notified and fell out of compliance on reporting. A single misunderstanding of a statement by NMFS that all of his permit [sic] were to be issued together . . . results in 600 violations. When the issue came to light, he produced his records and showed what he had purchased and from whom. GCLE indicated an intent to fine him $6,000,000, and suspend his permits for 2 1/2 years, but eventually settled the case for

$750,000 – which he has been paying for years. . . .

"Somewhat uncharacteristic of the American judicial system with its supposed due process protections; there is less judicial involvement, or common sense, required in NOAA's taking of a man's business assets, home and ability to earn a living, than in a challenge to a parking ticket issued on federal land."

The Plot Thickens

Ouellette's testimony was not mere allegation. He furnished documentary evidence to back his statements.

Notwithstanding the Congressional investigation, NOAA continued to target the Gloucester Seafood Display Auction: a fact that had been disclosed in Zinser's report to Lubchenco. NOAA committed a federal offense when it used fabricated information to obtain a search warrant to inspect the auction house's cold storage facility, office building, and associated property. To NOAA's great chagrin, law enforcement agents found nothing incriminating to bolster its case.

By this time, NOAA had already cited the auction house with 59 violations. Although the appeals court denied that much of the evidence was factual, and dismissed the charges, NOAA nonetheless imposed fines that totaled *ten times* the amount that such penalties ordinarily drew for such minor infractions. Lubchenco agreed with the decision to impose the fines.

The lack of a yellowtail letter of authorization was the excuse that NOAA used to issue many of these violation notices. More than a dozen commercial anglers who dealt exclusively with the auction house were cited *retroactively* for allegedly not possessing an LOA three years earlier, when the LOA was in effect.

NOAA went a step farther. After Lubchenco upheld NOAA's recommendation to continue its vengeful campaign against the auction house, NOAA engaged in a press release crusade, claiming that the auction was about to be closed, so anglers were warned to sell their fish elsewhere.

NOAA's unethical scare tactics were premature. The

auction house case was under appeal in federal court. NOAA had no right to predict the court's findings, any more than the media had the right to sway public opinion by pronouncing a person guilty of a crime before a jury has reached its verdict. But unscrupulous pandering was NOAA's stock-in-trade: another stuffed rabbit to pull out of its hat, especially when its house of cards was on the verge of collapse.

District Court Judge Douglas Woodlock slapped NOAA's collective wrist on two counts: he reprimanded NOAA for its underhanded media blitz, and for its announcement to impose penalties before the judge rendered his opinion.

NOAA shrugged off the court's admonishment as if it were swatting an annoying mosquito.

This meanness, this vindictiveness, ran rampant throughout NOAA. NOAA conducted its business not by being fair or by helping to promote the fishing industry, but like a leech that sucked blood from its victims in order to promote its moneygrubbing agenda. NOAA clearly had only its own interests at heart and not those of the American people. It was this rake-off scheme in which the auction house was embroiled. Anglers who habitually dealt with the auction house were dying a slow death through associational fallout.

Relief was on the way . . .

The Inspector General stepped into the fracas. He determined that NOAA's abnormally excessive penalties were "contrary to the interest of justice," and that they were designed to "put the auction out of business."

The Gloucester Seafood Display Auction had the last laugh. After reviewing ten-years-worth of allegations, the court ruled in favor of the auction house.

Secretary of Commerce Gary Locke not only affirmed exoneration, but he formally apologized to the auction house and promised restitution for its legal expenses. He made the same affirmation and promise with regard to scalloper Lawrence Yacubian: another target on NOAA's hit list. Over the long haul, Yacubian's legal expenses totaled more than $328,000.

Not to be outdone, when NOAA assigned Administrative Law Judges to hear the cases for reimbursement, it assigned the same ones who had presided over the trials for alleged violations, and who had found the defendants guilty on all counts. Clearly this was a conflict of interest, especially as one judge – Parlen McKenna – as well as the prosecuting attorneys in the Yacubian case, were among those who took the all-expenses-paid trip to Malaysia immediately after finding Yacubian guilty.

Yacubian's attorney, Pamela Lafreniere, demanded that McKenna recuse himself, which he did.

Paul Muniz, attorney for the auction house, did not follow Lafreniere's lead immediately, but he found that the judges against the auction house – Walter Brudzinski and Michael Devine – were dragging their feet. Muniz stated, "It is not surprising that NOAA would want to delay these proceedings indefinitely and avoid paying what is rightly owed to those who they unjustly and unfairly prosecuted."

An equitable solution was long in coming, in no little part due to Lubchenco's last-ditch face-saving circumvention in which, acting as administrative appeals judge in order to exert her authority, she conferred a guilty verdict against the auction house, but reduced the sentence to a $10,000 fine and a ten-day closure – both of which Locke overruled.

In light of NOAA's hardball manipulations of the law, justice could not be found within the administration.

Sorry, Charlie

One would think that after being struck such a resounding blow regarding its unethical behavior toward the commercial fishing industry, NOAA would back off its money-making schemes and toe the fishing line. One would be wrong. NOAA was nothing if not tenacious. With its administration mired in pulling money out of the air – er, water – it kept on doing what it had always done: taking money from anglers who risked their lives at sea to earn a buck.

NOAA was undaunted by past courtroom failures.

NOAA's mantra was: impound the catch, sell the fish, issue a violation, keep all the proceeds. NOAA seemed to believe that the sole reason for the existence of the commercial fishing industry was to earn money by fishing so that NOAA could take it away by bureaucratic fiat.

Case in point: Bluefin tuna is worth really big bucks. In early 2011, one tuna that weighed 745 pounds sold at auction for $396,000. Hard to believe, but true.

Now consider commercial fishing operator Carlos Rafael. He owned a small fleet of fishing trawlers. When one of these trawlers hauled in its net, crewmembers found a Bluefin tuna among the other, smaller fish. This monster weighed 881 pounds. The tuna was dead – a result of being dragged through the water column for a couple of hours – but chipped ice that was packed around the body kept the meat fresh.

Assuming a proportionate amount of dollars per pound of the 745-pounder, Rafael's tuna could be worth more than $450,000 on the open market. That would go a long way toward making up for his losses in previous years, and help to defray the costs of boat mortgages, maintenance, repairs, fuel, insurance, dockage, crew salaries, and income taxes. He might even turn a profit for the year.

Rafael was in possession of fifteen tuna permits that were spread across his fleet. In accordance with marine fishery regulations, he duly called in the catch on the official Bluefin tuna hotline.

Agents of NOAA's Office of Law Enforcement – the same OLE that was under such strict scrutiny and censure in the preceding sections – were waiting at the wharf when the trawler docked, on November 12, 2012. They confiscated the fish under the pretense that it had been caught in a net instead of by rod and reel.

What was NOAA going to do with the dead tuna? Sell it on consignment overseas, and pocket the ill-gotten gains. NOAA has learned that it is safer and easier to catch fish by means of seizure than by any kind of fishing tackle. This method required no capital investment; not even a boat.

In a way Rafael was lucky. NOAA did not cite him with a violation.

I saw firsthand the results of NOAA's regulatory policy of confiscating collateral catch and citing the unfortunate catchers with unpredictably high fines. I was walking along the beach on the Outer Banks of North Carolina when my attention was arrested by three large gray shapes on the sand below the high-water mark, where they had been deposited by the receding tide.

Approaching slowly because of the awful stench, I soon identified the shapes as dead, putrefying tuna. At first I was caught off guard. I wondered why these fish had committed suicide by beaching themselves. Then the awful truth dawned upon me.

These tuna had been caught by accident at sea. Their bodies had been dumped overboard because the risk of being fined hundreds of thousands of dollars for possessing a regulated species that was out of season or overweight or snagged by means that were not considered sporting, was assured by NOAA's policy on the matter.

The concepts of "forgiveness" or "extenuating circumstances" were absent from NOAA's vocabulary because these commonsense notions did not fill NOAA's coffers with the hard-earned income of commercial anglers.

It was better to let unauthorized tuna rot on the beach – spreading disease as the bodies decomposed where children dug sand castles – than to entertain the hope that NOAA might see reason.

The Biomass Wasteland

Senator John Kerry had much to say about NOAA's Gestapo practices: "NOAA's excessive penalties and retaliatory enforcement actions have caused deep distrust among our fishermen."

Kerry referred to the Dale Jones scandal as "an exclamation point and an underline of what was already a frayed relationship." Jones was the OLE director who not only had his own NOAA-furnished vehicle, but who took free trips on public transportation by dint of being an armed enforcement officer. "We need a full accounting of what happened so we can put the pieces back together and move forward."

As the previous section clearly shown, NOAA has demonstrated no intention of rescinding its unscrupulous ways. Quite the opposite. National Marine Fisheries Service Director Eric Schwaab and NOAA Chief Counsel Lois Schiffer sent a memo to Jane Lubchenco in which they suggested that NOAA would be better served if it ignored the excessive penalties that had been imposed on commercial anglers, and disavowed unwarranted legal actions against same.

Possibly it was this memo that led to NOAA's mass shredding maneuver.

Equally as bad as not punishing NOAA evildoers was the irreparable harm that NOAA did – and was continuing to do – to the commercial fishing industry, and to the American people who relied on that industry to furnish seafood for the dinner table.

According to the New England fishing caucus, "In 2007 (the last year for which we have data), only 27 percent of the total allowable catch was harvested because of regulatory measures designed to protect the weakest stocks. Thus, 73 percent of the allowable, sustainable catch was left in the ocean, costing our fishermen and our coastal economies approximately $500 million.

"Without an emergency action to adjust the 2010 allocation levels for these stocks, fishermen will yet again be forced to walk away from abundant species within the groundfishery, leading to significant job loss and tens or even thousands of millions of dollars in forfeited revenue."

Not only did NOAA not redress this economic disaster, but Lubchenco called for a *reduction* in the fishing fleet by more than 50% – not only putting more people out of work (commercial anglers at sea as well as land-based businesses that provide associated services such as fish cleaning, warehousing, wholesaling, food preparation, distribution, cooking, canning, and so on) but driving up market prices, so that restaurants and supermarkets must charge more for the difficult-to-obtain product.

Malfeasance – the Official NOAA Watchword

NOAA cares nothing about the fish-scales of justice. NOAA is in the business of exploiting legislation to its own best advantage, so that its employees can drive free vehicles and go on expensive junkets that the anglers and taxpayers who are paying for these illegal perquisites can ill afford.

A proven criminal agency such as NOAA is not the kind of governmental body that should be entrusted with controlling a national industry.

A proven criminal agency such as NOAA is not the kind of governmental body that should be entrusted with controlling marine resources of any kind.

A proven criminal agency such as NOAA is not the kind of governmental body that should be entrusted with controlling maritime, historical, cultural, and archaeological resources.

A proven criminal agency such as NOAA should not be allowed to function at all in a free democratic society in which the citizens are guaranteed by their hard-won Constitution to have the right to vote such a governmental body out of existence, when those citizens become dissatisfied with that agency's felonious conduct.

Subterfuge 501
NOAA's Lark:
Miscellaneous
Capers and Shenanigans

Takeover of the FAA

NOAA is authorized by Congress to manage and regulate ocean resources. The Federal Aviation Administration is authorized by the same body to manage and regulate national airspace.

NOAA is not empowered to extend its regulatory authority into areas that are already managed by competing government agencies or administrations. Yet in its bid to expand its ever-widening sphere of influence, NOAA has recently presumed to regulate airspace that is the province of the FAA.

This creeping encroachment began when NOAA contrived to create restricted airspace in the vicinity of four West Coast sanctuaries, on the supposition that wildlife might be "disturbed" by the engine noise of low-flying aircraft.

According to NOAA's ruling of January 26, 2012, "The regulations for each sanctuary now establish a rebuttable presumption that flying motorized aircraft below the existing minimum altitudes within any of the existing zones results in the disturbance of marine mammals or seabirds. This means that if a pilot were observed flying below the established altitude within a designated zone, it would be presumed that marine mammals or seabirds had been disturbed and that a violation had been committed. This presumption of disturbance could be overcome by contrary evidence that disturbance did not, in fact, occur (e.g., evidence that no marine mammals or seabirds were present in the area at the time of the low overflight)."

A minimum altitude of 1,000 feet was prescribed for the Channel Islands, Gulf of the Farallones, and Monterey Bay; 2,000 feet for the Olympic Coast.

I should not need to point out that the presumption of guilt violates one of the most fundamental principles of American law: that a person is presumed innocent until he is proven guilty beyond reasonable doubt.

If you have not skipped over the previous four chapters, then you should also be aware that NOAA further violates the Sixth Amendment of the Bill of Rights, which states, "In all criminal prosecutions, the accused shall enjoy the right to a speedy and public trial, by an impartial jury of the State and district wherein the crime shall have been committed."

Whenever NOAA charges a person with the commission of a crime, that person is denied due process by dint of the fact that his fate is determined not by a jury of his peers, as prescribed by the Constitution, but by an Administrative Law Judge who is paid by NOAA, and who receives bonuses in the form of free airfare, lodging, transportation, and so on, for finding people guilty so they can be forced to pay exorbitant fines.

NOAA treats the Constitution of the United States with evident disdain.

Furthermore, NOAA's self-serving regulation begs several important questions. First, exactly who is empowered to make the accusation against the pilot? The regulations do not specify any particular law enforcement agency; nor do the regulations specify that the accuser even has to *be* a law enforcement officer. The accuser could be anyone: a private citizen, for example, with a grudge against the pilot in question. Anyone can call a NOAA office and lay an accusation. It then becomes the burden of the pilot to prove his innocence beyond all unreasonable doubt.

Second, by what method is an aircraft's location and altitude ascertained? Can the accuser simply eyeball an aircraft in the sky and guesstimate that it has crossed an invisible border and is flying below the minimum altitude. What kind of observational instrument accuracy is needed to distinguish between 995 feet and 1,005 feet, from a ground observer who may have viewed the aircraft from a distant oblique angle?

Third, how can the pilot of a private aircraft establish his innocence? Small private planes and ultralights are not equipped with flight recorders to keep a running tab of location and altitude. Unless the pilot videotapes his entire flight with a downward-facing camera, he would be unable to prove that no "protected" animals were present during his overflight; or if there were, that they were not disturbed by his passage. Absent confirmatory proof, an ALJ would automatically find the defendant guilty, and collect an undetermined amount of money: NOAA's notice in the Federal Register established no limits on how much an alleged violator may be fined.

You begin to see the problems that NOAA has overlooked in its eagerness to create a controlled environment in which an unwary pilot can be nabbed by uncertain means, and forced to fatten NOAA's coffers without recourse to appeal. The absurdities of this quagmire do not matter to NOAA because guilt is presumed (and presumptuous). NOAA does not have to prove that a violation occurred; it only has to make an unsupported accusation. The pilot has the onus of furnishing hard-core evidence of his innocence: evidence that by its very nature is impossible to obtain after the fact.

Unfriendly Skies

Usurping the authority of the FAA has more far-reaching repercussions than simply opening a bank account so that unsuspecting pilots can be coerced into enriching NOAA and the very judges and attorneys who prosecute them.

For one thing, NOAA's overflight regulations are not indicated on current FAA aeronautical charts; nor are they provided anywhere in Federal Aviation Regulations printed matter. This means that unless a pilot has read the tens of thousands of pages of the Federal Register, in which NOAA's new regulations are buried, he can be caught unawares.

For another thing, the FAA does not require pilots to keep aeronautical charts or a copy of the Federal Aviation Regulations on board. There are no fences in the sky. Thus a pilot without charts or printed matter has no way of knowing when he is encroaching on a NOAA preserve.

Even if every aircraft was required to keep aeronautical charts or a copy of the Federal Aviation Regulations on board, can you imagine the pilot of an ultralight unfolding a chart in a hundred-mile-per-hour wind? And where would he stash printed regulations? If he did manage to find space to store printed regulations, how could he read them in the open air while keeping his hands and eyes on his controls? Ultralights do not have cockpits or copilots.

Hot-air balloons are considered to be noise-producing aircraft because of the noise that is made by the burner and by the combustion of propane. Balloons are subject to the vagaries of the wind. A balloon can easily be blown over an invisible border despite the pilot's willingness to turn away. Furthermore, a balloon may not be able to generate enough hot air or drop enough ballast to fly above the restricted altitude.

Aeronautical charts are already overly cluttered with symbols and written instructions that cannot be assimilated at a glance. Adding new information to designate sanctuary boundaries and airspace that is not restricted to a universal flyover, but restricted only to an altitude limitation, would require a whole new array of symbols and written instructions, adding immeasurably to the complexity of charts while leaving some information open to interpretation.

In some cases NOAA altitude restrictions conflict with traffic patterns that are designated by the FAA: for example, for those airports that are located near sanctuaries. NOAA's prohibition against low-altitude overflights effectively precludes aircraft from taking off and landing at those airports, because a high-altitude approach does not allow a pilot sufficient time to drop drastically into approach position before overshooting the runway, and because low-powered aircraft are not able to gain sufficient altitude to rise above the restriction limit before reaching the sanctuary.

Nevertheless, NOAA allows for no exemptions.

Enforcement of low-altitude fly-bys has also created serious safety hazards for pilots. Airports are sometimes socked in by fog, covered with clouds that create a low-altitude ceiling, or suffer adverse wind and weather conditions that force pilots to make long, low approaches in order to avoid crashing their aircraft. The FAA *requires* pilots to fly 500 feet below a cloud ceiling. Yet to do so at airports that are located near sanctuaries would violate NOAA's low-altitude restriction.

NOAA's response to this dilemma: "If weather conditions are such that maintaining visual flight rules (VFR) cannot be achieved while avoiding the flight ceiling, rather than violating the overflight regulations the pilot could instead choose to do any of the following: (1) Avoid flying over sanctuary waters by flying inland; (2) fly instrument flight rules (IFR) through the clouds; or (3) fly above the clouds."

In other words: no ifs, and, or buts. NOAA expects its regulations to be held sacrosanct; enforcement is its only priority. Pilots are threatened with severe penalties if they do not stay away from sanctuaries, even if doing so endangers life, limb, aircraft, and people on the ground who might be killed or injured by a crashing plane.

NOAA repudiates any and all forms of reasonableness that violate its regulations. It recognizes no such concept as extenuating circumstances. If collateral damage includes human sacrifice, so be it: as long as no wild animals are disturbed in the process.

NOAA's Incestuous Seal of Approval

It is important to note that none of the species that NOAA seeks to protect from disturbance is endangered. They are common seals, sea lions, sea elephants, and feathered friends such as seagulls: that most cosmopolitan of birds that is a chronic annoyance not only along thousands of miles of American coastline, but on inland lakes, ponds, and reservoirs. The ubiquitous seagull even inhabits shopping mall parking lots in my home-town of Philadelphia. As for marine mammals, they in-habit not only sanctuaries, but every other unoccupied niche along the entire western seaboard; and occupied niches as well.

The primary purpose of the Marine Mammal Protec-tion Act was to limit the number of individuals that could be culled from herds (particularly cetaceans: whales and porpoises), and to prevent disruption of their life cycle (particularly pinnipeds: seals, sea lions, and sea elephants, but including otters). Life cycle interfer-ence refers to breeding, migration, feeding, and shelter-ing in their natural habitats.

In promulgating its noise reduction regulations, NOAA furnished no documentation or scientific evidence to support its contention that wildlife was harmed by nearby engine operation, which was no louder than nat-urally occurring thunder from lightning storms.

When it was recommended to NOAA that it was un-der obligation to prepare an environment impact state-ment before proposing new regulations, NOAA respond-ed thus: "The amendments to the sanctuary regulations in the four national marine sanctuaries identified in this notice do not have significant environmental impacts and are categorically excluded from the need to prepare an environmental assessment pursuant to the National Environmental Policy Act. Specifically, the proposed amendments to the regulations are legal in nature, es-tablishing a rebuttable presumption regarding distur-bance below a certain level and are thus categorically excluded by NOAA Administrative Order 216-6 Section 6.03c.3(i)."

How can NOAA state categorically that the new reg-ulations have no environmental impacts if it never con-ducted any studies to support its position? Its statement is totally without basis.

NOAA then cited its own in-house order as justification for exclusion from having to prepare an Environmental Impact Statement. If every government agency excluded itself from Congressionally mandated laws, *no* EIS would *ever* be prepared.

NOAA not only acted above the law, but by its hostile wording it went as far as to flaunt the law.

By circumventing an environmental impact study, NOAA did not have to assess associated impacts such as safety and economic considerations.

Noise Reduction Ratio Absurdity

The Aircraft Owners and Pilots Association represents more than 400,000 members who ostensibly could be affected by NOAA's infringement of FAA territory. The AOPA was quick to point out the absurdity of NOAA's noise-reduction regulations when they were compared to the actual volume of noise that was generated by high-flying military and commercial aircraft.

The amount of noise that reached the ground from the overflight of a low-flying single-seat or two-seat private aircraft – such as an ultralight or a Piper Cub – was a minute fraction of the amount of noise that reached sanctuaries laterally from a jet or turboprop aircraft during takeoff and landing.

If NOAA continues to have its way, it will force the shutdown of the San Francisco International Airport – the seventh busiest airport in the country – because of its proximity to the proposed expanded boundaries of the Monterey Bay NMS.

The Seal of Fate

The manner in which NOAA has chosen to interpret the Marine Mammal Protection Act has long since surpassed the height of ludicrousness. I observed this first-hand on a visit to Crescent City, California, where mobs of aggressive sea lions had taken over the local marina. A situation that was shocking to an East Coaster like me was common knowledge to Californians.

Millions of West Coast residents in general, and tens of thousands of West Coast boat owners in particular, are eminently aware of the fact that seals, sea lions, and sea elephants are in no danger of extinction. Indeed, these superabundant marine populations are not only thriving in their natural habitats, but they are teeming in such masses that they are presently overrunning harbors and boat basins. They are a constant and ever-present nuisance.

These obnoxious marine mammals clamber onto wharves and finger piers, motorboats and sailing craft, sidewalks and beaches. They do not just visit; they inhabit. Like junkyard dogs, they bark and snort at passersby. They defecate everywhere, far worse than seagulls because of their mammoth size and voracious appetite.

Imagine the plight of the person who boards his boat to find his seat cushions chewed, clawed, and torn apart; the decks and cockpits filthy with rotting fish carcasses and large piles of excrement that lay stinking in the sun. But damage and health hazards are not the worst of the plight.

NOAA does not permit boat owners to chase off the invaders. Worse than that, owners are not even allowed to go near their boats if these destructive marine mammals are blocking the way.

You read that correctly. If any kind of marine mammal is roosting on the finger pier between the wharf and a person's boat, no one is allowed to board his boat if his approach disturbs the interlopers. This is what I saw myself in Crescent City: hordes of sea lions resting on the floating docks or cavorting nearby in the harbor.

NOAA enforcement officers were lurking out of sight, ready to nab anyone who got close enough to the wild sea lions to make them slip into the water, or raise their heads from their slumber, or twitch a flipper, or bark, or roll its eyes toward an approaching person. In other words, if a sea lion – and there were dozens on the pier and in the water – made any kind of movement that constituted awareness of a human being, that human being was liable to be fined as much as $50,000 per violation. And the violation could be multiplied by the number of

Subterfuge 501

animals that were "disturbed."

I would not have believed that such a situation was possible unless I had seen it with my own eyes. There were boat owners who had not been able to board their boats for weeks, because these sea lions did not just swim into the harbor for brief rest periods: they *lived* there! Only if every one of them went to sea for food at the same time was a boat owner permitted to have access to his property.

The scenario that I witnessed was being repeated thousands of times along the entire western seaboard.

The worst case scenario actually occurred. On at least one occasion, so many sea lions climbed onto a boat at dock that their combined weight tipped over the boat and sank it!

When Congressional leaders enacted legislation to protect marine mammals, they proposed to safeguard them in their natural environment. They did not intend – nor could they have anticipated – that these animals would overrun seashore resorts, or that property owners should be ousted from their possessions.

NOAA subverted the intent of the Act in order to effectuate another money-grubbing scheme.

A Whale of a Tale

In May of 1992, Lee Tepley and Lisa Costello were boating off the coast of Hawaii when they spotted a pod of pilot whales in the distance. Tepley maneuvered the boat so that it lay in the path of the swimming whales. He and Lisa jumped into the water wearing snorkeling gear. Tepley had a video camera inside a waterproof housing.

He switched on the camera as the pod of whales approached; he started taping. The whales swam past them, then stopped to play. It was an exhilarating experience – until one of the whales bit Costello's leg and dragged her down to a depth of 25 feet. The whale could hold its breath for an hour, but the woman could not. Tepley was powerless to do anything to help her. He kept the camera rolling on the tragedy in progress. Costello was slowly drowning.

As Costello's life was in the final stages of ebbing away, the whale took her to the surface and let her go. She gasped for air. Tepley helped her onto the boat. They were both relieved after a close call with death.

This was real life, not a television melodrama. The couple later appeared on a news broadcast, where they related their near-death experience. Tepley's footage was shown nationwide to an enthralled audience.

After the program, both Tepley and Costello were cited for violating the Marine Mammal Protection Act. NOAA's Administrative Law Judge Hugh Dolan – the same one who presided over two of my *Monitor* cases – found the defendants guilty of interfering with the whales by placing themselves in their path. They were fined $10,000.

The whales got away scot free.

Although I have mentioned it elsewhere I must repeat myself, not only because of the significance to the case in point, but because of its relevance to NOAA's on-going history of unscrupulous conduct: the pair was tried by a NOAA-paid judge without the benefit of a jury. This kind of trial is unconstitutional. Article III, Section 2 of the Constitution of the United States asserts explicitly, "The Trial of all Crimes, except in Cases of Impeachment, shall be by Jury."

This assertion is repeated in Amendment 6 of the Bill of Rights: "In all criminal prosecutions, the accused shall enjoy the right to a speedy and public trial, by an impartial jury."

Nowhere does the Constitution equivocate about a trial by jury.

The reason for a jury trial is twofold: jurors are unbiased, and they have no monetary incentive to find a defendant guilty.

NOAA viciously enforces the letter of the law without giving consideration to the intent of the law. NOAA treats the Marine Mammal Protection Act the same way it treats the various fishing regulations: as a private source of revenue that its employees can spend on themselves, so they can enjoy benefits and perquisites above and beyond their pay grade.

Examples of NOAA's abuses in this regard are legion. In this slender volume I have touched upon only a few of them, to give the flavor of administrative abuse that runs rampant throughout the agency, and that is growing by leaps and bounds: all without the country's voters having any say in the matter.

When NOAA wants to do something, it does not ask for permission from the voters or their representatives; it just goes ahead and does it.

NOAA is self-regulated, which in reality means that it is *un*regulated. It operates beyond the pale of the voters' reach.

Scales out of Balance

Every chemist knows that a gas expands until it fills all available space. Likewise, every politician knows that government agencies expand forever when they are allowed to go unchecked.

NOAA is in the process of expanding both its territory and its control. It operates autonomously, without a system of checks and balances. It constantly abuses its authority. It exercises autocratic control of its dominion.

NOAA utilizes deceptive practices when possible, or outright lies when deception it too weak an artifice. It lays false charges against anglers and fish auctions. It seizes fish from the anglers who caught them. It confiscates vessels on allegation without conviction. It imposes fines that far exceed the alleged violation. It denies defendants due process of law. It employs oppressive tactics to intimidate and cajole those people who do not recognize its authority.

And like a cancer, it wants to grow exponentially without any controls placed on its growth or authority.

Thunder at Thunder Bay

The Thunder Bay NMS website lists a number of government agencies that allegedly favored expansion of the sanctuary. Yet the website did not list the hundreds of organizations and individuals who submitted letters of protest that opposed expansion. This calculated concealment of facts gives the illusion that expansion was universally favored, and that no one opposed it.

At one of the 2012 scoping meetings for the Monitor NMS, David Alberg went to great lengths to express how NOAA had postponed its plan to expand the Thunder Bay sanctuary because the conditions at the time did not seem right, and instead declared a five-year moratorium on expansion. He gave the impression that NOAA had acted on its own, out of divine benevolence.

What he did *not* say was a mouthful: that Michigan voters and the governor of the State refused to allow the expansion. Michigan could do this because the State owns the submerged bottomlands.

Alberg's pretense cleverly contrived to conceal the true reason that NOAA declared the moratorium. Furthermore, both Alberg and the sanctuary website neglected to mention the government bodies and organizations that *opposed* the sanctuary: the Michigan Department of Natural Resources, the Michigan Department of Environmental Quality, the Alpena Department of Natural Resources, the Presque Isle County Board of Commissioners, the Michigan Salmon and Steelhead Fisherman's Association (MSSFA), the Michigan United Conservation Clubs, and the Thunder Bay Steelheaders, to name just a few. Congressional representative Bart Stupak also opposed the sanctuary.

I am not the only one to voice the truth about NOAA's dishonest propaganda campaign. Perhaps Jim Vandermaas, president of the MSSFA, did the best and most succinct job of summarizing NOAA's unilateral process: "Focus groups are being deliberately and very selectively stacked to achieve the goals that NOAA . . . wants to reach. . . . Along with them is the 'powerful' backing of Michigan State University because of the 'raw pork' they expect to get in the form of grant funding, along with the position of sanctuary manager. NOAA wants total control. . . . It's the only result they will be satisfied with."

Another reason for locals to oppose expansion was NOAA's refusal to guarantee in writing that no user fees would ever be implemented. Michigan residents pointed to the Florida Keys NMS as an example of what NOAA did (and will do) once it took control of the resource: it instantly increased user fees by 400%, it strictly controlled access to selected shipwrecks, it banned certain types of diving activity, it severely restricted fishing, and it found numerous excuses to punish visitors by imposing excessive fines for minor infractions: not as outrageously as it did to Massachusetts anglers, but still unwarranted by the degree of disobedience, especially in light of the fact that many of the restrictions were purposely designed not to protect a resource but to achieve an atmosphere (or hydrosphere) in which violations could easily be cited by law enforcement agents but difficult to defend.

In other words, NOAA instituted severe constraints that were never discussed in the formalization process. According to the *Florida Keys Keynoter*, "The vast majority of commercial fishermen, small-business owners, marine interests and property owners [did] not want NOAA's program in the Keys. Apparently, the groups opposed to the designation were not allowed to attend the meetings."

I could write another book about how NOAA overruled sweeping opposition from Floridians, but that book should be written by an author who has greater experience in local happenings. Bent as it was on territorial domination, NOAA gave no consideration at all to the voice of the stakeholders.

Florida residents took to posting signs along the highway and wearing buttons and T-shirts that read "SAY NO TO NOAA." Michigan residents followed suit and did the same.

Michigan stakeholders pointed another finger at NOAA's conduct in its West Coast sanctuaries. A handful of scuba divers were tied up in court for years, and were fined hundreds of thousands of dollars, because an undercover agent claimed to have seen them fanning the sand with their hands. In NOAA's opinion, hand-fanning constituted a disturbance of the seabed – notwithstanding that every minor offshore storm causes a thousand times more disturbance, and erases all sign of prior disturbance.

NOAA used the same excuse in Florida to prevent treasure salvors from moving sand with prop wash deflectors – again, notwithstanding that the next hurricane to pass through the Keys would completely obliterate every vestige of previous sand dispersal.

In Michigan, local government now needs NOAA's permission to dredge shipping channels that have become choked with sediment, because dredging alters the bottomland. NOAA is sometimes reluctant to give such permission, the result of which traps boats in affected harbors, and prevents boats on the lake from entering those harbors.

Violent storms brew quickly on the Great Lakes. When one appears on the horizon, mariners dash to the nearest harbor for protection. As the timeworn saying goes, "Any port in a storm." But NOAA's restrictions put mariners at risk because some of those harbors are no longer available. NOAA has placed the sanctity of mud above the safety of human lives.

Despite all this opposition, at the May 19, 2009 meeting of the Monitor NMS Sanctuary Advisory Council, superintendent of the Thunder Bay NMS Jeff Gray declared, "In 2007, boundary expansion was the number one request and was supported by the entire community and full Advisory Council." This statement is pure bunk, baloney, and another pejorative that begins with B.

Gray also declared, "There was a buoy system installed on many of the wreck sites." The statement is true but misleading because the buoy system existed before Thunder Bay became a sanctuary. I know this firsthand because I have been diving on shipwrecks in Thunder Bay since the 1980's. NOAA cannot not take credit for this pre-existing system.

Gray further declared, "TBNMS . . . are [sic] working

with every branch of the government." The Thunder Bay sanctuary most certainly was *not* working with those branches of the government that opposed the sanctuary, as noted above.

To the question, "Why does NOAA want to expand the sanctuary?" Gray made his most ingenuous comment of all: "In the case of TBNMS, it was not NOAA, but rather the community, through TBNMS Advisory Council, that wanted to expand the Sanctuary."

As I have pointed out more than once, Sanctuary Advisory Councils are in-house constructs whose choice of members is based on their favoritism toward NOAA, and whose members must swear an oath of allegiance to further NOAA's goals. Thus Gray's statement flies in the face of the reality that the "community" did not want to expand the sanctuary; rather, NOAA's covert adjunct only *claimed* that the community wanted expansion, as a surreptitious way to fool congressional representatives into believing an untruth that would lead toward furthering NOAA's goals of territorial expansion and total control of the underwater world.

All this goes to show how far a sanctuary superintendent was willing to go in providing false information for public consumption.

NOAA compounded the misconceptions that Gray declared, by posting on the Thunder Bay NMS website: "During the sanctuary's management plan review in 2006, NOAA received comments encouraging expanding the sanctuary's boundary to include the waters adjacent to Alcona and Presque Isle counties. Several local government and non-governmental organizations passed resolutions or submitted letters of support for boundary expansion. In 2007, the Thunder Bay Sanctuary Advisory Council adopted a resolution supporting expanded boundaries."

Once again, NOAA resorted to reporting a one-sided view of the expansion issue by eliminating all mention of the government bodies, non-government organizations, and numerous individuals who staunchly opposed expansion. Once again, NOAA deceived the public and their State and federal representatives by implying that everyone favored expansion and that no one opposed it.

Many "concerned" recreational divers sent letters to NOAA to ask questions about the implications of expansion. Not one received an answer; their letters of "concern" were simply pigeonholed.

The list of NOAA's lies, deceptions, and administrative abuses is endless. It would take a set of encyclopedia to detail them all.

An agency that is as dishonest and disreputable as NOAA should not be suffered to exist in a free democratic society.

California Here I Come

The National Park Service, a NOAA partner, is aiding and abetting NOAA's lunacy by shutting down a 100-year-old family-owned oyster business called the Drakes Bay Oyster Company. Despite the fact that in 2007, the NPS featured the company and its employees as "outstanding environmental stewards," high-ranking officials concocted a scheme to fake evidence that the company caused pollution which resulted in depopulation of local harbor seal herds.

This is another one of those political intrigues that would take a book to describe in depth. The case is currently in litigation, with NPS personnel accused of submitting fraudulent data. I apologize for such a cursory examination of the facts, but this is only case among many in which federal agencies are castigating hardworking Americans with criminal intent. This particular case is the most egregious. Here are the highlights of a case in which the *outline* alone – documenting manifold instances of scientific misconduct on the part of the NPS – is 44 pages in length.

Despite a thriving seal population, in 2006 the NPS published a fictitious report that oyster feces was harming the environment by stifling eelgrass and killing the fish on which the seals feed; no supporting documentation was included in this finding. In fact, NPS background data clearly showed no reduction in the fish or seal population, and a doubling of growth of eelgrass (in which fish hide).

The NPS made the fictitious claim that on one particular day, oyster company boat traffic disturbed roosting seals. Investigation proved that the day in question was Sunday, when the company was closed and no one was working; in addition to which the sandbars on which the seals habitually roosted were submerged that day.

The NPS then made false assertions that seals were so disturbed by oyster gathering activity that they were unable to birth pups on nearby sandbars. This assertion was made without an actual count of seals and pups. Even if fewer pups were born on these sandbars, no one checked to determine if the number of pups born on other sandbars increased. Seals are wild animals whose movements are not restricted by bureaucratic fiat. The NPS refused to honor FOIA requests for substantiating documentation.

Three years of photographic evidence proved beyond a shadow of doubt that local seal populations were stable. Yet the NPS suppressed this information because it contradicted its engineered deductions.

The NPS fabricated evidence, then released a report that insisted, "the impact on the harbor seals is a national emergency."

The NPS made accusations that were not only unsubstantiated, but were contrary to the agency's own data. Other NPS data were manipulated in order to achieve a false perception that was not warranted by the facts.

In the midst of this turmoil, NOAA partnered with the NPS on the harbor seal issue. I suppose this proves the adage about honor among thieves. This conspiracy appears to be part of a long-term goal to put the company out of business as part of the "conglomerization" of West Coast sanctuaries.

Mega-sanctuaries

The handwriting is on the wall for all who care to read. NOAA is in the process of taking over the all the submarine property that lies adjacent to the United States.

Already in the works is a diabolical scheme to increase the size of four existing sanctuaries: an eightfold expansion of Thunder Bay NMS in Lake Huron, expansion of Stellwagen Bank NMS to encompass all the international waters off the coast of Massachusetts, expansion of the Monitor NMS to encompass all the international waters off the coast of North Carolina, and the creation of a super-sanctuary off the coast of California by combining three existing sanctuaries and trebling their size.

It is but a short step from there to expanding these super-sanctuaries into two gigantic mega-sanctuaries: one on the east coast spreading from Canada to Florida, thence into the Gulf of Mexico; and one on the west coast spreading from Canada to Mexico.

American citizens face a two-ocean war that rivals that of World War Two, only now the enemies are not the hostile foreign nations of Germany and Japan, but domestic egomaniacal forces that are fighting to dominate Americans from within.

And this is to say nothing about the noncontiguous States of Alaska and Hawaii, with the conquest of Hawaii already in progress.

Thanks to NOAA, the erosion of freedom in the United States is accelerating at an ever-quickening pace.

NOAA's Der Tag is on the underwater horizon.

What will be NOAA's next territorial demand?

Baltic Sea, watch out.

Index

THE LUSITANIA CONTROVERSIES
THE TWO-VOLUME
HISTORY OF WRECK-DIVING

There is more to a book than its title. There is the subtitle. A subtitle is an explanatory device which describes the topic of a book more fully than its title. A case in point is The Lusitania Controversies. At first glance the title implies the sole subject of the Lusitania. But each of the two volumes possesses a subtitle which explains in greater detail the global premise of which the Lusitania is but a part.

Together, both volumes present the entire history of wreck-diving, from its meager beginnings in the 1950's to the advent of technical diving in the 1990's.

Book One is subtitled Atrocity of War and a Wreck-Diving History. One quarter of the volume is devoted to the construction, career, sinking, and aftermath of the Lusitania. Three quarters are devoted to the history of wreck-diving and to autobiographical experiences of the author, who became an essential element in wreck-diving and a pioneer in technical diving. Coverage extends to 1979, and includes a section on the author's first Doria trip, in 1974.

Book Two is subtitled Dangerous Descents into Shipwrecks and Law. This volume continues the history of wreck-diving from 1980; describes numerous dives on ever-deeper shipwrecks; a number of incredible penetrations into the vast interior of the Andrea Doria, including the recovery of two bodies; and details the beginning of mixed-gas diving to the point at which an expedition to the Lusitania became practical. The volume concludes with a detailed description of the 1994 Lusitania expedition (of which the author was a part) and subsequent legal activities.

The two volumes are larger than the sum of their parts. They comprise biographical content with incredible underwater adventures: some hair-raising, others deadly, all exciting: a fascinating excursion into the real world of wreck-diving and the evolution of the activity.

Books by the Author

The Popular Dive Guide Series

Shipwrecks of Massachusetts: North
Shipwrecks of Massachusetts: South
Shipwrecks of Rhode Island and Connecticut
Shipwrecks of New York
Shipwrecks of New Jersey (1988)
Shipwrecks of New Jersey: North
Shipwrecks of New Jersey: Central
Shipwrecks of New Jersey: South
Shipwrecks of Delaware and Maryland (1990 Edition)
Shipwrecks of Delaware and Maryland (2002 Edition)
Shipwrecks of Virginia
Shipwrecks of North Carolina: Diamond Shoals North
Shipwrecks of North Carolina: Hatteras Inlet South
Shipwrecks of South Carolina and Georgia

Shipwreck and Nautical History

Andrea Doria: Dive to an Era
Deep, Dark, and Dangerous: Adventures and Reflections on the Andrea Doria
Great Lakes Shipwrecks: a Photographic Odyssey
The Fuhrer's U-boats in American Waters
Ironclad Legacy: Battles of the USS Monitor
The Kaiser's U-boats in American Waters
The Lusitania Controversies: (Book One)
       Atrocity of War and a Wreck-Diving History
The Lusitania Controversies: (Book Two)
       Dangerous Descents into Shipwrecks and Law
The Nautical Cyclopedia
NOAA's Ark: the Rise of the Fourth Reich
Shadow Divers Exposed: the Real Saga of the U-869
Shipwreck Heresies
The Shipwreck Research Handbook
Shipwreck Sagas
Stolen Heritage: Grand Theft of Hamilton and Scourge
Track of the Gray Wolf
Underwater Reflections
USS San Diego: the Last Armored Cruiser
Wreck Diving Adventures

Dive Training
Primary Wreck Diving Guide
Advanced Wreck Diving Guide
The Advanced Wreck Diving Handbook
Ultimate Wreck Diving Guide
The Technical Diving Handbook

Nonfiction
The Absurdity Principle
Wilderness Canoeing

Science Fiction
A Different Universe
A Different Dimension
A Different Continuum
Entropy (a novel of conceptual breakthrough)
A Journey to the Center of the Earth
The Mold
Return to Mars
Silent Autumn
Subaqueous
The Time Dragons Trilogy
A Time for Dragons
Dragons Past
No Future for Dragons

Sci-Fi Action/Adventure Novels
Memory Lane   *Mind Set*
The Peking Papers

Supernatural Horror Novel
The Lurking: Curse of the Jersey Devil

Vietnam Novel: *Lonely Conflict*

Videotape or DVD
The Battle for the USS Monitor

**Visit the GGP website for availability of titles:
http://www.ggentile.com**

www.ingramcontent.com/pod-product-compliance
Lightning Source LLC
Chambersburg PA
CBHW062209270326
41930CB00009B/1688